More Meditations of a Militant Moderate

More Meditations of a Militant Moderate

Peter H. Schuck

ANTHEM PRESS

Anthem Press
An imprint of Wimbledon Publishing Company
www.anthempress.com

This edition first published in UK and USA 2026
by ANTHEM PRESS
75–76 Blackfriars Road, London SE1 8HA, UK
or PO Box 9779, London SW19 7ZG, UK
and
244 Madison Ave #116, New York, NY 10016, USA

First published in the UK and USA by Anthem Press in 2023

© 2026 Peter H. Schuck

The author asserts the moral right to be identified as the author of this work.

All rights reserved. Without limiting the rights under copyright reserved above, no part of this publication may be reproduced, stored or introduced into a retrieval system, or transmitted, in any form or by any means (electronic, mechanical, photocopying, recording or otherwise), without the prior written permission of both the copyright owner and the above publisher of this book.

British Library Cataloguing-in-Publication Data
A catalogue record for this book is available from the British Library.

Library of Congress Control Number: 2026930325

ISBN-13: 978-1-83999-946-8 (Pbk)
ISBN-10: 1-83999-946-2 (Pbk)

This title is also available as an eBook.

TABLE OF CONTENTS

Part 1: Preface and Part 1   1
    Introduction to Part 1   1
    Militant Moderation   2
    The Supreme Court's Abortion Decision   7

Part 2: American Exceptionalism   11
    Introduction to Part 2   11
    The Anatomy of American Exceptionalism   12
    Remembering James Q. Wilson   27
    In Diversity We (Sorta) Trust   29

Part 3: Civic Discourse   35
    Introduction to Part 3   35
    The Widening Gaps between Our Politics and Civil Society   36
    Searching for Public Courage   39
    The Shackling of the Progressive Mind   41
    Cancel Culture Has a Lot to Answer For   45
    Thinking Clearly about Sexual Harassment   48
    Taking a Knee: How to Squander a Teaching Moment   51
    Five Realities of Tribal Politics   53
    Principles to Guide a Nation Through Issues that Divide Us   55
    Racism and Racialism Are Different   57
    What Systemic Racism Systematically Downplays   59
    Meritocracy   71
    Diversity, Equity, and Inclusiveness: Their Coherence Requires Line-Drawing   75
    What I Learned from the Icelandic Ash Cloud   81

Part 4: The Misbegotten Trump Presidency   85
    Introduction to Part 4   85
    Limerick   85
    Trump's Refugee Limits Betray Past Republican Presidents and the Founders   89

The Real Problem with Trump's National Emergency Plan 91
The Court Ruled Correctly on the Travel Ban 93
Trump's "Horrifying Lies" About Lori Klausutis May Cross a Legal Line 95

Part 5: Campus Follies — 97
Introduction to Part 5 97
What the President of Yale Should Have Said 98
Free Speech—Where Are the Adults in the Room? 101
Assessing Affirmative Action 105
Six Reasons Why Student Loans Are a Looming Disaster 123
The Garden of College Excellence Is Growing Weeds 127
The Commencement Disinvitation Season 131
On Sexual Assault Policy, Trust Colleges Not Uncle Sam 133
Valdosta and the Future of the Authoritarian Campus 136

Part 6: Immigrants, Citizens, and Refugees — 139
Introduction to Part 6 139
Democrats' Vulnerability and Opportunity on Immigration Policy 140
Birthright of a Nation 145
Refugee Burden-Sharing: A Modest Proposal 147

Part 1

PREFACE AND PART 1

Introduction to Part 1

Eighteen years ago, I published *Meditations of a Militant Moderate*. My purpose then was to collect in one place more than three dozen of my short essays on various questions bearing on the public interest, essays that had appeared during the previous 25 years in many leading national and academic publications The earliest, a *New York Times* op-ed, "Rethinking Liberalism," was written in the wake of Ronald Reagan's first election and suggested that liberals' insights about how the natural world works were deeply inconsistent with their views on social policy dynamics. The latest were a group of 2005 essays on diverse topics. I hoped that these essays would enlighten my readers about what I considered some of the crucial issues facing American society during a quarter-century of great change.

Today, the world that prompted those essays seems distant. American society has been convulsed by wars, pandemics, presidential impeachments, economic recessions, the internet, fundamental changes in media and interpersonal communications, global environmental challenges, a narrowly-averted attempt at a coup in Washington, and polarizing changes in our political parties with an utterly transformed Republican Party absorbing and normalizing far-right elements while Democrats have been challenged by "progressive" insurgencies from the left. In mid-July 2022, the *New York Times* reported a nationwide poll finding that a majority of American voters across nearly all demographics and ideologies believe their system of government does not work, with 58% of those interviewed saying that our democracy needs major reforms or a complete overhaul.

These convulsions have been manifested in countless ways. Many of them were crystallized in the presidency and continuing influence of Donald Trump on many aspects of Americans life, but some changes were quite independent and remain so. The writings collected here touch on only some of these factors, of course, but they are among the most salient ones for understanding what American society has become. The remainder of this Preface, also

Part 1 of the book, presents two essays written in 2022. The first explains why I continue to consider myself a "militant moderate" even—or especially—in these turbulent times. The second piece is unpublished. I present it as a moderate reaction to the literally precedent-shattering Supreme Court decision in late June 2022 overruling *Roe v. Wade*.

The rest of the book, parts 2-6, consists of 30 additional essays and two poems. I have omitted footnotes; they can be found in the original published versions cited after each article. Because these essays are quite recent, I have revised them only minimally, with necessary updates or in response to points raised by two anonymous outside readers. Part 2 concerns American exceptionalism. Part 3 is the longest, consisting of many articles that contribute to different aspects of our vital national conversation on civic and political issues. Part 4 consists of pieces (including a limerick) written during the first presidential administration of Donald J. Trump. There, I strongly criticize him on legal, policy, and political grounds but I want to be clear from the very outset that I regard him as a dangerous, utterly immoral, and perhaps criminal politician. Part 5 ("Campus Follies") presents commentaries about various academic issues. Part 6 focuses on immigration policy, the debate over birthright citizenship, and my novel proposal for dealing with large refugee flows.

My topical and academic writings have addressed a very wide range of subjects, so I had to be very selective in deciding which ones to include in this short volume. Readers interested in my reflections on a host of other issues may wish to consult my comprehensive publication list at https://law.yale.edu/sites/default/files/documents/faculty/phsvita.pdf

I wish to acknowledge the useful comments of the outside readers and the fine administrative assistance of Miriam Benson of the Yale Law School staff who helped me to pull these disparate writings together and assemble them in this book. I thank the original publishers of these essays for permission to republish them here. NYU Law School generously provided me an office and computer support.

* * *

Militant Moderation*

Back in 2006, I published a collection of writings under the title *Meditations of a Militant Moderate*. The alliterative appeal of the title aside, the idea was to celebrate a mode of thinking about public issues—fact-based, respectful of conflicting values, collaborative, solution-oriented—that seemed endangered. Today, this aspiration seems more elusive than ever.

---

* *American Purpose*, 3/16/2022; https://www.americanpurpose.com/articles/militant-moderation/

Our need for a more moderate form of discourse and politics is, alas, much more urgent today than it was in 2006. Then, the national conversation about politics was fraught, to be sure. President George W. Bush, whose victory in 2000 had depended on a few Supreme Court justices, was increasingly unpopular. The shock of September 11 was still fresh in our collective mind. The war in Iraq, after a lightening-swift initial victory (but no weapons of mass destruction to seize), was metastasizing into seemingly endless savagery throughout the Middle East and Afghanistan. Corporate scandals involving Enron and others had shaken public confidence in our business institutions. Congress, still smarting from the bitterness of a presidential impeachment and the scorched-earth tactics engineered by then-House Speaker Newt Gingrich, had become more partisan than at any time since the Civil War.

Our public discourse has steadily coarsened since then. In ideological and personal confrontations, martial analogies applied to domestic politics no longer seem hyperbolic. The animosity and vituperation that now divide partisans, fellow citizens, their neighbors—and even family members—have reached apparently unprecedented levels. Just before the 2020 elections, nearly 40 percent of Democrats and 40 percent of Republicans said that they would be somewhat or very upset at the prospect of their child marrying a person from the opposite political party. The sharp partisan divisions over Covid vaccinations and the sometimes violent divisions evident in the wake of January 6 have likely sharpened these divisions. Perhaps most alarming is the rising support throughout the system for partisan violence against political opponents. The almost routine resort to criminal sanctions against political opponents—used both by and against Donald Trump, former President and declared candidate for another term—is another sign of these extremist, "banana republic" tendencies.

This more open acceptance of violent rhetoric and behavior, and the inclination to criminalize political competition, are manifestly illiberal and antidemocratic; they tend to chill debate, stifle competition, discourage many civic-minded citizens from actively participating in public affairs, raise the stakes in decision outcomes, and seed the entire political realm with corrosive cynicism and mediocrity. Militancy there is aplenty, but it is not remotely moderate.

What, then, is the case for an alternative stance—moderation—toward fellow citizens who in their views, aspirations, and actions seem increasingly to be rejecting it? First, one must clarify what moderation means. We can begin by recalling—and rejecting—a famously pithy formulation proclaimed by presidential candidate Barry Goldwater in 1964: "Extremism in the defense of liberty is no vice," while "moderation in the pursuit of justice is no virtue." In a liberal democracy, both of these sentiments are wrong for one fundamental reason: the notions of justice and liberty have no uncontested meaning; they must always be defined through public debate over—and application to—specific situations that entail inescapable trade-offs among values that compete both normatively and empirically for our allegiance.

In contrast, the notion of militant moderation is both coherent and attractive—even though it does not dictate policy outcomes in specific disputes or on a left-right continuum. "Moderation" refers to an orientation to a substantive issue relative to other possible orientations to that issue, while "militancy" denotes a high level of conviction about how issues should be resolved, and a willingness to advocate and act on that conviction. Moderation might also include endorsing liberal means to conservative ends, or vice versa. So much for definitions.

But why might one think that moderation is a virtue in the first place? After all, we all know of complaisant people who will pay almost any price to avoid controversy. Some people, including certain politicians, seek compromise for its own sake. This stance might be because they believe (or act as if they believe) that the truth of any matter in dispute is always located somewhere in between contending positions. The same stance, however, might be for another reason—one sometimes held by decision-makers who have already invested lots of time and resources in trying to find a solution: They may believe that almost *any* solution is better than an impasse. On the other hand, radical evil and heroic goodness do exist; some extreme positions are actually correct; and even incorrect extremes can exert salutary pressures on status quos that rest on little more than political inertia and embedded injustice.

Today, the virtues of moderation in our politics and in civil society need more emphasis and celebration than perhaps at any point since the Vietnam War and Watergate. But again, what are those virtues? The defense of moderation in political and social life more generally goes back to Aristotle, who offered its (literally) classic defense. The nobility of individual character, he argued, depends on mediating between the antipodal excesses of human conduct and feeling to which we humans are inclined. For him, cowardice, rashness, surliness, and flattery are vices while courage and friendliness are virtues. Moderate temperament and disposition, in his view, are constitutive not only of private morality but of civic virtue and social health. His ideal of the golden mean was meant to cultivate the character needed by a good society and healthy polity.

Yet moderation is most valuable precisely when Aristotelian virtue is in short supply, which seems to be the case today when even teaching virtue in our public schools is hotly contested. Under current conditions, then, the case for moderation must be made mainly on policy grounds. When the questions at issue are daunting for political or substantive reasons, neither simple ideology nor simple morality provides much useful guidance for the hard work of problem-solving. Ideology (other than that of pragmatism) lacks the suppleness needed to apprehend and act upon complex, fluid social facts. Morality, for its part, usually cuts in more than one direction. Ideology and morality, then, can be useful starting points for pursuing policy solutions, but the roads that they mark quickly run out when they encounter complexity, conflict, and implementation challenges.

President Biden's experience so far in swiftly enacting and implementing certain of his policy priorities while failing on others reveals both the demands and the political virtues of a moderate course—in this case, necessitated by razor-thin majorities and with provisions that provide future protection to both parties. His huge American Rescue Plan won early passage despite its $1.9+ trillion price tag because it promised to spread the money to every congressional district and thus benefit a very broad swath of the American public, while spreading the costs over many years through more opaque, long-term deficit spending rather than through higher, more visible taxes in the short term.

In sharp but telling contrast, his Build Back Better plan and voting rights legislation have foundered because they raise sharp ideological and partisan issues—questions of both principle and electoral advantage. These are harder to compromise over (although incumbent-protecting electoral maps may foster such consensus). If any ground is to be gained in enacting these especially divisive bills, the legislators will probably have to focus on certain provisions—amending the Electoral Count Act, for example—that are more procedural in nature and whose partisan impacts are more likely to even out over time. In every way but rhetorically, Biden has had to abandon much of the progressive agenda—the Green New Deal, redistributive tax and social spending policies—that helped win him the Democratic nomination.

These forms of moderation fly under the flag of *incrementalism*, which is perhaps moderation's most familiar form in political life. But although moderation is ubiquitous, it is seldom exciting; it rarely makes the heart race or the spirit soar. Unlike scientists and engineers who often discover new facts and techniques enabling them to solve problems with large social payoffs, public policymakers must work with a limited set of familiar tools. They generally offer old wine in new bottles, as their opponents are only too eager to point out.

One can embrace militant moderation, then, for many reasons—none of them exhilarating, but all indispensable to the health of a complex, extraordinarily diverse democracy like ours. Today, powerful actors of all ideological stripes—from the 2020 election deniers on the Right to the "cancel culture" and systemic racism diehards on the Left—are all too eager to suppress that diversity through belligerent demands for Procrustean conformity to one or another view.

Moderate optimists might believe that the nation's political temperament remains firmly moored to the moderate liberal tradition famously celebrated by sociopolitical sages like Harvard's Louis Hartz and Arthur Schlesinger, Jr., in the 1950s and 1960s, which repudiated the presidential candidacies of both Goldwater and George McGovern. This tradition favored private, lightly regulated markets; a stable two-party system controlled by party professionals; a "civic religion" of constitutionalism and patriotism; strong roles for the states even in federally-run schemes; and a diverse, vital civil society of private firms, flourishing religions, solid families, robustly protected free speech, and a vast independent sector. Even Ronald Reagan and the Bush presidencies' nominal conservatism could fit fairly comfortably within this moderate, classically liberal framework.

That world survives today mostly in nostalgic memory. The two parties are weak, unable or unwilling to control their most extreme factions. The Trump presidency tested, and often crossed, vital constitutional guardrails, stretching the rule of law beyond recognition and often treating the government as his personal plaything. Trump's refusal to acknowledge his electoral defeat in the face of compelling evidence created a constitutional crisis and fostered an insurrection whose criminal character continues to haunt the nation. The Republican Party has ceased to be a loyal opposition even as it fosters treasonous conspiracy theories. Religious membership has withered, along with already fragile levels of family cohesion. The federal debt exceeds previous levels, with fiscal crises looming in Social Security and Medicare for which the only solutions are sacrifices—however modest—that the polity at present seems unwilling to make. Shared values seem scarce, and young Americans' knowledge about and commitment to nonviolent democracy is worryingly limited. The pandemic has revealed American society as sharply divided over the most fundamental precepts of public health and civic obligation to protect one's neighbors against a common threat.

The militant moderate's role today, then, is to stand athwart history and yell—what? Not "Stop!" (as William F. Buckley urged conservatives to do), nor "Bring on the revolution!" (as Leftists often exhort society to do). Experience teaches that these stances lead to uncertainty, disruption, futility, divisiveness, irrationality, and too often blood on the floor. A militant moderation urges us, instead, to reason together to determine which compromises must be made in the public interest, how their net benefits can be maximized and fairly distributed, and how they can then be implemented. Insisting in this technocratic spirit that the alternatives are likely worse is not a glorious battle cry. But it is the truth.

The Supreme Court's Abortion Decision

The Supreme Court's decision in *Dobbs v. Jackson Women's Health Organization* is destined to join a handful of other Court judgments in our nation's history that were so bitterly divisive that they became rallying cries for sustained, bellicose campaigns on both sides. *Dobbs* is not *Dred Scot*—Americans are deeply divided but will not take up arms against each other over this. Even *Brown v. Board of Education*, which held legally segregated systems of public education unconstitutional, isn't quite analogous. Massive resistance to *Brown* continued for many years, and not just in the South; even seven decades later, entrenched segregated housing patterns continue to confound its implementation.

Dobbs is different. It ensures that the abortion wars will be waged continuously and aggressively in every state, indeed in every community. In those states that ban abortion, women seeking to terminate their pregnancies but who lack other options such as interstate travel, mail-order abortifacients, or other self-induced remedies will seek to evade the ban as best they can while anti-abortion activists will further hone their harassment techniques. Many of these harassment techniques will raise their own legal issues, spawning new litigation. So much for the notion that *Dobbs* has "settled" even just the legal aspects of the abortion issue once and for all—and even in those states that purport to ban the practice entirely. *Dobbs* changed where the battles are being waged and thus the political terms of engagement.

One's analysis of the majority opinion in *Dobbs* would ordinarily track one's views of the merits of the underlying policy dispute—that is, the question of whether abortion should be widely, if not unconditionally, available to any woman who desires it. If one's answer to that question is yes, then the state's only legitimate role is to assure that the service is delivered to an informed woman by competent practitioners who can assure the woman's health and safety, and that unnecessary barriers to her access are dismantled. Abortion opponents, of course, disagree vehemently with this limited notion of the state's interest in the matter, insisting that the value of life is infinite and cannot be destroyed by even a flawless procedure. This assertion, of course, simply begs the question of when life begins for valuation purposes—a central issue in the abortion wars—and (for many antagonists) when a fetus is capable of feeling pain. At the same time, abortion opponents are actively seeking to narrow the existing exceptions such as for rape and incest even in restrictive laws.

I am an ardent advocate of women's broad access to abortion services, for the usual reasons. The decision to bear a child is among the most momentous—and private—decisions in one's life. To force that role upon an unwilling mother is among the most oppressive conditions that one can imagine; such coercion deeply offends core liberal values, and its consequences for the mother and the unwanted child—physical, psychological, marital, financial, and otherwise—may be very severe. Moreover, this interest of the mother is vastly greater when the fetus is the result of rape, incest, or other form of aggression or overreaching by the father who will eschew the burden of parenting the child. The state's interest in compelling her to give birth against her will is non-existent or at most trivial. Other than the military draft—which burden the draftee shares with many other similarly situated people and is ordinarily imposed by the government for nationally compelling reasons—or criminal punishment, I can think of no comparable burden that is imposed on free citizens. And when the state imposes this burden at the behest principally of religious groups deploying a theologically and historically dubious doctrine (I follow Garry Wills' analysis here)—namely, that the interests of a pre-viable fetus outweigh those of the mother who does not wish to carry it to birth—the state is acting even more illiberally and arbitrarily.

These reasons amply justify a woman's right to procure an abortion—but not as a constitutionally grounded right, much less a constitutionally compelled one. Instead, my argument supports a woman's access to abortion as a policy matter—one available not by constitutional fiat but instead by statute, regulation, insurance coverage, or otherwise in the marketplace. *Roe*'s constitutional grounding—in a liberty interest inferred from the Due Process Clause of the Fourteenth Amendment at a time when a women's independent civil and political rights more generally were essentially non-existent—was weak at its inception and only grew weaker in the ensuing years with the incessant attacks on both its reasoning and its result. Indeed, *Roe* itself suggested its novelty, which was obvious in the fact that no firmly-grounded precedents clearly foreshadowed it. Much has been made of the salient fact that leading constitutional scholars such as Yale's John Hart Ely denounced *Roe*'s reasoning from the outset, that it has never been well-settled law, and that the most prominent feminist lawyer in the country, the iconic Ruth Bader Ginsburg, disparaged it not just for its weak grounding but also for the political backlash that it immediately unleashed which interrupted the momentum of state-level liberalization. From a practical point of view, of course, *Roe* did enable countless women to obtain abortions legally for almost fifty years—an immense and precious achievement.

Henceforth, then, the struggle over abortion will be conducted largely, though not entirely, at the state level just as it largely was before *Roe* came down. (State-granted local autonomy is possible but seems unlikely.) Given *Dobbs* and the conservative majority that will control the House beginning in January 2023 and so produce an abortion policy stalemate in the Congress, this state-level focus is the best that pro-choice forces can hope for at present.

But quite apart from that tactical consideration, the states are also the constitutionally appropriate venue for the political struggles over abortion that are continually being waged. This state-centered locus of the abortion issue is fully consonant with our constitutional system—a position that puts me at odds with many other choice advocates who preferred *Roe*'s federal constitutional grounding. I maintain that *Roe*'s half-century of federal court regulation of abortion policy has blinded many choice advocates to a central fact: under our governmental scheme, abortion (if it must be regulated at all rather than simply being a matter between the woman and her provider, as I prefer) *should* be a state law matter. This is true even though access to abortion is a vital (literally) interest for women and their families.

A common misconception about our constitutional system is the notion that important policy areas are and ought to be presumptively regulated by federal law. This notion, which elevates the value of national uniformity above all other considerations, is simply false. In fact, disparate state laws govern many matters of arguably even greater significance to the well-being of individuals and families than abortion: access to medical care, welfare for the poor, housing, education, domestic relations, privacy, labor law and employment, police protection, finance, property rights, recreation, and numerous other elements of individual and family well-being. (To this pervasive pattern of state-dominant policymaking, the big exceptions are Social Security retirement and Medicare). Despite their fundamental importance to well-being, these matters are *not* controlled by federal law and policy, much less guaranteed by the federal Constitution, and still less by the fuzzy, highly-contested doctrine of substantive due process. To be sure, federal law often affects and funds these areas, but they are predominantly governed by state laws, policies, and politics that are often quite disparate. In our system, state variation is the default rule—and an argument for uniformity must affirmatively overcome that default.

It is far from obvious that abortion policy can do so. Even ardent abortion rights advocates like me must concede a key fact: access to abortion in a woman's state of residence is not obviously more fundamental to her well-being and autonomy than many of the state-varying, life-shaping interests just listed. It is politics that prevents enactment of more abortion-permissive policies in the recalcitrant states—the same force that also prevents access to decent education, health care, and many other life-shaping interests that the Constitution leaves to state discretion. As Justice Alito pointed out in his majority opinion, "the percentage of women who register to vote and cast ballots is consistently higher than the percentage of men who do so." Indeed, 61% of women now characterize themselves as "pro-choice" while only 33% consider themselves "pro-life." Recent public opinion has consistently supported the availability of abortion—probably never more so than now—though many supporters still favor some restrictions on it. To note this strong trend, however, is certainly not to minimize the desperate plight of abortion-seeking women in states like Mississippi who cannot afford to travel to more permissive states. One hopes that mail-order abortifacients and private philanthropy will be equal to their needs.

The legal-political action, then, has moved back to the states where it probably should have been all along—and where (as Justice Ginsburg famously noted) liberalization was gaining ground when the Court decided *Roe*. Advocates of choice have many powerful arguments to deploy in favor of abortion rights, arguments that have prevailed legislatively in a growing number of states since *Dobbs* came down. I pray, then, that the advocates will mobilize to punish the mostly male state legislators (all too often beneficiaries of gerrymandering) who vote to restrict abortion. Pro-choice states should facilitate access to abortion by out-of-state women whose own states prohibit abortions or make access unduly difficult. Federal law should firmly protect access to mail-order and FDA-regulated abortion products, abortion services on federal facilities, and other federally-influenced avenues to abortion services. Pro-choice people like me have relied far too long on the vanishing breed of pro-choice Supreme Court justices to do our political work for us.

Part 2

AMERICAN EXCEPTIONALISM

Introduction to Part 2

The notion that America is an exceptional society has always been fraught—and never more so than today. The features of American life that used to inspire pride in so many of its people, especially its individualist ethos, high standard of living, openness to immigrants, and constitutional stability, now arouse in many other Americans harsh criticism and sometimes even contempt. We are a far more sharply-divided country in 2023 than we were in 2005—more rancorous, more ideologically self-segregated, more apprehensive and suspicious of fellow Americans, more prone to violence and threatening confrontations, and more mistrustful of our national government and many other communal institutions than most close observers can recall.

This Part consists of three essays that speak to American exceptionalism. The first is an unpublished paper that I wrote for a festschrift honoring James Q. Wilson, perhaps the most astute, broad-gauged, rigorous, and influential academic analyst of American society until his death in 2012. I had the privilege of co-editing with Professor Wilson a volume, *Understanding America: The Anatomy of an Exceptional Nation* (2008), which exploited the work of leading social scientists in many different fields to analyze just how distinctive the United States is in a wide range of institutional and policy domains. The essay summarizes their findings and Wilson's (and my own) gloss on those findings. Although that book was published 15 years ago, virtually all of its general findings, as distinct from specific numbers, remain accurate today. The book did not mention Obamacare, which took effect gradually beginning in 2010. The second piece is a *New York Times* op-ed I wrote about Wilson upon his death highlighting some of his other contributions to our understanding of American society. The third, much shorter essay is my analysis of an article by noted political scientist Robert Putnam, author of *Bowling Alone*. That much-discussed book famously contended that Americans increasingly isolated themselves in self-referential nodules that tended to minimize the kind of "bridging" social capital that characterizes healthy democratic communities and institutions. My analysis here reflects on how Putnam's article bears on his earlier book's thesis and thus on an important ingredient of American exceptionalism.

The Anatomy of American Exceptionalism*

Is our country unique? That question is difficult for the citizens of any nation to think about objectively. As a matter of common observation, every nation is different, just as every culture and individual is. And it is a simple truism that a proud citizen of any society is likely to think that his home is special. "I believe in American exceptionalism," President Obama famously said in a 2009 press conference, "just as I suspect that the Brits believe in British exceptionalism and the Greeks believe in Greek exceptionalism."

But most champions of American exceptionalism make a different claim about America than Obama did: It is more exceptional than other Western democracies in the sense that it is more of an outlier along more important dimensions of national life. This fact, of course, does not necessarily mean that it is better; some of our distinctiveness, such as crime rates, is lamentable. But some object to even descriptive claims of American exceptionalism—and for understandable reasons: Such claims seem to carry more than a whiff of the sense of superiority that I have just disclaimed and that many critics of American national pride are keen to debunk. The U.S., they point out, is now in relative decline in areas that we once dominated, such as public education, public health, voter participation—and even some sports! Other nations have indeed caught up with or exceeded some of our achievements, and more may do so in the future. Some disparage our global pre-eminence, past or current, by rooting it in violence and treachery rather than in anything unique and admirable in our character, culture, or achievements. Our vaunted standard of living, they maintain, is not rising as fast as it once did, and in any event it was built on the backs of the poor; our attainments pale before our gross social inequalities. Slavery, Indian removal, racism, and nativism, among other excrescences, blight our history. Vulgarity is a trademark of our popular culture, and working-class Americans are dying earlier than before.

But do these critiques provide an adequate and accurate account of American exceptionalism? In 2008, I had the honor of exploring this question with James Q. Wilson, one of the greatest students of American society. A scholar of everything from urban politics to crime and law enforcement, bureaucracy, regulation, drug policy, the role of intellectuals in public life, equality and elitism, the state of the family, moral reasoning, and human nature, Wilson (who died in 2012) combined an empiricism of small but telling details with an eye for deep distinctions and trends. So when we determined

---

* Unpublished

to compile a reader on what made America exceptional, we quickly decided on a distinctly "Wilsonian" approach to the subject.

Instead of discussing exceptionalism on the high level of generality at which it is usually addressed, we asked some of America's leading social scientists (plus a keen observer from abroad) to analyze as many important aspects of our national life as would fit in a single volume. Using the most solid empirical evidence, each author analyzed in detail a single area of public policy, institutional structure, or culture. Where possible, they discussed how the U.S. compares with other wealthy democracies.

The resulting book, *Understanding America: The Anatomy of an Exceptional Nation*, was published in 2008, and was one of Wilson's final projects. It offers both a source of insight into what is and is not distinctive or unique about America, and an example of how to think about a complex question about which objective analysis is difficult—partly because only experts tend to have the necessary comparative expertise and partly because we are often too immersed in our own system to see its deep structures. Key to the methodology, as to Wilson's decades of scholarship, was an insistent empiricism. Although America's principles and premises are vital to a nation midwifed by a liberal, Enlightenment-inspired Constitution, we focused our authors on America's institutions, political and policy choices, and culture. That is how Wilson taught generations of students and readers to understand America.

Years after the publication of <u>Understanding America</u>, and after Wilson's death, the question of American exceptionalism is even more pertinent and perplexing than ever, as we and our liberal democratic allies go our separate ways in so many areas. Answers provided by a Wilsonian approach can teach us a great deal about our country and how to shape its future.

What follows is a kind of summary of one of Wilson's final reflections on American life, building on the research of some of the students and colleagues he most admired. This essay cannot examine every one of the book's chapters, but seeks to present most of its key findings as they bear on exceptionalism. It also reveals Wilson's methodology in analyzing large, complex questions of this kind, drawing on those whose mastery of the facts in diverse areas of American life can help guide us to an understanding of our elusive, sometimes unwelcome exceptionalism.

Our Exceptional Politics

The American political system is perhaps the most obvious institutional way in which the United States stands apart from the rest of the developed world. This is probably what most people think of when considering American exceptionalism.

The U.S. Constitution is not only the oldest constitution among major developed countries, it is also the most terse and has been formally amended very infrequently—the first ten times with the Bill of Rights in 1791 almost immediately after ratification, and then only 17 more times in the subsequent 225 years. Although a model for many democratic constitutions during the 18th, 19th, and part of the 20th centuries, it is now something of an outlier, aped by relatively few countries.

Our political system self-consciously rejected other constitutional arrangements; it is, in this way, exceptional by design. As political scientist Nelson Polsby noted in *Understanding America*, the Framers sought "emphatically not a presidential system, where the chief executive rules more or less alone; nor was it a parliamentary system where the 'government' arises via party organization from a relatively passive legislature. Rather, they created a system in which president and Congress, as separate entities, must cooperate in the making of laws and in practice actively compete in exercising influence over the subordinate agencies of the permanent government."

In this competition, Congress's numerous controls, both formal and informal, over an administration's policy and implementation make it unquestionably the most powerful legislature in the world, at least with respect to domestic policy. Its powers over foreign policy, although less formidable, are still extensive. The executive's ability to check and balance Congress—mainly through the veto power, appointment of senior positions over the bureaucracy, discretion in how to interpret and implement laws, special presidential advantages in conducting foreign relations, and the ability as the sole nationally elected official to exert greater influence over public opinion—is considerable, to be sure. But in most other democratic political systems, where the chief executive utterly dominates the parliament, such presidential checking powers are largely unnecessary.

Because Congress is so powerful compared not only with foreign legislatures but also with America's other political institutions, its internal structure matters far more than it would in other systems. Polsby, perhaps the leading scholar on Congress in his time, noted that in other systems, the more numerous, more representative chamber is usually the most important by far, whereas the opposite is true in the U.S., where the smaller, more severely malapportioned Senate is first among equals.

Polsby also emphasized the remarkable complexity of our political system. One dimension of this complexity is the intricate, opaque interaction of separated powers, federalism, and judicial power. A second is the number, length, and cost of elections. As Jack Citrin noted in his chapter on our political culture: "Americans have more opportunities to vote than citizens of any other democracy. Staggered elections at set times; primary elections for nominating candidates; elections for judges, local administrators, and boards; and direct democracy at the state and local levels make for frequent trips to the polls to fill out truly long ballots." Partly for this reason, Citrin argued, Americans vote at much lower rates than the citizens of virtually every other democracy. (Other reasons for lower American turnout include the use of plurality voting rules, with its many "wasted" votes, rather than proportional representation, as well as differences in how turnout is calculated.)

A third contributor to political complexity is "the sheer size of the decision-making community in American government," which Polsby illustrated with an "ambassador's problem":

"An ambassador newly arrived in most of the world's capital cities can, over a reasonable length of time, get to know virtually everybody who is instrumental to governmental decision-making. Even in the most advanced and civilized democratic nations, there is a not-too-large group of parliamentarians and civil servants who, to all intents and purposes, run the country.... In the United States, that number is dauntingly large.... in part because policymaking is not contained within the government, or even within the interplay between the two political branches of government, but spills out into a great variety of intermediary organizations."

If America's political system is exceptional, so is its political culture. In his contribution to the volume, Citrin, like countless observers of American life at least since Alexis de Tocqueville, marveled at the country's distinctively liberal tradition. That tradition, Citrin argued, is manifest in "the absence of a strong socialist party, the weakness of the labor movement, the acceptance of economic inequality, and the limited development of government programs in the area of welfare and health care." Also distinctively liberal is the robust civil society that dominates more areas of social life in America than in any other country, performing numerous functions, including philanthropy (discussed below), that elsewhere are mainly performed by government.

This is surely in part because Americans are far more individualistic than Europeans. Even blacks and Hispanics, whose status in the individualist social order tends to be lower, are more like white Americans than Europeans in their optimism, emphasis on personal responsibility, skepticism about government income guarantees, support for private ownership of business, and belief that poverty is due more to lack of individual motivation than to unfair treatment by society. "Consistent with these attitudes," Citrin found, Americans pay lower taxes than most Europeans (although such comparisons are complicated by European value-added taxes and other factors). America also spends less on transfer payments such as pensions, unemployment insurance benefits, family allowances, and child care than other countries and is virtually the only wealthy democracy without a government-supported universal health care system. Moreover, the financing of Social Security and health care programs reflects the commitment to personal responsibility: individuals and their employers contribute to insurance funds. And unlike many European countries, America restricts the access of even legal immigrants to social services such as Medicare, with widespread public support.

Citrin's reference to our health-care system, of course, was written before the Affordable Care Act, but the design of that law actually reinforces his point: It is not universal but relies on sanctions to induce voluntary enrollment; it is largely administered by private insurers; and it is only partly government-supported. The book's chapter on our healthcare system, contributed by David Cutler and Patricia Keenan, identifies many other unique (some uniquely dysfunctional) aspects of that system.

Meaningful political power is also distributed between different levels of government, so that when it comes to domestic policy ours is a genuinely federal system. The United States is not alone, of course, in having an emphatically federal system in which some power is shared between the national government and sub-national units. But Martha Derthick, in her discussion of federalism in the book, contrasts America's version both with Europe's unitary states and with its federal states which, except for Switzerland, "tend to treat federalism as a form of decentralized unitary government rather than as a product of formerly separate sovereigns." America's federalism is comparable to Australia's in some respects, and is in fact less decentralized than Canada's system. But American federalism has several other exceptional features.

One is how it affects the party system. Polsby observed that a "significant reason that Americans make do with only two major political parties, unlike voters in other much smaller western European countries, who are accustomed to have what they perceive to be a far greater range of partisan choices, is because each of the two American major parties is in most respects a loose coalition of state parties." These coalitions are all structured differently, and they produce "close to a one-hundred-party system."

A second distinctive aspect of American federalism is the relative size of the national and sub-national governments. State and local governments, Derthick noted in 2008, employ vastly more people than the federal government does, and they still do today: State and local government payrolls stood at just under 19.1 million workers in 2013, compared with 2.7 million civilian federal workers, counting both part-time and full-time employees. California's government—in terms of employees, tax revenues, and other indices of size—is larger than those of most nations. Approximately 85% of federal employees work outside the Washington, D.C. area.

Decentralized Policies

American federalism accounts for the unique decentralization of some of our key policy sectors. Education and law enforcement are perhaps the two most important examples. Paul Peterson's analysis of the educational system emphasizes that local control of the public schools extends not only to their administration but, even more important, to their being financed primarily through local property taxes. The latter produces great and unjust inequalities in per-pupil spending, inequalities that federal programs targeting low-income children alleviate only marginally. Although American public schools were once the envy of the world, they are now mediocre, despite the following facts: America's parents are better educated, earn more, and devote more time to their children's instruction; U.S. schools have far more financial resources per pupil (in constant dollars) than ever before; and the number of professionals per pupil within the school buildings has grown steadily so that classes in 2005 had, on average, 10 fewer students than they did in 1960. In sharp contrast is the comparative excellence of American institutions of higher education, particularly liberal-arts colleges and research universities—a sector dominated by private institutions to a far greater extent than anywhere else. (For-profit educational institutions are also far more common here than elsewhere.)

American law enforcement is also more decentralized than elsewhere, as Wilson noted in his own contribution to the volume:

> "In Europe, the criminal justice system tends to be centralized, with national police forces and government ministries that oversee law enforcement. Though Great Britain has fifty-two police departments, America has at least seventeen thousand and maybe more....In America, every city, county, and state has its own police department; every county and many cities have their own elected district or city attorney; and every state has its own correctional system."

The main consequence of this more decentralized law-enforcement system, Wilson argued, is that it is far more sensitive to public attitudes and pressures about crime, which helps to explain our greater propensity for "tough on crime" measures, including capital punishment, high incarceration rates, long sentences, and other policies.

The U.S. has lower rates of most property crimes than many other democracies do, but a much higher murder rate. Indeed, Wilson observed, "the rate at which Americans kill each other without using guns by relying instead on fists, knives, and blows to the head is three times higher than the non-gun homicide rate in England." The same difference in fatality rates exists between New York City and London even when the motive is a robbery and no gun is used. "To put it bluntly, Americans are a more violent people than are the British, though the latter have been trying hard to catch up."

Jonathan Caulkins and Mark Kleiman, in their contribution to the volume, noted two other differences between the U.S. and European approaches to crime, both related to drugs. Although Americans use roughly equivalent amounts of drugs and probably less alcohol than citizens of comparable developed nations, they consume much more of one drug, cocaine, which is associated with high levels of crime and violence. And our criminal-justice system arrests and imprisons more drug offenders than European systems do (although this gap may narrow in the future). This is, again, in large part because law enforcement in America is far more answerable to local pressure and public opinion than it is in most other democracies.

Many of these distinctive features of American life are reflected in the management and the work of the government. The actual public bureaucracy, particularly at the federal level, is much smaller relative to the economy in America than in other liberal democracies. But at the same time, our system of administrative law delegates enormous power and discretion to federal agencies under political conditions that make it unusually difficult, especially when compared to European bureaucracies, for officials to establish the democratic legitimacy of their actions. Two of those conditions have already been mentioned: the separation of powers, which multiplies the sources of influence over the administrative system, and the fragmentation of decision-making, which leaves to state and local officials many of the most important public functions, including education, land-use regulation, criminal justice, transportation, tort law, occupational licensure, and much more.

At the same time, however, our federal bureaucracy is run to an exceptionally large extent by political appointees, who work to advance the cause of the elected president—and therefore tend to make the system more answerable to the public will but less independent and so in important ways less trusted. There are 3,000 politically appointed positions in the executive branch at the federal level; about half of those are senior officials—and these numbers have grown dramatically over time. This "layering" of political appointees over career bureaucrats contrasts sharply with many parliamentary governments where only the very top officials' positions change hands with a new government. In Denmark, for example, there is only a single political appointee—the minister—above the career civil servants in most departments of government. In the U.K., career civil servants operate just below the ministers and a small number of aides. As Donald Kettl observed in his chapter in the volume, this layering produces serious problems of competence and continuity in American government:

One is that some appointees lack detailed knowledge and long-term experience in the agencies they are charged with managing. The second is that, by dipping several layers into the bureaucracy, the risk of conflicts with career administrators multiplies. Finally, many of these political appointees serve for relatively short periods of time—often just eighteen months or a little more.

Two other exceptional aspects of American bureaucracy are officials' non-elite recruitment and training (compared, for example, with the U.K. and France), and the large extent to which the ordinary courts, which are constitutionally empowered to check the behavior of the other two branches and which afford easy access to those who want to challenge agency action, play a strong role in shaping administrative decisions.

In *Understanding America*, legal historian Lawrence Friedman identified a number of features of the legal system that distinguish ours from those in other developed democracies—including the dominant role of lawyers in American public and private life, a point emphasized by Tocqueville 180 years earlier. Americans' deep-seated suspicion of government, together with a highly fragmented and decentralized legal order, assigns vast authority to federal and state courts to constrain the actions of both agencies and legislatures—and in a real sense, to make law—through expansive judicial review. With the largest legal sector in the world (1.3 million lawyers in 2015 and growing faster than the overall population), it is also a system that is remarkably accessible to ordinary citizens and strongly oriented toward asserting and protecting individual rights at the expense of governmental and social claims.

More than in any other country, our legal system broadly protects expression of all kinds—not only political advocacy but speech-like behavior (like picketing and message-bearing clothing), commercial advertising, and defamatory, indecent, abusive, and outrageous utterances as well. And our legal culture is famously litigious and adversarial. As Friedman explains:

> "Other countries may have as much law as the United States...but they have much less lawyering. They are also less rights-conscious. They give more power and discretion to administrative agencies, and they make it harder to challenge those agencies in court. The vast proliferation of jokes about American lawyers, a genre which simply does not exist elsewhere, ironically suggests the greater salience of lawyers in the United States. Only the United States feels it is in the grip of a litigation crisis."

And it is not just the structure but also the core doctrines of our legal system that differ significantly from those of other nations, including those with common-law systems like ours. In the U.S., for example, far higher damage recoveries attract litigants from abroad if they can establish jurisdiction here, and U.S. public law is an outlier in rejecting proportionality as an explicit judicial methodology for rights adjudications (except in a few areas, including the First Amendment).

America's public life—our political institutions and practices, political culture, and legal system—is thus unique in some important respects that both reflect and shape our national character. As Robert Wuthnow explains in his contribution to the volume, Americans are also the most religious among large Western nations, although "researchers question whether religion here is quite as strong as such comparisons might suggest." Our religious practices reflect many of the very same features that mark the U.S. as exceptional in the secular realm: market competition, individualism, ethnic and racial diversity, privatism, ideological division, localism, evangelical and moralizing movements, global reach, and consumerism. Americans shop around for congregations, treating religion as a kind of consumption good. "American religion," Wuthnow observes, "is big business."

The sheer number and density of non-Western religions found here such as Hinduism and Taoism also set us apart. Much of this is due to immigration (although "attendance at worship services among foreign-born Americans is actually lower" than for the native-born). Religion's effect on American politics is profound. More than in other liberal democracies, "[p]undits and politicians show an almost inexhaustible interest in what preachers may be saying about public issues. They wonder whether one political party or another is better at mobilizing its religious base, and whether the personal conduct of public officials violates religious teachings."

Haves and Have-nots

Economic distinctiveness parallels our unique political system. In his contribution to *Understanding America*, Benjamin Friedman showed that the American economy is unlike those of other advanced democracies in achieving a sustained record of growth, job creation, technological innovation, capital investment, and a widespread distribution of ownership.

He attributed these achievements to a number of factors. First is the remarkable flexibility and competitiveness of American enterprises. Second, a relatively unregulated, highly mobile labor market imposes few constraints on firms, and that freedom rewards workers who can shift from dying industries to growing ones. And third, America is home to the world's leading financial markets, which in turn depend on sound regulation and supervision of financial institutions.

The American regulatory environment, compared with its more intrusive foreign counterparts, encourages entrepreneurship, new business formation, and job growth. America's comparative openness to immigration also contributes to these economic strengths, albeit by holding down low-skill wages somewhat. (Some critics believe that it also encourages recklessness and illegality.) Finally, a substantial share of American economic output is provided outside the for-profit market economy in the non-profit sector. The result of all this is a standard of living that has ranked at or near the world's highest for decades, far outranking all other countries of major size and geopolitical importance.

Friedman explained the features of America's economy that enable it to produce so much more per person than that of France, Germany, or Japan:

> "One fairly consistent part of the story...[is] simply that Americans work more....Of those who are of normal working age, more are employed in paying jobs than is true on average in the other G-7 countries, and those who hold jobs put in more time working....The productivity of American workers [is] also greater than that of workers in the other advanced economies, although less so than the simple difference in output would imply. One influence that helps make American workers more productive, even compared to those in Western Europe, is that they receive more schooling. On average Americans have nearly three more years of education than citizens of the other six G-7 countries.... American workers also have the advantage of more capital with which to do their jobs....[which] well exceeds what workers in any of the other G-7 economies have."

For example, Friedman noted, America had accumulated more than twice as much information-technology capital per person than the average of the other G-7 economies. He went on to explain the institutional reasons why America's economy exhibits these features more than other countries do. The American workplace operates under far fewer restrictions of the kind that make companies in Europe particularly reluctant to hire new workers. Labor unions are a far less influential force in the U.S. than in other countries: Only 14% of U.S. workers are covered by collective-bargaining agreements compared with more than half on average in the other G-7 countries, including more than 80% in Italy and more than 90% in France.

The income and other economic support that non-working citizens receive from government is also both less available and less generous in the U.S. than in most other advanced economies. Income earned from working is typically taxed at lower rates in America than in most other advanced countries.

Americans' intense work effort may also reflect deep cultural preferences. Finally, U.S. financial markets are larger, more diversified, more decentralized, more participatory, and thus operate more efficiently to raise capital than those elsewhere, and the American regulatory and monetary regimes reinforce these advantages. Such advantages, of course, do not obviate the significant challenges that the American economy faces. But they do help make America distinct—and likely explain why our recovery from the Great Recession has been more robust than those of other OECD countries.

Differences in taxation and labor policies are closely tied to differences in the nature of the safety net and social insurance, and these in turn reflect differences in the public's tolerance for inequality. The United States is plainly an exception on these fronts. Measuring and comparing poverty and inequality in different countries is a difficult task, for many reasons explained by Gary Burtless and Ron Haskins in their contribution to *Understanding America*, but by most criteria the U.S. is much more unequal than other OECD countries. To cite one measure, almost 11% of Americans received a net income below 40% of the U.S. median income—much more than the average percentage in other rich countries. Nor did using a higher poverty threshold change the result much. Our low-income population received smaller incomes than the poor in nearly all the other industrial countries, and the rich received much higher incomes than the rich anywhere else. The U.S. also had a high proportion of children in single-parent families, where they are more likely to be poor than if they lived with two parents.

Much the same is true of intergenerational mobility: The U.S. has only moderate income and occupational mobility compared with other rich countries, although including in the mobility calculations the large income gains by immigrants from poorer countries would reduce this disparity. The native-born, however, do not enjoy exceptional opportunities for upward mobility compared with people born in other rich countries. Particularly for those at the bottom of the income distribution, the United States is less successful than other rich countries in equalizing opportunities for children.

And by international standards, the programs the U.S. government has established to reduce poverty are relatively small. Among the seven largest industrial countries, the United States spends the smallest percentage of its national income on direct government provision of social-welfare benefits; we prefer instead to use, much more than those other countries do, a variety of tax preferences to induce the private provision of welfare benefits, especially health care and occupational pensions. And if anything, our welfare system has become more different from Europe's in recent decades, especially in the wake of the most significant modern reform of welfare, in 1996. "Although some European countries have moved toward the U.S. policy of pushing single mothers to work, no European government has been willing to impose the tough measures that are now common in the United States, such as time limits on benefit receipt or cessation of benefit payments for mothers who refuse to work," Burtless and Haskins noted.

Political support for government redistribution is much greater in Europe than in America. Americans care far more about alleviating poverty among those they consider deserving of help than they care about reducing inequality per se. These differences of attitude are clearly crucial to America's distinctive social policies. Burtless and Haskins pointed out that, "while almost two-thirds of Americans agree with the statement that 'income differences in the United States are too large,' policies aimed at reducing income differences command relatively little popular support." When Americans are asked to report their priorities, inequality ranks quite low, and much lower than it does in other advanced democracies. "A large majority of Americans believe that individuals should bear primary responsibility for supporting themselves," they note, "whereas voters in other rich countries are more inclined to believe that governments have an obligation to assure that everyone is provided for." But Americans also believe that upward mobility is much more prevalent in our country than it actually is—our faith in mobility stands out among developed nations, while our actual levels of mobility do not.

The flip side of lesser government support for the poor when compared with Europe's social programs is America's truly exceptional private philanthropy. As Arthur Brooks pointed out in his contribution to the volume, all developed economies have non-governmental sectors, but what sets the United States apart is the extent to which this sector provides key public services funded by massive private support. In the late 1990s, he notes, Europe's largest non-profit sector (in the United Kingdom) was about 14% of the size of the U.S. sector, and this difference has likely grown since then.

Even more exceptional, the vast majority of support for the U.S. non-profit sector is purely voluntary: Private charitable donations totaled more than $358 billion in 2014, about 2% of GDP, representing an increase for the fifth year in a row. About three-quarters of this voluntary giving is from living individuals; the rest comes from foundations, corporations, and bequests. As Brooks noted, "No developed country approaches American giving and volunteering levels." On a per-capita basis, Americans generally give about three times what the French do and seven times what the Germans do.

"These differences," Brooks wrote, "are not attributable to demographic characteristics such as education, income, age, sex, or marital status." And they reflect several deep differences between the U.S. and comparable societies in Europe. For example, government's larger role in European countries "crowds out" private philanthropy and volunteering more than in our less statist country. Brooks cited economists' estimates that a dollar in public support for social-welfare services displaces at least 25 cents in private giving and reduces private voluntarism as well. Another difference has to do with religious belief, which is the single most important predictor of charitable activity. In 2000, religious people were 10 percentage points more likely than secularists to give money to explicitly non-religious charities and 21 points more likely to volunteer, Brooks noted. Conservative citizens tend to be more charitable than liberal ones; people who believe that the government should not equalize incomes gave, on average and after controlling for demographic variables, four times as much money and other forms of philanthropy to charity as those who believe that the government should do more equalization.

Who We Are

Essential to the exceptional American belief in mobility is the American immigrant story. Even now that immigration is once again at the center of heated debates, the American approach to immigration and its place in our cultural self-understanding stands out among those of other nations. Indeed, if there is any one aspect of American life that even exceptionalism skeptics would concede is exceptional, it is immigration. As I noted in my own contribution to the volume, the U.S. is by far the leading destination for immigrants. The foreign-born population now exceeds 40 million, and the proportion of foreign-born Americans is roughly back at the record-setting 14% first reached a century ago (before sharp constraints on immigration brought it down to less than half that). A million more immigrants, the vast majority of them authorized, now arrive each year. About half the arrivals to the U.S. since 1965 have come from Latin America and more than a quarter from Asia—ethnic backgrounds very different from those of the national population a half-century ago.

A number of other OECD countries now have similarly high percentages of foreign-born residents, but for almost all of them—Australia since the late 1950s, Sweden since the 1990s—this has been a relatively recent development. By the same token, ethnic diversity in some of those countries is also great today, though not as great as ours.

Americans generally support legal immigration, not just because so many identify as the descendants of immigrants, but also because of the immense social gains that most Americans think it has produced: economic expansion and competitiveness, population growth, cultural diversity and enrichment, invigoration of religious communities, promotion of tolerance, a solidarity that is civic rather than primordial, and much more. They tend to admire legal immigrants both as a group and as individuals, and believe that they have been good for the country—although opinions about unauthorized immigrants are of course far more negative.

The pace of immigrants' social integration also sets the United States apart. By any definition, it is proceeding rapidly, although at rates that differ from group to group (and indeed from subgroup to subgroup). The U.S. economy, both formal and informal, produces a very low immigrant unemployment rate, unlike European economies where immigrants fare far worse. Hispanics and Asians and Pacific Islanders in the U.S. live longer than whites. Immigrants now acquire English fluency at roughly the same rate as earlier waves did. American-born children of immigrants learn English at school and strongly prefer it to their parents' native language; virtually all members of the second generation speak it proficiently by the end of high school; and the third generation is largely monolingual in English—and likes it that way. American law also makes citizenship relatively easy to acquire (and almost impossible to lose), which facilitates immigrants' integration and strengthens their new national identity.

Another significant index, as well as a key cause, of immigrant assimilation is the high rate of interethnic marriage, particularly between whites and Asian women and Hispanics, and the rapid residential integration of those groups into white-majority urban and suburban communities. Also important to their integration are the allure and ethnic diversity of a powerful mass media and popular culture, and the receptiveness of America's religious communities to newcomers who are re-invigorating and often transforming these communities.

Most unusual, from a comparative perspective, is the fact that—unlike virtually all other immigrant-receiving countries—no avowedly nativist political party or significant anti-immigrant movement existed in the U.S until Donald Trump's takeover of the Republican Party. With that very important exception (whose durability remains unclear), few prominent Republicans had supported restricting legal immigration below today's relatively high levels—although they all insist on more careful screening of refugees and other processed immigrants for terrorist ties.

Finally, America's unique success in integrating immigrants is also evidenced by the experience of Muslims, who express far more alienation in European societies than they do here. Some of this experiential and attitudinal difference reflects demographic patterns in the two regions. Muslims in the U.S. are highly diverse in terms of countries and regions of origin, languages, and even race (half of native-born Muslims, 20% of the total American Muslim population, are black). American Muslims are also more prosperous, educated, politically active, and integrated into the larger society (including in terms of citizenship) than their European counterparts; indeed,

American Muslims equal or exceed the income and education levels of the general population. The greater religiosity of Americans in general, noted earlier, makes for a more congenial environment for devout Muslims (and other immigrants) than the far more secular societies of Europe. The lower barriers in the U.S. to family-based immigration, entrepreneurship, and employment growth also play their part, as does the now-longstanding celebration of ethnic diversity in America.

This celebration of difference points to another important cultural distinction between the United States and many comparable nations. In her contribution to the volume, cultural historian and critic Martha Bayles pointed out that American popular culture is extraordinarily diverse and rich—and always has been. In a sense, this cultural diversity is itself one of our chief exports. It arouses some hostility, of course, particularly in more traditionalist (especially Muslim) societies, but it has been immensely influential in shaping a truly global popular culture.

The vibrancy of our popular culture has a lot to do with the history, character, and organization of the American mass media. And these, as S. Robert Lichter showed in his contribution to the volume, are all quite different than in other advanced democracies. The First Amendment, and the tradition of freedom from government censorship that produced it, have no real counterpart abroad: "In Europe, most newspapers and magazines began as organs of ideologically aligned groups such as political parties and churches, with which they retained connections into recent times. In the United States, most publishers had shed their partisan ties by the mid-nineteenth century. They were much more concerned with profit margins than group attachments," Lichter noted. "[T]he mass media in the United States have primarily been privately owned businesses....[which] have enjoyed unequalled freedom and government support, and electronic media have been regulated relatively lightly." He concluded that current conditions in the communications industry are making the American media "simultaneously more decentralized, diverse, competitive, and contentious" compared with Europe.

Wilsonian Exceptionalism

These general descriptive terms—decentralized, diverse, competitive, and contentious—actually describe what makes America unique on a whole host of fronts. Stepping back from the particulars, and from the descriptive analyses offered up by experts in specific segments of American life, one is struck by the way in which what makes America exceptional seems, again and again, to be its resistance to being homogenized and regulated by government.

Not only in his work on *Understanding America* but also in his vast body of work spanning half a century, James Q. Wilson frequently emphasized the significance of this diversity and libertarian streak. He drew subtle distinctions and analyzed the causes of exceptional outcomes while cautioning against over-generalizing from them. His brand of social science stayed close to the ground—to the facts, to the people's attitudes and behaviors, to complicated motives and patterns—rather than trafficking in simple explanations and easy abstractions. This distinctly Wilsonian approach to exceptionalism is especially valuable today. It demands that we carefully consider the many distinctive—and in some cases, unique—features of American life, while urging us to be skeptical about their applicability to other societies. The empirical evidence summarized here and presented extensively in *Understanding America* shows that, however one defines "exceptional," the term unquestionably applies to us in a purely descriptive sense.

Normatively, the picture is surely mixed. Some of our country's exceptional features—like its political stability, decentralization, competitiveness, successful integration of immigrants, vibrant media, and remarkably robust non-profit sector supported by unparalleled private philanthropy—are praiseworthy. Others, like our growing economic inequality, violence, child poverty, adversarial legal culture, and demoralized public bureaucracy, are deplorable. Fortunately, much of this is remediable, as Wilson would have reminded us. But, I think he would have added, some of it probably is not.

Remembering James Q. Wilson[*]

James Q. Wilson, who died last week at the age of 80, was widely considered the pre-eminent political scientist of the last 50 years. Curiously, the commentary surrounding his death has largely focused on his justly famous "broken windows" theory—and to a lesser extent, his penetrating 1993 book, *The Moral Sense*—yet these works are only a small part of his extraordinary contribution to sound thinking about government, politics and public policy.

Even more important, perhaps, are his groundbreaking analyses—first elucidated when he was just 30—of the most fundamental features of political behavior, whether by parties, bureaucracies, regulatory agencies, or other organizations. Unlike his work on law enforcement and other specific policies, these analyses are structural; they apply, other things being equal, to all

---

[*] *New York Times*, 3/10/2012; https://www.nytimes.com/2012/03/11/opinion/sunday/remembering-james-q-wilson.html

public policies and all political acts. Just as a powerful microscope illuminates the biological world, Mr. Wilson's writings provide enormous insight into how the political world works.

In the field of social science, where good theories generating important testable predictions are exceptionally rare, no one else has come close to matching his achievements.

In this work, Mr. Wilson showed that all organizations—political parties, social clubs, environmental groups, companies, and regulatory agencies—share one essential trait: They must attract the resources necessary to achieve their goals and survive (he called this "organizational maintenance") by offering incentives or inducements to join and support them.

He distinguished three types of incentives—solidary (that is, incentives that promote solidarity), material, and purposive—and he theorized that the specific type of incentive distributed by a particular group both shapes and constrains its behavior and effectiveness.

Thus, the Junior League provides solidary incentives by emphasizing the social status of and personal interactions among its members, while companies provide material incentives—i.e., money and other economic value—which buy them more tactical flexibility. In contrast, the Sierra Club's incentives are purposive, attracting members through its programmatic and visionary ideals. But such incentives also *constrain* purposive groups, which may lose support if they compromise those ideals by being too pragmatic.

In two early books, Mr. Wilson deployed this theory, along with intensive fieldwork, to show how such incentives help explain—and predict—the behavior of diverse political organizations. In his 1960 book, *Negro Politics*, he compared two diverse styles of politics of the most prominent black congressmen of the day, William Dawson and Adam Clayton Powell Jr. Mr. Dawson, loyal to Chicago Mayor Richard J. Daley, was a classic machine politician who attracted low-income voters by distributing material favors controlled by the machine—jobs, connections, economic benefits—while assiduously avoiding more controversial, policy-oriented appeals that might divide his constituency and displease ideologically diverse colleagues. Mr. Powell, from New York City, was the exact opposite: a flamboyant firebrand, he often played the race card to win re-election but was isolated in Congress and accomplished little programmatically. Mr. Wilson's analysis of the relationship between different organizational-political styles and outcomes helps explain, among other things, the challenges that minority politicians everywhere face today.

Two years later, in *The Amateur Democrat*, Mr. Wilson compared the disparate organizational strategies of Democratic political clubs in Los Angeles, New York and Chicago. The Chicago clubs were essentially cogs in Mayor

Daley's materialistic machine. The New York clubs were divided between organizational regulars and insurgent reformers—groups driven (and riven) by different incentive systems in a city whose politics, unlike Chicago's, could not centralize power enough to control policy outcomes.

The political style of the Los Angeles clubs was the most striking, as it prefigured a new kind of politics that has largely defined the Democratic Party ever since: it elevated the intra-party influence of "amateurs" over professional politicians, demanded ethnic and gender balance in internal party affairs, mistrusted central leadership and (until recently) avoided broad coalition building with business interests. This more ideological, protest-type mode (so evident in today's Republican Party as well) made it very difficult for them to unify and aggregate the power needed to govern effectively in a decentralized political system like ours.

Mr. Wilson later extended these theories to bureaucracy and regulation. In his 1989 work, *Bureaucracy*, he drew on numerous examples to show how bureaucracy is not one thing but many things, and that different agencies must deploy different incentive and task structures, which in turn explain a great deal of how they work, including how they define and pursue their goals, bargain with other groups, recruit expertise, and often fail. Likewise, in his 1980 book, *The Politics of Regulation*, he developed a new political taxonomy of regulation linked to a theory of how regulators build political support and manage their organizational constraints. This was more than a theory; he used it to predict, with stunning accuracy, how agencies would act in different situations.

Most impressive, however, is how Mr. Wilson succeeded in using these rigorously academic approaches to educate mass audiences, putting him in a small pantheon of public intellectuals with his friends Daniel Patrick Moynihan and Irving Kristol. In today's fraught times, we need his wisdom more than ever.

In Diversity We (Sorta) Trust[*]

America's unique level of diversity is widely celebrated, especially among well-educated, cosmopolitan people. Political leaders from both parties, professors and pundits of all stripes, savvy business executives, and most other members of the public believe that it is a major source of America's strength, dynamism, and creativity.

---

[*] *The American Lawyer*, December 2007

In truth, racial and ethnic diversity have little popular support outside the United States and Canada. The diversity ideal appears to be a distinctively, if not uniquely, American (or at least North American) theme. most of the democracies that now tolerate ethnic diversity have done so only recently—and perhaps only temporarily, until their anti-immigrant forces can mount an effective counterattack. Even in the U.S., diversity-mongering is a recent innovation, dating only to the aftermath of the civil rights movement in the late 1960s. Many Americans still oppose diversity, while many others support it only because they assume that it will be merely a temporary condition. Newcomers, they suppose, will quickly assimilate to American ways, shedding their distinctive ones. In most cases, they are right.

I am firmly convinced that ethno-racial diversity is good for American society, and that the law should protect it. This conviction, however, is more an article of my faith in the vitality and inclusiveness of American democracy and the rule of law than it is an unassailable fact. Reasons for skepticism abound. Nothing could be clearer, for example, than the timeless record of diversity-generated war, social conflict, enduring hatreds, oppression of "outsider" groups, and murderous communal violence, sometimes on a colossal scale. Just in the last century, the Armenian genocide, the Holocaust, the Muslim-Hindu carnage in India after partition, and the recent ethnic wars in Northern Ireland, the Balkans, Rwanda, and Congo remind us that 250 years after the Age of Enlightenment, the dark side of diversity is very much with us.

Are Americans right to think that we are somehow different, that we can escape the carnage and conflict that diversity has wrought in countless other societies since the beginning of time? Few questions are more vital for our society's future.

Optimists like me can cite our dedication to the equality protections of our Constitution (at least the modern, post–civil rights version), our rising levels of education and cosmopolitanism, our widespread ethos of tolerance, the fragmentation of political power, and the merciful absence of communal violence since the 1960s. (I am not including the assault on the Capitol on January 6, 2021, which occurred many years after this was written). Where diversity is concerned, American society seems to be a great, if incomplete, success story. Now, into this extraordinarily sensitive and important debate, comes Robert Putnam. A widely-respected political scientist at Harvard University's Kennedy School of Government, Putnam is the author of a much-discussed book, *Bowling Alone*, published in 1995. In that book, Putnam analyzed the nature of "social capital," which he defined as "social networks and the associated norms of reciprocity and trustworthiness." Putnam emphasized the enormous value of these networks, both for those who are in them, and for the rest of us. His boldest claim, drawn mostly from survey data, was that America's stock of social capital had significantly declined, that Americans who used to congregate and interact in communal activities (e.g., bowling leagues) were now "bowling alone." This claim was, and remains, highly controversial. For example, Putnam's critics cited the growth of soccer teams, book clubs, religious communities, and the like, arguing that social capital had not declined but merely changed form.

Putnam, who had speculated that increased TV watching might be reducing social capital, is now testing other causal theories. In a new article, he brings a mountain of social science data to bear on how diversity affects social capital. His core finding? As immigration and ethnic diversity increase, social capital and solidarity decrease.

An earlier generation of social scientists, Putnam points out, had been more optimistic. They advanced a "contact" theory, which posited that more intensive interaction among groups would foster greater trust, harmony, and feelings of community, as people learned that "we are all the same under the skin." Instead, Putnam concludes, the evidence seems to support a "conflict" theory, which holds that greater physical proximity among different ethnic groups causes increased suspicion among them, and a retreat to the security of narrower in-group loyalties. Putnam's most important and unexpected finding is that the more ethnically diverse a community is, the less people tend to trust others, including members of their own ethnic group in their own neighborhoods. This pattern, moreover, holds for every demographic and ethnic group and every definition of neighborhood. It also holds regardless of the degree of economic inequality within or among the groups. In Putnam's words, "inhabitants of diverse communities tend to withdraw from collective life, to distrust their neighbors, regardless of the color of their skin, to withdraw even from close friends, to expect the worst from their community and its leaders, to volunteer less, give less to charity and work on community projects less often, to register to vote less, to agitate for social reform more but have less faith that they can actually make a difference, and to huddle unhappily in front of the television."

Nevertheless, Putnam remains optimistic that ethnic diversity may eventually build social capital rather than erode it. He speculates that although many Americans retreat in the face of ethnic diversity, this may change over time as people become more comfortable with it. But where might this comfort come from if they are busy hunkering down? Putnam suggests that ethnic identity may give way to, or at least coexist with, more overarching identities such as occupation, consumption patterns, and neighborhood, that make ethnicity less salient to people. Citing improved race relations in the military, increased religious tolerance, and rising rates of ethnic intermarriage, Putnam contends "that in the short run there is a trade-off between diversity and community, but that over time wise policies (public and private) can ameliorate that trade-off." As examples of such policies, he mentions building more public facilities for common use, aiding local communities, encouraging churches to be more inclusive, and offering greater support for English instruction for immigrants.

Some of Putnam's readers are more skeptical. Political scientist James Q. Wilson reminds us that neighborhoods—where social capital must largely be built—are different than the military, churches, or professional sports (where integration has also been successful). Unlike those domains, he argues, neighborhoods lack the authority and discipline to induce people to desire more diversity there. He cites evidence—including Putnam's findings, economist Thomas Schelling's modeling of how neighborhoods' ethnic composition often changes to produce even less integration than their residents may want, and my own analysis of legally mandated residential integration by race and class in Yonkers—for the proposition that "people enter into more useful and fulfilling social networks in ethnically homogeneous areas."

Putnam's work is very important in providing a firm empirical confirmation of what many close students of diversity thought we already knew. Organizational economists, for example, have shown that diversity can raise the decision and governance costs of corporations, worker-owned firms, cooperatives, and nonprofit groups. If social capital manages to form in such organizations, the chronic indecision and embedded conflict generated by this diversity will likely squander it.

The truth is that the value of diversity, like the value of most everything else, is in the eye of the beholder. It is an acquired taste, and its attractiveness depends on social context. Those of us who celebrate it have a hard time understanding why others might find it threatening or disturbing or even hateful. As Putnam shows, however, this reaction is not necessarily racist or ethnocentric (although it may be); once triggered, it can cause one to turn away even from members of one's own group.

What does all this have to do with law? A great deal, as it turns out. Managing diversity wisely while also building, or at least maintaining, social capital is among the most compelling and difficult tasks facing all societies today. To accomplish this vital goal, we have a number of different but related tools to work with: politics, law, markets, social norms, and a wide variety of civil society institutions such as families, voluntary associations, and education. Each of these tools has its distinct advantages and disadvantages, of course, which is why we often deploy several, and sometimes all, of them when attempting to solve complex social problems like diversity-magnified conflict. The trick, however, is to combine them optimally in light of the nature and magnitude of the specific problem being addressed.

Law is essential for this task, but law—for a variety of reasons that lawyers understand very well—can be heavy-handed and counterproductive. Where the delicate task of diversity management is concerned, law must be used as a scalpel, not a bludgeon. Broadly speaking, law can do eight things with diversity: Law can import and assimilate it (as with immigration policy). Law can define and certify it (as with affirmative action). Law can subsidize diversity (as with housing) and mandate it (as with legally required integration). Law can protect existing and emergent diversities (under the First Amendment) and exploit them for the good (by using existing religious and other diversities and voucher-type programs to promote public policy goals, such as increasing the choice and quality of education).

My own study of diversity management in the U.S. suggests to me that the law is most legitimate and effective when used to import and assimilate diversity and to protect and exploit existing diversities. The best examples of the latter are laws that promote competition and that prohibit invidious discrimination. Law is least effective in managing diversity when the government seeks to define, certify, subsidize, and mandate it.

Where its goals are to manage diversity and build social capital, law should wherever possible create (or unleash) positive incentives rather than impose coercive and inevitably crude rules. For example, government gives tax-free status to nonprofit associations, which can then experiment with different types of associational and programmatic models, rather than having government choose the "best" model and then regulate it. Rules will be necessary, however, to protect diversity against discriminatory and monopolistic conduct. These principles are especially important in a liberal society like ours that relies so heavily on individual choice and market dynamics. Americans most resist government intervention in areas that they consider deeply private—notably, the decision to live in one neighborhood rather than another, and to interact with some people rather than others. (The fact that the government heavily subsidizes such housing choices does not much affect most Americans' view that this choice is essentially private.) More generally, the same is true of our choices about how much diversity we want, of which kind, with which individuals, and through which interactions.

Much in American culture—our individualism, our immigration, our religiosity, our First Amendment—demands and nourishes diversity. But we must struggle to understand what diversity actually means, how much it costs, whether and how law can effectively manage it, and when other social processes might do it better. The bad news is that we have only begun to ask these immensely difficult questions; Putnam's data should inform our thinking. The good news is that no other society in history has been better equipped to answer them than twenty-first-century America.

Part 3

CIVIC DISCOURSE

Introduction to Part 3

Civic (and civil) discourse is the grease that lubricates the gears of democracy. For Americans to respect, deliberate, and transact with one another, we must communicate meaningfully in both public and private domains. In the preface to this book, I discussed what this type of communication entails and why I have sought to promote and practice it. The moniker "militant moderate" simply attests to the importance I ascribe to this kind of communication and why I believe that the future of our sacred democracy depends on it.

This Part features thirteen articles, most of them op-ed pieces, which seek to bring these abstract notions down to earth. Some of these articles address general features of civic discourse. One, written before pandemic and inflation struck us, is the widening gap between the norms and practices that prevail in our politics, on the one hand, and those that prevail in our civil society, on the other. I explore this growing gap in one essay, and in another articulate principles that can guide us in closing this gap. Another feature of our discourse is the paucity of what I call public courage and clear thinking, especially about topics that tend to rile us up or engender our discomfort. One piece explores this problem in the context of sexual harassment conflicts. Another takes up the "tribal politics" phenomenon, by which I mean disputes that tend to divide us decisively along recurrent, tenaciously-held lines.

Several essays take up what has come to be called "cancel culture." Here, one's offense at a perceived practice or belief is taken as a license to simply dismiss or defame those who are thought to engage in that practice or hold that view. I present several examples of this. One particularly toxic example is the routine attribution of "systemic racism" to opponents or even to passive bystanders. This charge often serves as a conversation-stopper, a subject-changer, and a categorical dismissal of competing views. My longish essay on systemic racism, and a short, slightly overlapping one on the distinction between racism and racialism, together seek to dispel these destructive effects on a desperately-needed public debate over the causes of continuing black disadvantage. My review of a book by British essayist Douglas Murray reveals that this cancel culture problem extends well beyond issues of race in America to questions of gender identity in Britain which have parallels here.

Evasive ambiguity is another impediment to clear thinking and discourse, and my' article on diversity, equity, and inequality is intended to explain why these terms, which are so promiscuously deployed as virtue signals, generate such misunderstanding. Another kind of impediment to rational argument is explored in a piece on athletes' "taking a knee" as a form of silent protest. Such protests, I argue, communicate only a vague, unarticulated grievance which tends to increase misunderstanding rather than dispelling it. My review of a book on meritocracy explores some of the intricacies of that important concept.

Finally, I have included a poem in which I reflect on the global effects of an Icelandic ash cloud in 2010 as a reminder of how interrelated our world is—and thus the urgency of rational discourse across communities.

The Widening Gaps between Our Politics and Civil Society*

Why does our civil society—the domain of markets, nonprofit groups, families, religion, and neighborhood life—flourish while our national government increasingly fails at its most basic function of resolving conflict in ways that build on the strengths of our people? The same people inhabit both realms, yet the performance gap between these sectors is large and growing. If we hope to shrink it, we must first understand its sources.

Civil society's rising trajectory is remarkable. Our sweet-spot economy has expanded for nearly a decade. Unemployment and inflation are low. Stock markets have reached record highs. Real wage growth has resumed and poverty levels have declined for all groups, including children. Women now surpass men in education and many other important areas, and young black women are narrowing the earnings and education gap with their white counterparts. Most markets, including tech, are highly competitive; the Fortune 500 from 1955 have almost all died, merged, or shrunk. Although innovation is hard to measure (the number of patents is too crude), many technological breakthroughs are at hand such as more applications of artificial intelligence and new energy sources.

Civil society's successes extend well beyond the economy. Life expectancy for most Americans is rising. Crime continues its dramatic decline in most communities. Teen pregnancy is down. Young people stay in school longer.

---

* The Huffington Post, 12/08/2017, https://www.huffingtonpost.com/entry/the-widening-gap-between-our-politics-and-our-civil-society_us_5a2a16dbe4b069ec48ac30bd?ach

Faded cities are reviving, spurred by immigrant energies. Our environment is healthier. Poverty, as traditionally measured, has declined substantially but far more so if measured correctly, especially by poor people's standard of living. Civil rights protections for minorities have expanded. Our institutions of higher learning and research are still the gold standard. Americans, even if "bowling alone," are still the world's most civically engaged, public-spirited people. Our high and common cultures are creative and energetic.

Obviously, civil society's success does not extend to all Americans. Persistent pockets of deep poverty spawn weak families whose children suffer destructive conditions and blighted prospects. In these enclaves, abuse of drugs, alcohol, women, and children is epidemic. Violence, crime, and homelessness rates are appalling. Economic inequality has widened. Our daily interactions have coarsened. Some conservatives focus on legacy government policies (e.g., failing public schools, housing projects, and welfare programs), but most of them have deeper sources in social breakdowns and individual frailties. Fortunately, these civil society dysfunctions are relatively isolated and do not directly impair most Americans' quality of life.

Our national politics, in contrast, fails in its most basic mission—to bind a diverse, energetic, conflictual country together. Polarization, contempt for compromise, savagery toward opponents, congressional paralysis, gerrymandered districts, policy gridlock, and other pathologies are at levels unseen for generations. Congress periodically verges on shutting down the government and enacted the most important tax legislation since 1986 while largely ignoring or discrediting Congress's own scorekeeper on the bill, which few of them likely read. The party system is broken, with campaign finance, a major party function, migrating to unaccountable outsiders (partly due to past reforms). No healthy, responsible party would have nominated President Trump, who routinely flouted rectitude, dignity, and prudence and was the most unfit occupant of the office in our history. Nor would a healthy, responsible party use its firm grip on congressional power to enable his democracy-imperiling actions. With vital issues crowding the nation's agenda, this power has accomplished little of sound and fair policy (I include you, tax bill!). With eight years to come up with a palatable alternative to Obamacare (which actually borrowed some Republican ideas), the GOP failed to come up with one. And however one views the merits of Trump's vast deregulatory edicts, many are of doubtful legality and will be tied up in courts for years.

These political failures are by no means confined to Republican lawmakers. The Democrats, in power for most of the last 25 years, bear much responsibility for enacting far-reaching policies without bipartisan support and for issuing important regulations without legally-required public processes, further eroding public confidence in our political system. Americans have always been politically divided, going back to the bitter conflict over the Jay Treaty in George Washington's second term. (The "era of good feelings" over which James Monroe presided was brief, ushering in the "Jacksonian revolution" which sharply divided the country, destroyed the first party system, and ultimately led to the Civil War). Today, our political maladies may be worsening, as many young Americans are not only dangerously ignorant of our history but claim to be deeply disaffected—not just from Washington but also from some of our most basic constitutional values, such as non-violent tolerance for speech that offends them. Many say that they will not even bother to vote.

This returns us to the initial question: Why does our civil society largely prosper while both of our national parties are not meeting their most basic political responsibilities? (Our state and local parties are too diverse to be compared). My 2014 book, *Why Government Fails So Often, and How It Can Do Better* (Princeton U.P., 2014), probes this question but the short answer is this: the government operates under a distinct set of incentives and constraints which—this is the key point—seem almost designed for failure. The political arts are essential, but the constitutionally-granted power to compel opponents' compliance encourages over-reaching and abuse of this power. This power naturally attracts and magnifies people's most corrupting, aggrandizing, and irresponsible tendencies. In principle and mostly in practice, this system favors majority voters. But it also tends to favor already-powerful interests whose concentration enables them to organize more effectively and cheaply than larger groups that lack these organizational advantages and whose votes are therefore harder to mobilize. (Strong ideological commitments can sometimes overcome these organizational obstacles, as environmental groups often do).

Government (and voters) rely upon information that is often stale and distorted by political interests, which helps explain the near-immortality of so many clearly ineffective programs. (A recent example is the perverse biofuels subsidy that even Trump has been unable to kill). Power-wielding politicians are constrained only by the formal checks and balances (Madison called them "parchment barriers"), which they constantly strive to undermine. Politicians work within a distinct moral code that makes sense to them—partly because unlike civil society actors, they do not bear personally the costs of their failures. Practices like partisan gerrymandering and self-dealing are routine, yet strike ordinary people as deeply wrong. At the same time, voters are plagued by ignorance and indifference (some of it rational) and persistent biases (cognitive and otherwise).

Civil society, by definition, is not coercive in any conventional sense; it is driven largely by cooperative, voluntary, and sometimes altruistic incentives—a private, conventional morality practiced by most citizens most of the time.

This morality is shaped by widely-shared norms and is normally constrained by competition. Businesses must satisfy their customers or fail. Non-profits must compete for donors. Families and neighborhoods typically naturally nourish their own even amid daunting challenges. To prosper, these groups must be resourceful and savvy. Social penalties for being poorly-informed and passive are severe.

These different incentives, constraints, and moralities help explain why our private lives are usually so much more satisfying and hopeful than our politics. And as government's size, deficits, and regulatory reach expand, this gap is only growing. Perhaps we are fortunate that government's role in the U.S. is still limited relative to elsewhere: its share of GDP (14.4 percent) is much smaller than in, say, France (23.7 percent).

For the vast majority of our people, civil society flourishes—often in spite of our government. But the performance gap should trouble all of us, for the remedies must ultimately be political.

Searching for Public Courage*

The initial responses to President Trump's appalling words after the Charlottesville protest—equating white supremacist, anti-Semitic mayhem and murder with the conduct of that of the victims—raises an important question about public courage: why do our political leaders exhibit less of it than some of our corporate executives do?

I define public courage as one's readiness to risk significant personal loss or disadvantage in order to publicly affirm a lofty social value or principle. (Self-interested action may require sacrifice and produce socially desirable results, but it doesn't count as public courage). Our political leaders should regard public courage as a great virtue. Indeed, it is a hallmark of a morally vibrant democracy, one that our greatest politicians have practiced when it was needed. George Washington sacrificed his intense desire to return to private life in Mount Vernon to Americans' almost universal view that their fragile new polity needed his leadership to survive. Lincoln's prosecution of an unpopular Civil War almost cost him the presidency and did cost him his life. Franklin Roosevelt ran great political risks in guiding an isolationist country into World War II; only Pearl Harbor made the politics of entry manageable. Lyndon Johnson rightly predicted that his civil rights legislation would weaken his party for a generation. (Only a southern president, Jimmy

---

* The Huffington Post, 8/18/2017, https://www.huffpost.com/entry/political-courage-ceos-politicians_b_5996e6c4e4b0a2608a6bc5c5

Carter, briefly interrupted its decline). John McCain has pursued a number of compromises that he knew would be unpopular enough in Arizona to perhaps unseat him. Other instances of such political courage exist, but are few and far between.

Alas, political cowardice is the norm, particularly in the more electorally-sensitive House. Politicians usually define success as re-election. This requires them to mobilize their base—typically a small minority of unusually party loyalists and activists—so as to head off the intra-party primary challenges that today's gerrymandered districts attract. They do this by shunning unpopular positions, avoiding bad publicity, and running for cover when controversy arises. And once they win, they use these same tactics to prepare for the next election. They think of this not as cowardice but simply as faithful representation of their constituents. Against the risk that they may lose a primary or election anyway, they devise an exit strategy to assure them of lucrative opportunities in the private sector or appointive office that will magnify their later market value. Controversy, they know, will limit these opportunities.

These incentives help to explain why Republican politicians are so reluctant to call President Trump out for conduct and words that deeply offend large numbers of Americans and that the politicians surely reprehend in private. Harder to understand is why so many appointees to top public office, people with admirable, hard-won reputations for integrity and courage do not resign in public protest in this situation. Generals John Kelly and James Mattis, for example, have earned sterling reputations over a lifetime of honorable deeds and sacrifices, yet these reputations are tarnished when their silence enables or countenances this immoral behavior. Presumably, they entered high office at the acme of their careers, hoping to advance cherished public goals. They can best do so by making clear that they will resign if Trump subverts those goals, and then doing so with publicly-stated reasons if it comes to that. This would not entail financial sacrifice; quite the contrary. Yet only two Cabinet secretaries have resigned on publicly-stated principles in the last century (Cyrus Vance in 1980 over Iran policy, and William Jennings Bryan in 1915 over World War I).

In contrast, many business leaders have already resigned from Trump's advisory councils, and more will likely follow. They have fewer public responsibilities than political leaders do, but they may also have more to lose by being outspoken. When public figures denounce a president's action as a growing number of corporate chiefs have done, they risk offending their customers, shareholders, and workers, not to mention their supposed ally in the White House. Unlike politicians who can succeed merely by satisfying their voter base, corporate leaders must constantly expand their markets or risk losing their lucrative jobs and reputations.

The spectacle of seeing our political leaders lie supine before a president who clearly has little respect for them, their democratic responsibilities, and a constitutional ethos that they all have sworn to defend, is disturbing. Some well-explained resignations, or at least rebukes, are long overdue. It should not fall to our business elites and other citizens to have to lead the way.

The Shackling of the Progressive Mind[*]

The leitmotif of young British commentator Douglas Murray's thought-provoking book, *The Madness of Crowds: Gender, Race and Identity* is well captured in his frontispiece quotation of G.K. Chesterton: "The special mark of the modern world is not that it is skeptical, but that it is dogmatic without knowing it." Murray's timing with this book could not have been better—both when published in 2019 and today. Its publication roughly coincided with a spate of bestselling books—Robin DiAngelo's *White Fragility* (2020), Ibram X. Kendi's *How to be an Antiracist* (2019), Ta-Nehisi Coates' *Between the World and Me* (2015)—that seek to educate whites about their racism (both vicious and clueless) and even to signal to people of color about their own toxic acquiescences. As if on cue, these books, with their closed, self-referential, echo chamber arguments, have perfectly illustrated Murray's critique. Two years later, that critique is even more compelling—and its apparent ineffectiveness even more dismaying.

Murray's principal target is identity warriors (as I shall call them) and their smugly dogmatic definitions of the groups they claim to represent. Their definitions deny or suppress the profound within-group differences that exist—and do so in harmful, even brutal ways. Murray shows how identity warriors misrepresent four groups: gays, women, racial minorities, and transsexuals.

In lively, blessedly non-academic prose, Murray recounts incidents in which self-appointed identity warriors (again, my term) have combined lies, gross hyperbole, and other obfuscating tools of "cancel culture" and character assassination to attack those who define their groups somewhat differently. Identity warriors first insist that there is only one legitimate way to be gay, feminist, Black, or trans; and next, that only they and their allies exemplify it. Finally, they politicize these arbitrarily crabbed versions of identity. Their typical method is to suppress crucial scientific facts about the subject groups while causing them reputational, psychological, and sometimes even physical harm.

---

[*] American Purpose, 12/1/2021; https://www.americanpurpose.com/articles/the-shackling-of-the-american-mind/

Murray's attack on identity warriors strikes at the coherence of their own identity claims, beginning with the core concepts they use to characterize their group identities in public presentations. "Social justice" is the master concept they deploy, presumably because few will dare to object to it in principle (except libertarians, perhaps). They practice identity politics, which neatly allocates people to discrete caucuses based on the four abovementioned characteristics. In the identity wars, these characteristics are the only salient attributes of group membership, conferring on them moral superiority, historical claims, or social insights unavailable to outsiders.

Murray is correct that these peremptory, misguided notions now dominate our mainstream public and private discourse. They have displaced understandings of reality that were taken for granted until "just now," and stigmatize all who fail to fall swiftly into line behind these novel claims as unregenerate, knuckle-dragging, hate-filled bigots. People desperate to avoid "cancellation" tolerate many claims that are vacuous, irrational, toxic to respectful discourse, and oppressive once they gain social authority. Too often, then, the identity wars leave a political residue of mindless solidarities, angry retributions, and implacable hostilities—the "madness of crowds" of the book's title.

Murray first applies his critique to the identity warriors' portrayal of gay people. Although proudly gay himself, he rejects a group identity built exclusively and dogmatically around gayness. Citing many intriguing examples of mainstream media devoting too much attention to the sexual preferences of people in the news, Murray wonders whether the media is not just hoping to make up for lost time when it was still part of the problem, but also wanting to "[rub] things in the faces of those not yet up to speed with the changed mores of the age."

He opposes those who insist that gayness is inborn and fixed rather than (as Murray reads the science) a matter of individual choice reflecting a variety of factors—some possibly genetic—that may be fluid over time and circumstance. What makes one gay, he convincingly shows, remains scientifically uncertain. He also rejects the notion that LGBT is in fact a cohesive community of identity. He presents evidence that lesbians and gays have little use for one another, that they entertain doubts about whether bisexuals are really members of the club, and that the Ls, Gs, and Bs in fact strongly disagree about "whether the T's are the same thing as everybody else or an insult to them."

Murray's deep skepticism about the homogeneity and identity (however defined) of these groups also extends to the other groups that he analyzes. But before making this pivot, he examines the foundational concepts of newish orthodoxies—neo-Marxism, radical political economy, and literary theory—that supposedly constitute them as coherent groups. Of the latter, he archly observes, "It is one curiosity of academia in recent decades that it has found almost nothing it does not wish to deconstruct, apart from itself." Murray predicts that future, better-informed generations will scoff at our simplistic, dogmatic stance toward transsexuality.

Even the "women" group exemplifies Murray's relentlessly individuating analysis, as he points to several social patterns that complicate and confuse our conceptions of women. First, the male-female relationship is inherently fraught, complicated by the raw chemistry of their interreactions; the power of carnal and psychological desire; power struggles; role conflicts; and other complications that were familiar obsessions of the ancients and that have been explored in arts and culture ever since. Simplistic generalizations about women obscure more than they clarify.

Second, Murray notes the epithet of "privilege" that feminist militants now hurl not just at men (another group monolithically defined) but also at other women who lack one or more of the (ironically privileged) intersectional attributes. (Identity militants also treat these "privileged" attributes as monolithic.) Third, Murray targets the misandry of many radical feminists, which he sees as yet another obstacle to rational discussion. Finally, Murray doubts that our gender endowment ("hardware") is really, as the identity militants claim, just malleable software. "They expect [us] to radically alter our lives and societies on the basis of claims that our instincts all tell us cannot possibly be true." Not just our instincts, one should add, but our science also tells us this.

Murray decries how Silicon Valley encourages dishonesty about and manipulation of gays, women, racial minorities, and transsexuals by presenting as fair, objective, and apolitically neutral whatever dubious data users and advertisers pump into its platforms. Social media has also "collapse[d] the barrier between private and public language," he notes, which has permanently conflated people's pasts and presents, and made forgiveness and amity more difficult even to pursue, much less achieve.

On race, Murray argues that "the greatest backsliding on Dr. King's dream" comes not from racists, who are strongly denounced in almost all corners of society, but from those who claim to advance King's ideal by insisting that White racism is the deepest, most universal practice of all—all the while deploying words and actions that King would find repellent. Murray cites egregious examples of intolerance and intimidation in the name of anti-racism—especially on campuses where "cultural appropriation" is a mantra-like indictment of anyone shameless (or syncretic) enough to borrow from other traditions. There, where conservative faculty members are as rare as hen's teeth, guilt-mongers with radical agendas use the noble ideal of anti-racism to justify their own racism against a putatively monolithic group (Whites).

The radicals' uncompromising, tar-and-feathering, vastly exaggerating tactics work to multiply injustice and repel many possible allies.

Consider Murray's shocking account of the mob-like attacks on novelist Lionel Shriver for defending artists who choose to leave their birth-allotted, demographically prescribed zones. When people like Peter Thiel, Kanye West, Thomas Sowell, and others avow "conservative" ideas, the identity dictators expel them for that ultimate crime. In the same cowardly, partisan spirit, the Atlantic quickly expelled a newly hired conservative writer when Ta-Nehisi Coates accused him of racism. (After Murray's book was published, the *New York Times* fired James Bennet, its editorial page editor, for carrying an op-ed piece by a conservative Senator to which liberal *Times* readers and staffers objected.)

When future, better-informed generations reflect on our current practices and beliefs, Murray predicts that they will scoff at our simplistic, dogmatic stance toward transsexuality. Gender ambiguity is an ancient, often honored cultural meme. Some people, like the late writer Jan Morris, crave to change their sex despite the trauma and risks it entails. Although no biological difference for this new-body obsession has yet been identified, Murray claims, many trans activists stubbornly insist that they in fact are born this way and that sexual desire and other preferences have nothing to do with it.

Murray shows how many trans activists and their liberal allies have savagely attacked others who see sex change as simply a matter of individual choice among multiple contending factors. He also shows how the practical irreversibility of a trans surgery raises hard questions about the fraught parental decisions to change young children's gender—decisions that some activists have politicized as a morally compelled action. Activist certitudes about the nature of trans status have fractured the LGBTQ formation. Indeed, as Murray shows, they sometimes vilify even feminist icons like Germaine Greer who deviate from their catechism.

Murray's bracing book on the current gender, race, and identity wars denounces bigoted, politicized, weaponized certitudes on complex, socially divisive issues that science cannot resolve yet—or perhaps ever. The dogma, he shows, is way ahead of the data, and the true believers' furious assault on the skeptics produces a dense "fog of war" that pushes rational debate off the field. He illustrates well how the great danger in this warfare is a "vengeful" group-think that insists "that questions are settled which are unsettled, that matters are known which are unknown, and that we have a very good idea of how to structure a society along such inadequately argued lines." Equal rights are precious. So too, is a reasoned line-drawing that our current identity politics too often cannot abide.

Cancel Culture Has a Lot to Answer For*

Sometimes our most precious cultural institutions fail to live up to their high educational and moral commitments and responsibilities. These failures especially damage the social fabric because they tend to harm many people who rely on them and tarnish the high ideals that the institutions claim to exemplify.

An incident in early October involving MIT, a jewel in world academia's crown, presents an especially egregious instance of this institutional failing, aggravated by that university's cowardice in the face of intimidation and threats by self-righteous students and their faculty allies. MIT had invited Dorian Abbot, a University of Chicago geophysicist, to deliver the prestigious John Carlson Lecture on climate and the potential of life on other planets—a topic on which Abbot is a recognized expert. Unfortunately for Abbot and his intended audience, however, he had recently committed the campus equivalent of hara-kiri by taking seriously the norms of academic freedom which MIT and other schools claim to cherish.

Abbot, in online discussions of the growing "diversity, equity, and inclusion movement ("DEI" is the subject of an article on p. 75) on American campuses, had stressed "the importance of treating each person as an individual worthy of dignity and respect. In an academic context," he continued, "that means giving everyone a fair and equal opportunity when they apply for a position as well as allowing them to express their opinions openly, even if you disagree with them." And in a co-authored *Newsweek* op-ed in August, he had argued that DEI as currently practiced on campus "violates the ethical and legal principle of equal treatment" and "treats persons as merely means to an end, giving primacy to a statistic over the individuality of a human being."

Abbot proposed instead an alternative framework that he called Merit, Fairness, and Equality (MFE) whereby university applicants are treated as individuals and evaluated through a rigorous and unbiased process based on their merit and qualifications alone. His MFE norm rejected legacy and athletic admission advantages, "which significantly favor white applicants." For these heretical views, he was pilloried by groups of students who demanded that MIT withdraw its lecture invitation. Ten days later, the chairman of the sponsoring MIT department did just that.

Here we have, quite literally, an instance of "cancellation culture"—one that seeks to impose a kind of annihilation or social death. Advocates for

---

* Quillette, 10/21/2021, https://quillette.com/2021/10/21/cancel-culture-has-a-lot-to-answer-for/

speech, actions, or positions that their critics deem unacceptable increasingly use the term to describe those critics' efforts to suppress, marginalize, boycott, and otherwise punish their adversaries. In Abbot's case, denying him a prominent platform for his views on DEI (and perhaps other issues) was a classic cancellation effort.

The Abbot incident also reveals cancellation's potential expansiveness. After all, his lecture topic, while socially and scientifically important, had nothing whatsoever to do with the protesters' demand for DEI. Even so, their cancellation scheme almost succeeded. In a lucky break for Abbot, he ended up delivering the canceled lecture—not at MIT but at Princeton. There, some faculty led by conservative political theorist Robbie George immediately stepped up and offered to sponsor it. Indeed, Abbot's luck was even more dramatic: the *New York Times* and other leading media gave the incident some prominence, thousands of students signed up for Abbot's Princeton lecture, and his cancellation by MIT earned him a distinction bestowed by the American Council of Trustees and Alumni, which named him a Hero of Intellectual Freedom!

This remarkable turnabout—a kind of moral jiu-jitsu in which Abbot was able to convert his vulnerability to a mob's demands into a larger forum for his message—should gladden the hearts and minds of the many people who deplore the forces of cancellation. All too commonly, such pressures for conformity are strictly reinforced by hierarchy, fear of social isolation and other informal sanctions, and the ubiquitous hostage-taking of reputation.

What is it about the DEI movement—its tenets, its action agenda, and its fierce, adamant champions—that has enabled it to gain such influence with students and some faculty on so many campuses? My close observation of the growing movement at Yale and elsewhere has convinced me of a number of related explanations. First, universities are massive entities whose leaders are obsessed by the need to raise ever larger endowments (Harvard's increased by $11.3 billion, or 40 percent, last year; Washington University in St. Louis gained 65 percent!) to fund ever more expansion, construction, academic and non-academic programs, and salaries. As such, they resolutely strive to create an impression of order on campus. But cancellations cause spasms of disruption, violence, and negative publicity that can affect their exceedingly important public rankings. Dissident students know that university leaders at the most prestigious schools (with rare but notable exceptions like Robert Zimmer and Geoffrey Stone of the University of Chicago) are prepared to pay a dear price to secure campus peace. And since they and their faculty are overwhelmingly liberal politically—almost 90 percent identify with and often contribute to the Democratic Party—they tend to sympathize with the protesters' agendas, even when more radical than their own.

This brings me to the second point about DEI. Its ideals are rhetorically appealing only so long as they remain undefined. Who, after all, can be against "diversity" and "inclusion," at least in the abstract? The reality, however, is that as abstractions these concepts are merely aspirational and essentially empty. What they actually mean in practice—and what the cancellation cadres plainly mean by them—is strict regimes of affirmative action based on race, ethnicity, gender, and a few other attributes. These attributes, cancel culture insists, must be used in college admissions, job hiring, sports teams, instrumental ensembles, art projects, and all manner of groups regardless of the actual distribution of preferences, talents, interests, and availabilities among the supposed beneficiaries. In a striking example, the Art Institute of Chicago just announced that it was dismissing all of its docents and starting over because too many of them are white women.

Cancel culture typically prescribes affirmative action as the means to install diversity in all activities that it values. But affirmative action means very different things to different people. It ranges from greater outreach to unrepresented groups—which Americans largely favor—to numerical quotas for minority groups, which most, including most black Americans, largely oppose. The same distinction applies to inclusion and equity; many of us endorse them in the abstract but often disagree when faced with specific applications.

Cancel culture is different—and actually yields less genuine diversity. For example, its orthodoxies often contradict minority communities' actual, intense desires for greater police presence and enforcement in their neighborhoods. These same orthodoxies also impede more effective discipline of unruly and violent students where such discipline might enable their children to learn and pursue pathways to a brighter future. Cancel culture's zombie-like insistence that white racism today is still the main reason for continuing poverty, high violent crime rates, poor health conditions, domestic turmoil, and chronic family dissolution in troubled inner-city communities is a perverse distraction from, and even a denial of, the more important causes and possible remedies for these tragic, debilitating conditions.

The MIT fiasco should remind us how much cancel culture has to answer for. Although this culture's activists are relatively few and its rhetoric is often risible in its hyperbole, its militants on college campuses sometimes have an outsize effect on others: cruelly blighted reputations, perverse policy agendas, stigmatization of moderate Democrats, and much more. But Princeton's swift response to Abbot's cancellation by providing an alternative, honored forum, also suggests a hopeful, low-cost remedy, consistent with free speech and liberal academic values. MIT should be ashamed of its craven support for bullying—and perhaps other more principled institutions will heed this simple example.

Thinking Clearly about Sexual Harassment[*]

A torrent of sexual harassment revelations has launched a long-overdue discussion of a perennial social plague afflicting countless women, girls, and boys. (Adult men are occasionally victimized as well). We have many courageous women and the #MeToo movement to thank for bringing this issue into the open where it is being discussed among friends, by policymakers, at workplaces, and in our families and other social milieus.

The quality of this long-deferred public debate will depend on at least three things: (1) how accurately we identify the causes of sexual harassment; (2) how carefully we distinguish among the different behaviors now lumped under this portmanteau phrase; and (3) how wisely we design measures to assess, punish, and prevent those behaviors.

Causes. Sexual harassment has several causes. The first is lust, sheer animal attractions between men and women. Lust is inevitable (for psycho-biochemical reasons), pleasurable (if indulged in mutually desired and gratifying ways), and necessary (to perpetuate our species). But our grotesquely sexualized popular culture dangerously stokes and magnifies this lust. Second, a pervasive power imbalance converts this lust into opportunities for exploitative, almost onanistic self-gratification by aggressive, narcissistic men against more vulnerable women. Third, harassment can reflect genuine misunderstandings, mixed signals, interpersonal clumsiness, and loss of ordinary self-control due to excessive drinking, substance abuse, and other factors. These causes cannot be eliminated but can be ameliorated—as crime, poverty, and teenage pregnancy have been.

Drawing distinctions. Much public discussion of sexual harassment treats it as all of a piece deserving of undifferentiated condemnation and punishment. But it isn't this simple. Many women affirm what should be obvious: the term is being applied to a variety of behaviors and situations whose moral offense and harmful effects are quite different. Yet *New York Times* columnist Bret Stephens and actor Matt Damon have been pilloried for making the same point.

The law already does some of this line-drawing. Centuries of legislative and judicial decisions have elaborated important defining concepts like force, battery, consent, autonomy, and reasonable fear for one's bodily or psychic integrity. Sexual assault, so defined, is both a crime subject to penal sanctions, and a tort subject to monetary sanctions. These laws can deter and punish

---

[*] Huffington Post, 1/1/2018, https://www.huffpost.com/entry/thinking-clearly-about-sexual-harassment_b_5a4a9e12e4b06d1621ba2f62

harassment but much of it is neither criminal nor tortious and so goes unremedied. More line-drawing is essential.

Kathleen Kelley Reardon, a management professor and blogger, recently offered guidance, describing a "spectrum of sexual misconduct at work" ranging from the inoffensive to the "egregious." She deems "common off the cuff compliments on such things as hair style and dress" to be non-offensive. But this category should also include sarcasm, digs, and words that hurt people's feelings. In our free-wheeling society, in which we interact with people whom we know only superficially, our exchanges need breathing space and spontaneity. We should endeavor not to offend, of course, but in the course of lively exchanges, our comments and intentions can easily be misunderstood and resented. The offended person should candidly tell the speaker that she objects, and why. Although this might deepen the resentment, an exchange that exhumes the real individuals buried beneath the superficial chit-chat might instead yield more rewarding interactions. Context matters.

Reardon next lists "awkward/mildly offensive" comments exemplified by "comments on gender differences." But here too, she condemns too broadly. While legal and social equality for women and sexual minorities advances, many gender differences persist, deeply rooted in biology and culture. These differences enrich our lives and our experiences of one another. We should not be discouraged from discussing them, even if some comments are unwelcome to those convinced that differences are "merely" constructs of a deeply unequal society. Jokes about gender differences may be crude or unfunny but even annoying jokes can contain some insight about our relationships—for example, that men and women often do see things differently. If one is offended, one should inform the speaker that it's not funny, or even walk out.

More offensive, according to Reardon, are acts like "holding a woman's arm while talking," "uninvited hugs," "patronizing/dismissive/exclusionary behavior toward women," and "implying or stating that women are distracted by family." Even here, reasonable people may disagree about what is actually going on. The meaning of such acts largely depends, again, on their context, which is often ambiguous. How is one to know whether a friendly hug of a woman whom one has met before is "invited" or not? Inquiring would destroy the gesture's warmth and spontaneity. Remaining aloof is safer but such common interactions are simply too variable to be regulated unless they are genuinely fearful or oppressive, which they seldom are.

Does Reardon's norm against "exclusionary behavior" condemn social gatherings in which the men and women commonly talk among their gender peers, presumably out of choice? And why is it offensive to suggest that a woman is distracted by her family when research clearly shows that she does in fact end up spending much more time than her husband in managing their children? Again, Reardon's admirable wish to avoid demeaning or sidetracking women gives too little weight to context. Thus we should view such a comment by a job interviewer (offensive and possibly illegal) differently than one by a neighbor or garrulous massage therapist. Even more serious offenses, for Reardon, are comments that "devalue" women—denigrating them as a group or making demeaning reference to their physical attributes. Such comments may be crude, thoughtless, and insulting, but the remedy for the offended should be to refute and censure the comment rather than trying to silence the commenter by formally sanctioning his unwanted speech. A worrisome analogy occurs on too many campuses where opponents of controversial ideas try to censor them by insisting that they are pained by being exposed to them. Our line-drawing, then, should discourage offensiveness while not encouraging hyper-sensitivity and undue umbrage.

Some of Reardon's examples of "evident sexual misconduct" —grabbing, rude patting, and unwelcome holding or kissing of a woman; describing her as a "slut" or "frigid;" and accusing her of using her gender to advance her career—are not merely objectionable; they could well constitute a tortious assault, battery, or defamation. But her catalog of misconduct goes further. It condemns looking a woman up and down "in a sexually suggestive manner." Depending on what that phrase means, it might condemn admiring glances that—if they go no farther—do no real harm. She would also punish a man who ignores a woman's expressed disinterest in a relationship and continues to "hassle" her. Depending on what "hassle" means in a specific context, this may either protect the woman or condemn a kind of male persistence that if inoffensive has yielded many happy relationships.

Reardon's more "egregious sexual misconduct" examples are already criminal, tortious, or both—and rightly so. But the real challenge concerns whether and how we should regulate aggressive but non-violent conduct and less egregious behavior that still causes fear and offense. Here, line-drawing is much more challenging. People interact in infinitely varied ways and assess signals and meanings very differently. Again, context and intent matter. Most social norms are opaque and informally enforced. Safety and security are at stake, but so are other values. In this realm, then, adopting hard-and-fast rules is less desirable than clarifying social expectations about how we should behave in various situations, how we should communicate our desires, and how individuals and institutions should respond when those norms are allegedly violated.

Procedures. Consider how educational institutions have handled sexual harassment claims. We see that even benign, well-resourced schools are caught in a cultural crossfire. Their efforts to handle these disputes with campus-specific procedures and standards founder on the high stakes. Accusers demand protection and justice. The accused, facing the prospect of expulsion and criminal prosecution, demand rigorous procedural safeguards. Onlookers—other students, alumni, civil rights officials, ideologues of left and right, and the media—have their own fish to fry and are ready to pounce on these disputes however they are resolved. No one seems satisfied by the schools' makeshift arrangements.

Law enforcement agencies, for all their limitations, are far better equipped to handle these difficult disputes. Schools, workplaces, and other institutions should not adjudicate sexual harassment claims but should instead limit their role to determining whether the accuser has alleged facts that, if true, could constitute legally actionable harassment. If so, the institution should advise the accuser to consider taking her case to the police and obtaining a lawyer. It should release as little identifying information as possible until the matter is adjudicated or otherwise resolved. Judicial rulings, official pressures, and public demands have already strengthened institutions' existing incentives to prevent harassment, but more prevention efforts can surely be undertaken. Importantly, they can punish the heavy drinking and drug use that fuel much harassment and can denounce the hook-up culture. Law enforcement agencies should look to the best practices of other such agencies, which include allocating more resources to informal counseling of fearful accusers and improving fact-finding processes.

Harms to the career, dignitary, and security interests of harassment victims are hard to quantify or even identify in individual cases. Remedies for victims may seem arbitrary. Most likely receive nothing, not even an apology. Accusers may suffer informal blacklisting. Yet some others get payoffs that seem far higher than the actual harm they could have suffered, as when Bill O'Reilly paid Lis Wiehl $32 million. We should clarify what we mean by non-criminal sexual harassment, which procedures are fair and effective, and then ensure that both harassers and victims get what they deserve.

Taking a Knee: How to Squander a Teaching Moment[*]

The October 2 edition of the *New York Times* carried a David Leonhardt column entitled "Kneeling Versus Winning" in which he praises the many National Football League players who have been kneeling during the national anthem. His point is that it will take a lot more than this symbolic gesture to

---

[*] Huffington Post, 10/11/2017; https://www.huffpost.com/entry/taking-a-knee-how-to-squander-a-teaching-moment_b_59de5c86e4b0fdad73b17889

win their "political battle with President Trump" and to encourage them to do so.

But what is their battle about? Like many observers, Leonhardt seems to think he knows the answer to this question, but I for one am less certain—and the protests do little to inform me. Indeed, they do the very opposite by failing to communicate what it is they are protesting. Many fans will wonder what players whose average salary in 2011 was $1.9 million (a median of $770,000), according to *Forbes*, have to protest about. Well, they are Americans and about 70 percent of them are black, so they might plausibly be complaining about any of a number of conditions, behaviors, or policies—racism, police brutality against blacks, Trump's innumerable outrageous statements and actions, the many disadvantages of being black in America, the fact that only a quarter of NFL head coaches are black, the NFL's handling of concussions, and many others. But we, the audience, have no way of knowing which particular things they are protesting, so that we have no way of focusing our attention on the issue(s) that they might be raising—even though we might well want to support them if we knew. (At least I might!)

I am not the only one who is confused. People's feelings about the protests depend on what they think the protests are about, but they do not agree on what they are about, much less how they feel about the protests. On October 9, Five Thirty Eight reported that "a recent CBS/YouGov poll of over 1,300 respondents asked people—regardless of whether they agreed with the protests—what NFL players were trying to do by kneeling during the national anthem. A large majority (73 percent) of respondents said the players were trying to call attention to racism, and 69 percent said players were calling attention to police violence. But 40 percent said the protests were trying to disrespect the flag, while 33 percent said the goal was to disrespect the military. Not surprisingly, the poll found that people's attitudes toward players taking a knee differ a great deal when they are told that the protests are about race, patriotism, or free speech (the only three subjects that the pollsters mentioned)."

President Trump has unwittingly confirmed and increased this confusion by insisting (as usual, without any evidence) that the kneeling (and team executives' complicity) is about still other things: rejecting the flag, the military, and the country. (The Supreme Court, of course, held almost 30 years ago that even flag-burning, which is far more provocative than kneeling, is constitutionally protected expression, but my point is about muddied message, not legality).

Because the protests are altogether undifferentiated, unfocused, and uncommunicative (except in the grossest sense) concerning their content and targets, they are literally meaningless. Although they are potentially powerful movers of public opinion, their substantive content is so opaque that they do nothing to advance public dialogue and understanding. The civil rights crusaders whom Leonhardt invokes took pains to identify the particular injustices that they were fighting—segregated lunch counters, schools, churches, neighborhoods, jobs and the like—and the bigoted Americans and illegitimate laws and institutions that supported these injustices. This clarity, which is utterly absent when players silently take a knee, made it possible for the earlier civil rights protesters to fashion and sell specific remedies.

Because so many Americans watch the NFL (more than 110 million tuned in for each recent Super Bowl), the protesters have a far larger audience than any earlier group of protesters did. This is a magnificent teaching opportunity—but so far, they have largely squandered it.

Five Realities of Tribal Politics*

Chattering classes throughout the world are talking about identity politics, and with good reason. It is propelling the so-called populist movements, and the response to those movements, which are shaking the foundations of almost every society today. Whether a polity is democratic, authoritarian, or anarchic, it is awash with clamorous appeals to relatively narrow allegiances based on race, religion, class, social position, gender, ideology, party—and typically some combination of them.

In the United States, college campuses, where our future voters and leaders are seeded, are the breeding grounds for these sectarian dispositions. There, young people newly emancipated from their families' supervision are free to define themselves afresh. There, they are pressured by peers and professors alike, as well as social media, to endorse the orthodoxies of the tribe.

The notion that there are but two sides on important questions—right versus wrong, tolerant versus bigoted, progressive versus conservative—is an unfortunate feature of this war of words. The real world, when they finally enter it, will perhaps discipline their minds in ways that their campus lives have not, but the residue of ideologies already implanted there may continue to shape them as voters and fellow citizens. So, here's this professor's effort to clarify the nature of identitarian rhetoric.

I offer five propositions that may confound partisans on all sides. First, all politics is identity politics even though the identities that are emphasized constitute but a small part of who we really are. This is neither a new

---

* Minding the Campus, 3/12/2018; https://www.mindingthecampus.org/2018/03/12/5-ways-to-stop-identity-politics-from-tearing-america-apart/

phenomenon—bitter, seemingly unbridgeable divisions have often occurred in American history—nor the exclusive or even predominant preserve of the left or the right. In any democracy, electoral politics means, among other things, dividing people up rather than uniting them, which is much harder. Getting elected entails "rubbing raw the sores of discontent" and "mobilizing bias" (as two analysts have put it).

All human societies are tribal. As Amy Chua argues in a new book, *Political Tribes: Group Instinct and the Fate of Nations*, we all seek warmth and solidarity from those whom we think are like us in some important respects. But beyond a certain point, tribalism can be pathological. Half of Republicans and a third of Democrats say they would be upset if their child married a member of the other party, and these antipathies are steadily deepening. This growing polarization of the parties parallels clustering of partisans in states, localities, and even neighborhoods, and it is occurring *within* parties as well.

Second, the appeal to the traditional transcendent unifying norms—notably "American values" and "the American Dream"—are debatable; they no longer do the unifying work that they once did. This, even though almost all Americans, including the poor, enjoy a rising standard of living, properly measured. In truth, these appeals beg fundamental questions of morality and complex policy on which Americans significantly differ, so it is not surprising that we cannot agree about value-laden and empirically-contested issues like immigration, the government's role in healthcare, the integrity of law enforcement, abortion, gun control, and many more.

Third, even the terms and categories that we use to think about and discuss identity issues are over-simplified—in some areas grotesquely so. Occupying center stage is the subject of race. Although science long ago showed it to be a meaningless, misleading concept, both sides deploy it aggressively and simplistically to conceal inconvenient truths. The right contends that race is only a battleground because activist groups like Black Lives Matter, campus protesters, and other "outside agitators" exploit it. Leftist groups divide society into whites, blacks, and other people of color even though a significant share of Americans carry other ancestries, and intermarriage among these groups has greatly increased. Campus activists deem whites to be categorically "privileged," yet the vast majority of poor people are white or non-black, and over half of "Hispanics," many of them poor, self-identify as white. Only about a third of black students at Harvard had four grandparents descended from slaves; the great majority were West Indian and African immigrants or their children. The good news is that far more young people socialize and marry inter-racially unlike their more restricted grandparents, who in any event are dying out.

Fourth, identity-talk makes no serious effort to engage with the teachings of social science. Yet empirical facts, careful distinctions, and hard-eyed assessment of policy consequences could complicate the easy moralizing and aggressive guilt-mongering in which identitarians of all stripes wallow. For example, sociologist Orlando Patterson has shown that the life experiences of black men and black women are so different that to treat them as a single "community" is vastly, even tragically misguided. By the same token, "immigrants" are not a single category but rather a congeries of people with sharply different social, cultural, economic, and legal statuses—and hence identities. To speak of immigrants generically, as we all tend to do, obscures their differences and misleads our judgments about them.

Finally, identity-talk is almost always more certain of its own premises—and more ignorant or indifferent to those on the other side of the lines it draws—than it should be. Smugness in the face of contradiction is endemic. Cosmopolitan liberals, for example, feel beleaguered by what they take to be an oppressive conservative hinterland now controlling Washington and the country. (Here, the classic New Yorker cover lampooning this view comes to mind). Yet as others have observed, liberalism has actually won the culture war, which in the long run is far more consequential for how we think, live, and vote. Conservatives have their own grievances, intensified by their own blind spots. Their bitter attack on Obamacare (which borrowed from Republican ideas) despite their inability to propose a viable alternative while controlling the machinery of government is but one example; another is the ease with which evangelical Christians continue to support a president who flagrantly violates their most fundamental moral commitments.

Yes, we are tribal, and yes, our tribes are blinded by ignorance and self-righteousness. Perhaps this has always been true. But our politicians seemed simply better at unifying both the voters that they had just tactically divided, and the institutions fragmented by our Constitution. In the end, we must reduce the hold that our tribes have over us, and we must elect those who share this goal.

Principles to Guide a Nation Through Issues that Divide Us[*]

As a campaigner, President Trump expressed sympathy for allowing transgender students to use bathrooms, locker rooms, and other school

---

[*] Philadelphia Inquirer, 3/19/2017; https://www.inquirer.com/philly/opinion/20170319_Commentary__Principles_to_guide_a_nation_through_issues_that_divide_us.html

facilities corresponding to their chosen identity. This was a policy the Obama administration adopted in 2016, threatening to cut off funds if schools continued to require bathroom use according to students' sexual identity at birth. Trump quickly rescinded that policy, deferring to his attorney general over his education secretary.

This issue, which Trump seems eager to intensify, raises important legal and policy questions and feeds into the culture wars that already divide Americans.

Lower courts have divided over whether this situation is covered by Title IX, which in 1972 barred discrimination "on the basis of sex" in any federally funded education "program" or "activity." The main legal issues are whether "sex" included assignment to bathrooms based on gender identity at birth or by subjective choice; whether going to the bathroom is an education "program" or "activity;" and whether the traditional arrangements constitute "discrimination."

This dispute may go to the Supreme Court, although it may prefer waiting for a case based on Trump's policy.

The lawyers will search for the intent of Congress 45 years ago when few if any people considered transgender bathroom use. Advocates will emphasize that some transgender students have been bullied and criminally assaulted by fellow students for being different, leading in some cases to depression and even suicide. (Trump's policy affirms that schools must protect them from discrimination, bullying, and harassment, but advocates hope to restore the Obama policy).

It is unclear whether Title IX covers transgender bathroom and locker-room choice, but the more important question for the future is what a sound policy would look like—since the new Congress and president may seek to clarify or change the law.

In *One Nation Undecided (2017)*, I analyzed how we should think about such issues—poverty, immigration, campaign finance, affirmative action, and religious exemptions—going forward. Rigorously defining the bathroom issue is the first step. Advocates define it most broadly as one of human rights, equality, and dignity. But we should instead focus on the specific context of the conflicting claims. Transgender people want to affirm their gender identity during their few minutes of school bathroom use, and the law that already protects them against bullying and harassment must be enforced. Their demand for choice is important, but it is certainly not a constitutional right; courts extend such rights only to certain claims essential to individuals' liberty and well-being—and only after their claims are balanced against the legitimate claims of others.

Does preferring chosen-identity-based facilities meet this demanding constitutional test? I think not. Dignity and identity claims are not a trump (no pun intended) in conflicts like this where both sides can plausibly invoke those values.

Several possible approaches can help resolve such conflicts. One is the principle of choice. How hard would it be for schools to provide choice with stalls that better protect users' privacy, or provide nonsegregated bathrooms with signage putting people on notice when they enter?

A second approach (used in antidiscrimination and religious accommodation law) is to insist that any limit on transgenders' facility choices must be the "least restrictive alternative." Again, this may mean privacy-enhancing stalls and dual-sex bathrooms. Other solutions may be needed for locker rooms.

A third principle is probably the most important: federalism. Law professor Rick Hills invokes federalism to resolve "reasonable and deep disagreements" about practices in situations where no social and legal consensus provides a baseline for resolving conflicting rights claims. In such situations, Hills argues, national rules should be avoided in favor of state or even local solutions, thus allowing different arrangements and experiments. This is how our system handles most policy differences where constitutional rights are not at stake.

Rules on transgender use of facilities are a good example. Few Americans considered this a civil rights issue until very recently, and fewer still will view this as equivalent to racial or sex discrimination. Transgender people, whose identity is often scorned, have demonstrated admirable courage. Courageous or not, antidiscrimination law should protect them in employment, housing, public accommodations, and all other aspects of their lives. Fortunately, states and localities are increasingly doing this, and anti-transgender policies are meeting growing political and economic resistance.

Do most transgenders find the familiar facilities patterns stigmatizing—or just inconvenient? How acceptable will compromise approaches be to both transgender people and others? What are the real trade-offs? What is the actual relation between familiar facilities patterns and bullying or violence? Let's find out by allowing diverse approaches until we know the answers.

Racism and Racialism Are Different[*]

Our campuses, newspapers, sports commentary, and electronic media are filled with accusations of racism—most recently, against police departments and sports team owners. A WSJ/NBC poll conducted shortly after the highly

---

[*] Huffington Post, 12/22/2014; https://www.huffpost.com/entry/racism-and-racialism-are-_b_6368010

publicized police killings of unarmed black men finds that only 35% of blacks and 40% of whites think that race relations are very good or fairly good—a sharp drop from a 2013 Gallup poll in which 66% of blacks thought that race relations were very good or somewhat good. Even so, whites overwhelmingly favor racial equality even in the most intimate settings. (85% of whites support black/white marriage—twice the percentage as recently as 1990).

Can these two things—acute distress over race relations, and support for interracial marriage and equality—both be true? Several explanations for this possible paradox are possible. Perhaps whites more effectively conceal their anti-black bias from pollsters now, embedding it in social institutions. Perhaps they are unaware of their own bias, as some psychologists (including a new MacArthur genius award recipient) infer from experiments in which whites quickly exposed to identical black and white images respond more negatively to the black ones. Perhaps the genuine racists—former Los Angeles Clippers owner Donald Sterling, for example—are far more influential than their small share of the population would suggest.

Indeed, even if only one in ten Americans are racists, that is still a lot of people.

These explanations for the paradox surely have some validity, but another reason for the paradox seems even more likely: widespread confusion between racism, which is hostility to blacks based on their supposed inferiority, and what I call racialism, which is a heightened consciousness of the race of others. It is easy to conflate them; dictionaries often define them as synonyms, and distinguishing them empirically is very hard. But they are crucially different. Racism is irrational, contemptible, and toxic. Racialism is rational, morally neutral, and inevitable in a society with our history of slavery, discrimination, and white-black social differences in so many areas.

Whether people are animated by guilt, observation of blacks' pervasive disadvantages, or the racially stratified nature of almost all of our institutions, they would have to be mad or willfully blind not to be racialist—and callous not to sympathize with the plight of blacks and other subordinated groups.

If whites describe this social reality truthfully, they will inevitably say racialist things, which will seem racist to those unaware of the distinction or ideologically inclined to ignore it. Atlanta Hawks owner Bruce Levenson, for example, was forced to sell his team after he sent an email that on its face indicated only a belief that some white fans prefer white cheerleaders and neighboring seatholders to black ones, and that this may reduce Hawks' ticket sales. This belief may or may not be true (one hopes it isn't), but it could be true—and if so, Levenson should not have been pilloried for saying it. Absent evidence of his own hostility to blacks, merely opining on others' views and their financial effects is racialist, not racist. Similarly, the psychology experiments finding differences in split-second reactions to images of people of different races might reveal racism. But it might instead show only that the subjects were as racialist as most other whites (and probably most blacks as well) in their acute awareness of America's pervasive racial disparities. For all we know, they may ardently want to reduce those disparities. We all entertain many stereotypes, including racial ones, based on perceived probabilities, not hostility. Probabilities, by definition, are true much of the time but not always. Sometimes, we must make quick decisions with no information other than probabilities—but absent hostility, this bespeaks racialism, not racism. Jesse Jackson famously said that if he were walking down the street, heard footsteps behind him, and feared robbery, he would be relieved to see that the person was white. Life presents countless examples of such racialism. None of us can escape them, but we can resist using them invidiously. The law and our own moral beliefs tell us that we must treat people as individuals, not statistics. In the workplace, for example, employers are legally required to individualize hiring decisions rather than rely on stereotypes—even statistically accurate ones. But the law still distinguishes between racism and racialism by allowing employers who do not hire candidates from protected groups to negate the inference of bias by proving legitimate reasons for not hiring them in individual cases.

A just society must struggle to reduce unfair disparities between racial groups. At the same time, we should respect the difference between merely acknowledging disparities and wanting to maintain them out of hostility. It is often challenging to treat people as individuals rather than lazily apply negative group stereotypes. Fortunately, Americans of good will manage to do so every day, while running the risk that their mere awareness of the other's race will backfire. Accusing racialists of racism makes a tough problem much worse because it indicts everyone, blacks included. If mere awareness of race in a racially differentiated society condemns us, then we have no defense and no remedy; we are all guilty and helpless. This is a recipe for endless misunderstanding, recrimination, strife, and misplaced guilt—not social progress.

Our much-urged "conversation about race problems" should put this on the agenda.

What Systemic Racism Systematically Downplays[*]

For several years now, systemic racism has been among the most frequently-mentioned concepts in American discourse. The term and its

---

[*] National Affairs, Spring 2022; https://www.nationalaffairs.com/publications/detail/what-systemic-racism-systematically-downplays

equivalents—including "structural" and "institutional" racism—appeared in the *New York Times* and the *Washington Post* roughly ten times more often in 2019 than they did in 2013, and have greatly proliferated since then. The topic is now the subject of countless college courses, classroom discussions, books, articles, media programming, political speeches, and formal and informal conversations. It is safe to say that today, systemic racism has acquired the status of a cultural meme.

Progressive advocacy groups use claims of systemic racism to shape a distinctive political agenda and rhetoric, emphasizing certain themes and downplaying others. Though their commitments are understandable and often persuasive, their preoccupation with the concept tends to understate progress among the black middle class while distracting from, and even undermining, a far more compelling priority: the repair of so many broken black communities in low-income areas.

The language of systemic racism, however, does not seek to mobilize such repair, nor does it equip younger black Americans with the tools to pursue the many genuinely equal opportunities that now exist. So while it is important to take the systemic-racism thesis seriously, it is also crucial to consider what it leaves out, as well as what it obscures.

Clarifying the Concepts

Before discussing the imperative of individual and community repair, I shall briefly clarify the notion of systemic racism itself, which plays a central, though largely unexamined and analytically undisciplined, role in our national debate.

The term "racism" is serviceably clear in its meaning, if not its application. It is the belief that one race—a human grouping distinguishable according to its inherited physical characteristics, particularly skin color—is inferior to another race, justifying stigma, separation, or mistreatment of various kinds. This concept differs from what I shall call "racialism," which refers to a heightened consciousness of the race of another person or group.

Racism is invidious, hostile, and demeaning. It denies the inherent equality of all human beings and represents the corrosive attitude that those who denounce systemic racism have in mind. Racialism, by contrast, is morally neutral, arguably rational, and—in a society with our history of race-based slavery, discrimination, and continued social differences between whites and blacks—probably inevitable. Ongoing racial disparities mean that people are often conscious of and call attention to another's race for reasons that lack the animus of racism, and indeed are often benign. Regardless of whether observers are animated by perceptions of blacks' continued disadvantages in our society, the racially stratified nature of so many of our institutions, or guilt over America's history of race-based enslavement and subjugation, they would have to be obtuse or willfully blind not to be racialist—not to mention callous in failing to sympathize with the plight of many black Americans.

Ordinarily, one cannot easily detect another person's feelings about black disadvantage in America, much less know whether those feelings are animated by racism or racialism. Since they are both states of mind, distinguishing between them empirically is especially difficult. Some advocates may not care much about detecting this attitudinal distinction, so long as blacks' disadvantage persists and whites fail to do what they should to eliminate it. But if whites' attitudes are the very essence of systemic racism, then the distinction between racism and racialism matters greatly.

So what makes racism—a conviction held by an individual—"systemic"? Definitions of the term vary, but they tend to hinge on the claim that racism is not simply an attitude held by some individuals. Instead, it is a form of discrimination inherent in policies, practices, social institutions, cultural mores, and environmental characteristics that place minority racial groups at a disadvantage relative to the racial majority. "Systemic" means that such bias is not only widespread, but practically inescapable.

In America, systemic racism is said to manifest in a socially pervasive bias against blacks that is threaded through all of our major institutions. Most, if not all, accounts of systemic racism build on both an observation of a population-level disparity—such as the differences between blacks' and whites' income or achievement levels in school—and a causal account of that divergence. Each of these variables raises thorny analytical questions that require solid data to answer. In order to compare how blacks and whites are treated by police or teachers, for example, one needs to know the behavioral base rates of the two groups; comparing blacks' and whites' arrest rates or differences in school-disciplinary actions is meaningless unless we know and can compare how the two groups actually behaved on the street or in the classroom. Yet such data are often hard to come by. Simplifying the task by presuming that the base rates are the same begs the question at issue, as does assuming that the base rates differ due to pervasive racism and its continuing effects on the black population—a central premise of the systemic-racism thesis.

Adherents of this thesis identify its manifestations in numerous, if not all, domains of American life. One popular video series focuses on eight indicia of the phenomenon: the wealth gap, employment disparities, housing discrimination, and differences in rates of government surveillance, incarceration, drug arrests, immigration arrests, and infant mortality. The Fair Fight Initiative lists a similar array of social conditions in which blacks are said to be systematically and chronically disadvantaged due to five widespread forms of racism: internalized, interpersonal, individual, institutional, and structural.

Those who denounce systemic racism see the cumulative subordination of blacks throughout history as forming a racist substructure that underlies, and thus permeates, our society, producing the disparities outlined above. Such racism is said to be so deeply embedded in our most powerful institutions and cultural mores that it will persist even without new infusions of racism at the individual level. This claim is pivotal and appears in its pure form in the December 2020 issue of Academic Medicine: "[I]f we are White," the article states, "we are a big part of the problem. We are part of the reason that structural racism imprisons and oppresses people of color every day, everywhere they go, and no matter what they do." Equal treatment now and in the future may soften the effects of systemic racism, but such treatment can never fully eliminate the harm.

Systemic racism is said to pose continuing barriers to blacks' ability to improve their socioeconomic lot—impediments that they have limited capacity to overcome thanks to the structurally racist milieu in which they operate. By the same token, it is not clear from this account what whites can do to rid themselves of their own inherent racism or purge the system of its bias—unless it is to support policies such as affirmative action that black leaders favor but that are highly controversial on their merits. Systemic racism's underlying premises, then, imply little agency on either side of the racial divide.

Systemic Racism Versus Inequality

The notion of systemic racism resonates with many Americans today, largely because racism was indeed systemic in the United States in the not-so-distant past. Slavery, which had been a feature of human civilization for millennia, took on a decidedly racial bent as millions of Africans were shipped to the New World as slaves. The United States eventually outlawed the trans-Atlantic slave trade in 1808, but race-based slavery continued to proliferate domestically for decades, most notably (albeit not exclusively) in the South. The ratification of the 13th Amendment on the heels of a bloody civil war brought an end to slavery as a matter of law in 1865. It would take another century, however, before black Americans were fully recognized as citizens entitled to equal civil rights under the law.

The long history of *de jure* slavery, segregation, and categorical subordination of blacks in America may have formally ended with the civil-rights revolution of the 1960s, but even then, some of the movement's fundamentally liberal reforms—particularly racial integration of schools, voting, public services, and accommodations—generated massive resistance, followed by slow, grudging, formalistic compliance in the South. Even in the North, efforts to integrate schools, housing, and other social domains spawned considerable public resistance. Almost three generations, decades of affirmative action, and trillions of anti-poverty dollars later, many Americans of all races remain painfully aware of continuing racial injustice and embedded inequality. This surely explains why 84% of Americans polled by the Pew Research Center in 2021 felt that more needed to be done to ensure racial equality.

But present inequality between blacks and whites, particularly in a historically stratified society like the United States, is not necessarily due to ongoing systemic racism. Black and white Americans remain unequal on a host of social indicators, to be sure. But whether each of these inequalities violates particular principles of justice poses other, more difficult analytical and normative issues that systemic-racism claimants seldom squarely address.

An important and deeply challenging feature of racism is that it is easy, and often tempting, to accuse another of harboring racist beliefs, but difficult—perhaps even impossible—for the accused to disprove the allegation. Charges of systemic racism are especially tricky to refute, as activists claim that race-based discrimination can be so subtle, so covert, and so entrenched in a culture or an institution's fundamental structure that those who operate under it may not even recognize their complicity in the subjugation of racial minorities. Again, given our society's long history of de jure racism and the complexities of causality over time, this claim of complicity is practically irrefutable, making such accusations easy to make—and abuse.

The best that the skeptic of this account can do is identify good reasons to doubt that racism in America today is truly systemic. As it turns out, there are at least four such reasons, the first of which is that rates of racist beliefs among individual Americans have declined over time. Public polling about white-black intermarriage, residential proximity, and other interactions shows dramatic increases in tolerant attitudes among whites since the 1960s. Although white-supremacist hate groups often loudly avow their racist beliefs, they remain a tiny, isolated fraction of the population, and are almost universally reviled by the political left and center as well as many on the right eager to distance themselves from fringe elements.

Of course, people harboring bigoted views often hide them in public, especially in social environments where racism is highly stigmatized. Answers in a survey are not proof that people do not hold racist views, although they do show that people are at least ashamed to admit them. That said, rates of behaviors related to or motivated by racism have fallen as well. In 2020, the FBI found that although the largest category of hate crimes (61.8%) were based on race/ethnicity/ancestry bias, the number of these incidents was under 6,000 nationwide. In a population of over 330 million, this surely does not qualify as systemic.

Second, the cohort of the U.S. population that has been most likely to hold racist views is slowly but inexorably dying out, to be gradually replaced by generations who tend to be far more accepting of racial differences. Though this theory is subject to some dispute, it is undeniable that members of younger generations seem to harbor less overtly racist beliefs than those of older generations. As these young Americans assume leadership roles in our nation's core institutions, their views will affect those institutions' structures, policies, and actions, as well as the people they influence. That virtually every major American institution in recent years has explicitly committed to combatting systemic racism suggests that we are already witnessing this trend taking shape.

A third reason to doubt the systemic-racism thesis is that anti-racist protests and highly publicized punishments of racist incidents have made racism much more newsworthy than it was in decades past. As a result, public discussion of the subject occurs much more often in our communities and traditional media today than it once did—and the tenor of this discourse is almost invariably opposed to racism. To the extent that systemic racism is inherently implicit or invisible, there is less room for it to hide now than there was in the past.

Additional public developments have likely heightened awareness of, as well as shame over, racism's role in our history. These include the 1619 Project (the book derived from which is on the best-seller list at the time of this writing), officially sanctioned removals of statues and other historical symbols linked to racism, highly publicized convictions of police officers and civilians for hateful crimes against blacks like George Floyd and Ahmaud Arbery, and numerous "cancel culture" incidents in prominent institutions ranging from local governments, schools, and museums to professional groups, athletic leagues, religious communities, and others. As I have written elsewhere, this practice of "canceling" individuals is often shameful and reprehensible. But it does demonstrate how deeply stigmatized racism is in American society.

It is possible, of course, that these developments have simply driven much hitherto overt racism further underground. But if so, such furtive racism—the sort of racism that dare not speak its name—would be the very antithesis of systemic.

Indeed, these incidents and others have made many white Americans desperate to avoid being associated with criticisms of blacks. The Democratic Party in particular has embraced a tactical silence on the matter, and for perfectly straightforward reasons: Given Latino defections during the 2020 elections, blacks are now the party's only reliable racial or ethnic constituency. Under these conditions, the party's white activists are less willing than ever to risk offending black leaders and voters. Meanwhile, Republican-controlled state legislatures and governors—realizing that blacks overwhelmingly vote Democratic—gerrymander legislative seats to minimize black constituents' political potency. If they believed black votes were truly up for grabs, they would surely compete for them—a logical circularity that Republicans may yet break, as they have done with Latinos.

Even if one were to ignore these compelling facts and insist that systemic racism remains widespread in today's America, there are good reasons to doubt that it represents the primary driver of continuing black disadvantage. For starters, the impressive upward mobility of other non-white groups—including immigrants of color—continues to confound the systemic-racism thesis. The most economically successful of these groups are Asians, particularly Chinese, Japanese, and Koreans—many of whom began life in America without American blacks' English-language advantage. In a recent study, researchers led by Raj Chetty—a leading analyst of economic mobility among different racial and ethnic groups—found that Hispanic and Asian Americans are closing much of the income gap with white Americans, while the upward mobility of lower-class black Americans has not kept pace.

Perhaps most discrediting of the ongoing systemic-racism account is the fact that black immigrants' economic mobility is much greater than that of blacks born in the United States. The median household income of the rapidly growing cohort of black immigrants is about 30% higher than that of American-born blacks. If systemic racism were the primary driver of blacks' disadvantages in America, we would expect it to hold back this population as well. Yet it seems not to have done so. Causal factors other than systemic racism, then, must be contributing significantly to black disadvantage in areas where it persists.

Seeking Remedies in the Wrong Places

Downplaying systemic racism as a major cause of continuing black disadvantages still leaves those disadvantages in place, of course. And for all too many of the most important social indicators, American blacks are significantly worse off on average than whites. This is true in terms of their lower income and net worth, as well as their higher rates of poverty, homelessness, criminal arrest, incarceration, marital instability, mortality, morbidity, and many other measures of social health.

Addressing these conditions should be among the highest priorities of public policy and civic and community action. Reformers frequently propose strategies to do just that. Some proposals are contained in pending legislation, and wisely target poverty across the board. A refundable child tax credit is perhaps the most compelling example, although it must be carefully crafted to minimize perverse incentives that tend to encourage the fractured-family complications discussed below. Refining and simplifying the Earned Income Tax Credit would also go a long way toward making the credit more accessible to more low-income workers. Efforts to reinforce the "success sequence" of high-school completion and delayed marriage and childbearing (discussed below) should be redoubled, as should those aimed at expanding school choice through vouchers, charter schools, and other innovative alternatives. Meanwhile, racism, systemic or otherwise, must be fought wherever it is detected or suspected, both legally and socially.

My focus here, however, is not to evaluate these and other specific policy remedies, as I have done in other publications. Instead, I would like to call attention to some of the problems and opportunities that the current preoccupation with systemic racism obscures, and may even aggravate. The following discussion has two purposes, the first of which is to detail some of the facts that impede blacks struggling to escape poverty's depredations. The second is to discredit the idea, which seems ubiquitous among reformers and activists on the left, that systemic racism continues to be a, if not the, principal cause of these enormous problems. As I emphasize above, systemic racism was indeed a most shameful, tragic feature of American history, and there is no doubt that some elements of its terrible legacy remain. But to say that ongoing systemic racism is the primary driver of current disparities between black and white Americans today is to distract attention from what may actually be causing or worsening the problem. It also likely contributes to a sense of despair that hobbles efforts to pursue meaningful change.

The first social factor contributing to socioeconomic disparities between blacks and whites in America is the fragility of the black family. Families represent the core of any healthy society, and the steady decline of two-parent households among Americans of all races is probably the most important, and most troubling, social trend that has materialized since World War II. For black families in particular, the development has been devastating.

In terms of family formation, black men today are far less likely than white men to get married. And unlike higher-income white men, who are more likely to marry than low-income white men, educated, economically prosperous black men are no more likely to marry than their poorer black counterparts. In fact, these men are less likely than poor blacks to have ever married at all.

For those who do marry, the statistics remain grim. Black men experience greater rates of divorce and separation than white men, and when their marriages dissolve, they are far less likely to remarry. Meanwhile, black women typically spend only 22% of their lives married—half the percentage of white women. And while unmarried women often cohabit with men, prominent marriage scholar Andrew Cherlin has found that these relationships tend to be relatively short-lived.

The breakup of marriages among black couples, combined with their failure to form in the first place, has had a predictably tragic impact on black children. Even as racism—both institutional and individual—in America has declined over the past century, the incidence of out-of-wedlock births within the black community has soared. According to the most recent National Vital Statistics data, 70% of black children were born to an unmarried mother in 2020—triple the rate Daniel Patrick Moynihan cited when he first sounded the alarm over the deteriorating state of the black family in 1965. For whites in 2020, the rate was just over 28%. (Moynihan's report placed it at 3% in 1963.)

The best predictor of low prospects for children, regardless of race, is growing up in a single-parent household. Over half of all poor children come from female-headed households, while a child raised without a father at home is four to five times more likely to be poor than a child of married parents. As family expert Kay Hymowitz has shown, these broken families often consist of "a revolving cast of stepparents, half-siblings, stepsiblings...and short-term romantic partners." Such instability, she observes, "can be every bit as damaging to children as poverty itself."

All of these elements—family and custodial chaos, low marriage rates, and high divorce rates—contribute to the persistence of disproportionate levels of poverty among black children. That these and other troubling trends in black family life have worsened at a time of diminishing racism, rising economic gains, and escalating political power among black Americans strongly suggests that systemic racism, whatever the term might mean, cannot persuasively explain them. Indeed, the fact that many of these same trends are also corroding impoverished white families while leaving black immigrants (whose marriage rates are over 70% higher than those of native-born blacks) relatively untouched indicates that racism, systemic or otherwise, is not the primary driving force behind the patterns described.

A second factor contributing to socioeconomic disparities between black and white Americans is isolation. Poor blacks are isolated in several ways that tend to keep them impoverished. The digital divide, for example, deprives them of information and social connections. But a related, and perhaps even more limiting, form of isolation is geographic—some of which reflects systemic racism of the past. As researchers like Harvard's William Julius Wilson have observed, blacks tend to live in areas of low economic growth, modest wage levels, and high unemployment, which limits their access to institutions and resources that contribute to upward mobility. Extensive research by Chetty and others suggests that these geographic elements are predictive of future economic prospects.

Blacks' isolation is not limited to geography, however; they tend to be socially isolated as well. Upward mobility depends heavily on people's social capital—their embeddedness in social networks and institutions—which helps them gain the kind of experience, reputation, and relationships that they can use to their advantage. Orlando Patterson's work on social networks provides dismaying insight into how social isolation perpetuates poverty among black Americans, even as a large black middle class has emerged against great odds. According to his research, blacks' networks are smaller, denser, and include remarkably few kinsmen compared to those of other races; indeed, almost half of black individuals surveyed had no kinsmen in their networks at all. In a finding he characterized as "truly startling," Patterson observed no relationship whatsoever between network density and education levels among this population. In other words, greater levels of education—which, as sociologist Robert Putnam has found, tend to correlate with larger social networks in the general population—did not extend blacks' ties by much. Again, ongoing systemic racism is not the likely culprit here.

A third factor contributing to continuing black-white disparities in America is schooling. Years of education and skills training are strongly correlated with wealth and income, and in recent decades, blacks have made significant gains in their rates of high-school graduation (which hovered around 25% in 1965 and are now at 88%) and college enrollment (38% in 2018, compared with roughly 15% in 1968). This progress is laudable, but high-school graduation statistics conceal large proficiency shortfalls in English and math.

At the same time, blacks' college-graduation rates continue to lag behind those of whites. One significant factor behind this continued disparity is black students' greater likelihood of dropping out of post-secondary school, which frequently saddles them with substantial student-loan debt but no credentials. Those who do graduate often leave with credentials that are too meager to sustain a promising occupational future.

At the primary- and secondary-school levels, black students are disproportionately cited for misconduct, which leads to higher drop-out rates and what some advocates decry as a "school-to-prison pipeline." Civil-rights officials in Barack Obama's Department of Education (many of whom have been restored during President Joe Biden's term) blame these discrepancies on racial bias among school administrators and teachers—accusations these groups stridently deny. John Ogbu and other educational researchers, by contrast, have pointed to an "oppositional culture" among many black students that manifests itself in less time spent on homework, high rates of truancy, elevated drop-out rates, and greater indiscipline. The latter in particular harms classroom learning for other students and has increased teacher attrition rates in many urban schools, which further undermines educational progress in black neighborhoods. The remedies for these conditions are elusive, but they surely lie to a large extent within the black community and black families.

A fourth factor contributing to social and economic disparities between blacks and whites is crime. Heightened levels of criminal activity continue to plague impoverished urban neighborhoods, where blacks not only disproportionately represent the perpetrators, but also the victims. Those who decry systemic racism often point to higher rates of incarceration as the main driving force behind disproportionate rates of black poverty. And indeed, this factor clearly contributes to racial socioeconomic disparities. Imprisonment, especially for long periods of time, ruptures a person's ties with his family and community—both of which offer legitimate sources of upward mobility. It also harms his future employment prospects, as many employers screen for applicants with criminal records. And as systemic-racism theorists almost invariably point out, blacks in America are imprisoned at much higher rates than whites.

Activists insist that these disparities call for large-scale decarceration, but releasing or diverting those convicted of minor offenses would have little real impact on incarceration rates. People whose only offense is drug use almost never go to prison today, and if they do, they rarely spend much time there. Moreover, recidivism rates in the United States are extraordinarily high: Two-thirds of those released from prison are arrested for a new crime within three years, while half end up re-incarcerated. Given that the victims of these crimes tend to be overwhelmingly black themselves, the costs of de-incarceration would fall most heavily on the black community. The same is true of "defund the police" measures, which many activists called for during mass protests against highly publicized police shootings of unarmed black individuals in 2020 and 2021. Wiser public officials—many of whom are black themselves—have opposed these demands.

Historically speaking, much of the damage to black families and communities had occurred long before black incarceration rates began their rapid rise several decades ago, suggesting that these elevated rates were at least in part a result, rather than a cause, of those communities' socioeconomic decline. To be sure, the two trends have likely precipitated a vicious cycle, whereby increased poverty begets increased incarceration and vice versa. Yet the order of the trends indicates that poverty—abetted by familial breakdown—was the leading impetus.

Fifth, many people—black and otherwise—find themselves in an impoverished state for a reason they may admit to themselves and others: They have made poor choices in the past that continue to harm them in the present. Observers who make this point are often accused of lacking compassion, "blaming the victim," and ignoring the structural causes of behavior. Such causes obviously matter, but any analysis that fails to consider the role of self-harming choices misses an important clue to what causes and sustains some poverty in black communities—and also what might reduce it.

By "poor choices," I am referring to decisions that squander or shut out opportunities to better one's prospects in the future. Some of these behaviors, like excessive gambling or the abuse of alcohol or tobacco, are merely self-destructive. Others, such as the abuse of illicit drugs, are also punishable by law. If detected, they will foreclose many paths out of poverty.

Most poor choices, however, are simply shortsighted; they sacrifice the real possibility of future, durable gains for more immediate, transitory ones. Common examples include chronic truancy; mingling with anti-social people; ignoring schoolwork in favor of television, the internet, or video games; engaging in habitual indiscipline; dropping out of school; excessive borrowing and spending; parenting children whom one cannot afford or care for; and quitting jobs or training programs from which one could acquire useful skills, experience, or certifications. Here, too, systemic racism's causal role is obscure. Though external remedies may help at the margins, solutions to these largely self-inflicted conditions must also include a change in individuals' behavior.

Indeed, studies have long shown that simple prudence and self-discipline—of which almost anyone is capable—can nearly eliminate the prospect of poverty for black and white teenagers alike. The so-called "success sequence" analyzed by Brookings Institution scholars—finishing high school, marrying after the age of 20, and doing both before having a child—reduces the risk of falling into poverty to 2%; failure to follow this path raises it to 75%.

To reiterate, racism was indeed a systemic phenomenon for most of America's history. And where racism persists, it remains a pernicious force in American life. But the insistence that racism continues to be both systemic and endemic, and that it alone or primarily accounts for ongoing disadvantages in black communities, is unpersuasive. The claim neither accords with crucial social realities nor points toward constructive solutions to the serious problems afflicting black Americans. As long as would-be reformers and their audiences take systemic racism as their principal target, real progress toward genuine and necessary policy and cultural solutions will be even more elusive.

Agents of Change

The challenge we confront today is to identify and overcome those obstacles to black Americans' progress that were placed there not only by racist systems of the past and programmatic failures of the present, but also by behaviors over which they and their communities have some control today. All three of these elements are crucial.

The vast array of federal and state policies that have been established and expanded for decades to address the challenges black Americans face have not sufficiently accomplished their missions. For better and for worse, the community's main challenges and opportunities today lie closer to home—in families, schools, workplaces, health practices, local mobilization, and well-targeted self-interest. This is one battleground where the future struggle must be waged and won.

Meritocracy[*]

More than 60 years ago, a British sociologist named Michael Young published *The Rise of the Meritocracy*. This justly-celebrated work was a satiric meditation on what a society in which political power and other advantages are held by the meritorious would be like. Young's meritocracy was dystopian, so it is no small irony that people today tend to speak of meritocracy approvingly, almost always signaling that it is a morally justified, even admirable basis for earning and allocating economic and other social advantages.

Daniel Markovits' ambitious, passionate, and provocative new book, *The Meritocracy Trap*, rejects this social judgment. In his very first line, he announces that merit—the belief "that social and economic rewards should track achievement rather than breeding"—"is a sham", a "counterfeit virtue, a false idol". His peroration condemns it as "an ideological conceit, constructed to launder a fundamentally unjust allocation of advantage," one that "undermines social solidarity," "corrupts democratic self-government," and "clearly serves no one's interests". In between is a painstakingly researched, immensely learned analysis of the admirable roots but (in his view) toxic effects of meritocracy in America. That the author of this disciplined jeremiad is perhaps the sweetest and mildest of my Yale Law School colleagues is an added surprise and perverse pleasure.

His detailed argument—supported by 90 pages of discursive endnotes and statistical appendices—is easily summarized. In sharp contrast with past regimes of hierarchy grounded in a warrior caste, aristocracy, land ownership, and then industrial organization, today's system of power and class advantage is grounded in merit, which has driven a radical increase in inequality between the "one-percenters" and the middle class. Poverty, he asserts, is "real and scandalous" but the War on Poverty largely succeeded

---

[*] *The Forum*, 3/5/2020, https://www.degruyter.com/document/doi/10.1515/for-2019-0043/pdf.

in protecting the poor from deep deprivation; poverty, even abject poverty, "is by any measure both narrower and shallower than in the past". His central—but dubious—point about poverty is that it is not today's distinctive form of maldistribution.

The winners have earned their advantage through rigorous training, technical skill, innovation, Stakhanovite dedication, merciless work schedules, and uncanny self-discipline. Nor are they simply clipping coupons. "Labor income," he explains, "now figures prominently even at the very sharpest peak of the distribution. Eight of the ten richest Americans today owe their wealth not to inheritance or to returns on inherited capital but rather to compensation earned through entrepreneurial or managerial labor". And as we shall see, they relentlessly transmit these qualities to their children whom they have programmed to carry these advantages forward. But lest we envy the one-percenters, Markovits insists repeatedly that they actually pay a grievous, soul-crushing price in the coin of anxiety, spiritual emptiness, anomie, and estrangement. These suffering overachievers know this but can't (or won't) get off their dispiriting, exhausting treadmill.* They end up (in William Deresiewicz's phrase) as "excellent sheep". They "do not just work too long and too hard; they also work in the wrong style—with the wrong motives and at the wrong tasks."

These "high-class conscripts" preside over a hollowed-out middle class of hopeless workers with too much credit-card debt and listless time on their

---

* Speaking of the treadmill, the author does not mention the famous welcome to generations of Yale Law School students by Dean (now Judge) Guido Calabresi urging them to "get off the treadmill" now that they had worked their way up to the academic summit where unlimited professional opportunities awaited them if they chose but exhorting them to pursue richer, deeper lives with less professional anxiety. Markovits tells us that they seldom do so, citing a 2014 survey of Yale Law students reporting widespread "mental health challenges" of various sorts and dissatisfaction with Yale's handling of these challenges. But Calabresi's memorable presentation of this moral option to remarkably mature, sophisticated women and men raises for me (though apparently not for Markovits) a fundamental question: perhaps their career choices years later are about as well-informed as such choices can ever be (although he obviously chose otherwise for himself) and they managed to meet those challenges, leading satisfying lives on the whole. I also accord less significance than he clearly does to their grousing about how hard they work and their desire – famously cited by almost every retiring politician – to spend more time with their families. (If so, their solution is as obvious as it is rarely chosen). As one who knows perhaps even more Yale Law graduates than Markovits (because I am older and taught there longer), I do not recognize the dismal, alienated portrait of them that he paints. (Louis Menand makes the same point in his September 30, 2019 *New Yorker* review of the book). In a private email, Markovits asserts that my depiction of them "is out of date." Possibly, but I suspect that the 2014 study about students' anxiety has little effect on their career choices over time.

hands—and no future. Worse, these losers worship at the same sturdy altar of merit constructed by the winners; they accept their fate as fair, justified, and inevitable. (This is precisely the perverse, literally demoralizing surrender that Young had predicted). Markovits dates this dystopia back to the 1970s when the "Great Compression" unraveled, ending a halcyon era when one of every three workers belonged to a union and could afford a comfortable, upwardly mobile life and retirement, a period when the non-poor experienced only modest differences in incomes, housing sizes, debt levels, education, and other accoutrements of post-war prosperity. Then, he tells us, "midcentury Americans self-consciously embraced this democratic merger and celebrated their classless society, including its popular culture".

What, then, has brought us to our current crisis where we teeter on the brink of a "class war"? Markovits emphasizes three interrelated factors. He uses the transformation of St. Clair Shores, a Detroit suburb, to illustrate and humanize the devastating dynamic. First, research and innovation (much of it subsidized by federal taxpayers) powered new, transformative technologies which were mastered by an increasingly cosmopolitan-international elite of MBAs, technologists, giant law firms, consultants, financiers, think tanks, and corporate raiders. Second, Markovits asserts, these new "masters of the universe" exploited law and politics to first establish, and then firmly to embed, bastions of privilege and wealth. Until John Kenneth Galbraith, Gabriel Kolko, Michael Harrington, and others spoiled the fun with their grim diagnoses and dire portents, this waxing tide did seem to be lifting all boats (not just yachts) until it ceased to do so as stratification set in.

This brings Markovits to his third factor: the new masters systematically distanced themselves from the "rest" of society. This separation began with their assortative mating. (He fails to mention the possible genetic advantages that they confer on their children; this omission avoids an academic minefield). The separation continues with their procreation (almost always within marriage); less stressful pregnancies; declining divorce rates (90% of children in the top 5% of zip codes live with both their biological parents); more time spent reading, speaking, and imparting organizational and emotional skills to their children while providing offspring vastly superior academic and experiential experiences from pre-K through college and graduate and professional schools. These excess investments in human capital made in a typical rich household over and above even middle-class ones, he reports, are equivalent to a traditional inheritance of roughly $10 million per child—a massive transfer of human capital that is "effectively exempted from gift and inheritance taxes".

The result—potentially lethal for a democracy and surely a factor in Trump's election—is that "the rich and the rest each lead lives that the other could hardly recognize and cannot understand", leading these lives in communities isolated from each other in numerous ways including health, pollution, life expectancy, crime, debt, consumption, and countless other variables—even "good teeth". This was not inevitable; Germany's educational and work trends "have taken nearly opposite paths". Strikingly, Markovits avoids making moral judgments about any of the choices that the "rest" have made, choices that might have contributed to their grim stasis; indeed, he claims to "make almost no moral judgments anywhere in the book". Like me, many readers will doubt this claim.

For Markovits, the chasm in educational preparation and career mobilization between the "best and the rest" is now almost unbridgeable:

> Economic inequality today produces greater educational inequality than American apartheid once did. [It] separates the rich not just from the poor but also, increasingly from the middle class.... By the time children apply to college, the differences are greater still ....

> Rich children now outscore middle-class children on the SAT by twice as much as middle class children outscore children raised in poverty Only about one in 200 children from the poorest third of households achieves SAT scores at Yale's mean.

In contrast, he maintains, the bottom and middle of the distribution are growing more equal; the income gap between the merely rich and the exceptionally rich has become immense; indeed, "eliminating the poor and the middle class from the distribution would actually increase inequality." As just noted, this baleful depiction does not accord the non-rich much agency; their own life choices seem to have no moral or consequential role in their grim social conditions. Their fates, it seems, are simply the detritus that the winners' choices leave behind.

Markovits evidently admires the one-percenters' earned achievements and does not propose to reverse them. Instead, he wants to debunk their claims of merit and redistribute their fruits. But he fails to reveal what should replace merit in his distributive justice vision. Reflexive references to "equality," of course, provide no meaningful standard of justice absent a rigorous definition of equality and a methodology for achieving it. The closest he comes to providing this is when he proposes to discount the economic gains generated by meritocratic innovation by the reduced productivity of non-elite workers that meritocratic innovation causes. He asserts that the net economic contribution of the elite to society has thus been "near zero," implying very large "costs of inequality". But despite the centrality of this claim to his thesis, his long supporting endnote does not prove it; the endnote shows only that economic productivity has risen at a lower rate since the 1970s than it did during the earlier Great Compression. Although true, its cause is actually one of macroeconomics' great mysteries and the subject of vast but inconclusive technical debate. It tells us little about how to define inequality for policy purposes, much less how to reduce it.

The path forward, he says, requires reforms that transcend progressives' approaches, claiming (unfairly, in my view) that their objections to meritocracy's social depradations are too tactical and limited:

> "... only when they discriminate against minorities or working mothers, or mask the operation of insider networks and cultural capital, rather than because they are simply, directly, and generally inhumane. In effect, this tells the elite to keep its nose to the grindstone in order to validate its privilege ... driv[ing] the middle class into the arms of demagogues and the elite to resort to ineffectual gimmicks".

Instead, he wants to capitalize on the harmony between "middle-class aspirations to recover lost income and status and elite aspiration to restore authentic freedom". This harmony—along with some proposals to change the payroll tax and to condition private schools' and universities' tax exemption on enrolling many more lower-income students—is Markovits' *deus ex machina*. Nothing in the rest of his book provides any reason to expect this harmony, much less explain how it would work. Masters of the universe at Goldman Sachs, Apple, and Yale Law School will not be transfigured from workaholics to egalitarian beachcombers. Would America really be a better or fairer place if they were?

Diversity, Equity, and Inclusiveness: Their Coherence Requires Line-Drawing*

In the last decade, three concepts—diversity, equity, and inclusiveness—have become so politically and organizationally compelling that their initials—D, E, and I—are now a familiar shorthand for institutional self-righteousness. D, E, and I (sometimes joined by A for accessibility) constitute the latest form of virtue signaling; they represent the normative commitments that organizations evidently think the public expects them to practice in their internal and external activities. Groups in a remarkable variety of fields now even designate DEI officials or committees, units that are deputized to

---

* *American Purpose*, September 7, 2022, https://www.americanpurpose.com/articles/drawing-the-line-on-diversity-equity-and-inclusion/

implement these three norms throughout the organization's outreach, governance, programming, staffing, and other activities.†

Given the "DEIfication" of organizational life, one might expect these three norms to be clear-cut and widely understood by those within the organizations who must apply and enforce them, and by the larger social audience to which these signals are being transmitted. But if, as I suspect, D, E, and I are essentially undefined and deeply ambiguous, someone seeking to understand how these values would apply to particular situations will likely be disappointed.

In a recent superficial test of my suspicion, I found earnest expressions of commitment to those values but no explanation of their meanings, criteria, or boundaries, when I visited the websites of three units at Yale University that claim to have D, E, and I programs: its Office of Diversity and Inclusion, its Office of Institutional Equity and Accessibility, and the Medical School's own Office of Diversity, Equity, and Inclusion. My guess—and it is only a guess—is that many other institutions exercise a similar calculated ambiguity, perhaps because the more explicit they are about what the terms mean, the more likely it is that they will attract criticism, backlash, and even legal challenges.

The deep ambiguities of D, E, and I are neither accidental nor surprising. Much of their attractiveness to an organization lies precisely in how they can elicit widespread public approval without the organization having to commit itself in advance to any meaningful constraints on its actions. This may help explain the baleful finding of a recent *Economist* survey of research on D, E, and I programs' effects: They often backfired; and mainly, they benefited white males.

Once one begins to specify the content of D, E, and I, deep disagreements almost inevitably surface. After all, the meaning or application of each of these terms is genuinely controversial—certainly as applied to specific cases, but even in general. This controversiality is why entities which claim D, E, and I as precious organizational values should add a fourth concept: line-drawing, or L. Indeed, L is essential to the intellectual coherence of D, E, and I. Absent L, the terms D, E, and I are essentially empty, lacking substantive moral content. In contrast, L by its very nature requires the decisionmaker to exercise discrete judgments and commitments, imposing on the

---

† *I do not discuss here another form of organizational virtue signaling known as ESG, for environmental, social, and governance. ESG mainly targets investors and other public and private monitors of corporate activity, often via glossy publications. A recent analysis finds that all of the Fortune 500 companies claim to practice ESG. Legal challenges to ESG disclosures are pending.*

organization a standard with moral content as an essential clarifying feature of its self-description.

We can see this by examining the line-drawing necessary to render D, E, and I meaningful and coherent. But before making the case for line-drawing, we must recognize that when D, E, and I policy architects do explicitly draw their lines, such efforts may be more than clarifying; they may be oppressive, perverse, and even unconstitutional. In a recent example recounted in *City Journal*, the California Community College system has published a DEIA policy that defines which values the system's employees must teach, think, and exemplify in order to demonstrate their "cultural competency" for purposes of job evaluation and tenure. This system's line-drawings, which demand adherence to highly dubious and illiberal principles, are drawn directly from the far Left's ideological playbook, including systemic racism and state-engineered equality. They almost certainly violate academic freedom and probably the First Amendment rights of faculty and staff as well.

(There is another problem with much DEI line-drawing, one that Harvard economist Roland Fryer has recently criticized. Citing examples from DEI claims of wage and other forms of discrimination, he shows how such claims are often analytically and empirically weak, relying on often misleading data and methodologies.)

Diversity

When an organization claims to be diverse or committed to diversity, what is it claiming? This turns out to be a complicated, question-begging issue. Diverse with respect to which features? And compared with what? How is diversity measured? And most important for this purpose: What values does this diversity confer on the organization? This question of values is where line-drawing comes in. Until the organization breaks down the undifferentiated notion of diversity into discrete elements of its application, the observer remains utterly in the dark about what the diversity means for this organization, why the organization values it, and the tradeoffs with other values that it might entail.

The example of affirmative action policy in higher education admissions helps to clarify this basic point about line-drawing. Twenty years ago, I systematically analyzed this very question, asking what "diversity value" ethno-racial preferences conferred on colleges and universities that administer them. Today, the programs' basic elements remain essentially the same except in the rare cases where the courts have rejected them, as with the University of Michigan undergraduate admissions program.

To answer this question, we need to know which particular aspects of individuals or communities the program designers think confer the relevant, desired diversity value, and which aspects do not. In drawing these lines, the programs clearly deem certain personal characteristics to confer high diversity value—especially race (and within race, especially Blackness) and ethnicity (and within ethnicity, Latinoness). Whether Asians in general, or individual Asian subgroups in particular, are thought to confer diversity value for purposes of these programs is uncertain; it is a central issue in a case now pending before the Supreme Court. Equally clear is that Whites and other ethnic groups or sub-groups do not receive any special consideration under these programs, nor do candidates' religious and political affiliations—an especially striking omission given how salient such affiliations are to one's viewpoints on a broad range of issues. The standard justification for diversity-oriented affirmative action, after all, is to foster viewpoint differences for the intellectual benefits that thinking about such differences may generate. A priori (which is how programs select the groups to be preferred), doesn't the perspective of a Muslim or fundamentalist Christian or Orthodox Jewish applicant have at least as much diversity value as that of a middle-class Black or Latino?

The need for line-drawing to verify, measure, or optimize diversity-value in any community, moreover, goes far beyond deciding who shall be admitted to it. In the collegiate context, for example, diversity-value may vary substantially depending on whether one measures it in a venue-specific way—that is, according to the number of the so-called diverse students who are present in a particular classroom, course, dormitory, or major.

An altogether different kind of line-drawing is required to determine how much viewpoint diversity exists in any particular academic setting. After all, nominal diversity seems rather meaningless unless it produces actual disagreement and debate. In my own pedagogical experience (shared by colleagues whom I have consulted on this point), ethno-racially diverse students in a classroom are no more or less likely to call attention to the racial implications or resonances of an issue than are other, non-diverse (ethno-racially speaking) students. Of course, student (and faculty) diversity may be desirable for other reasons—say, to encourage minority-group enjoyment of the socioeconomic status benefits that affirmative action is supposed to confer after graduation.

My point, however, is that such benefit is not generated because of what goes on in classrooms and other campus venues. Indeed, sociologist Orlando Patterson (an affirmative action supporter) ruefully conceded years ago that "no group of people now seems more committed to segregation than Afro-American students and young professionals." Again, the general rubric of diversity serves to conceal or confuse the different kinds and distribution of benefits and costs that the policy entails.

Accordingly, both the notion of diversity and the value that institutions do and should ascribe to it depend on many contextual factors—that is, on line-drawing.

Equity

Equity (or fairness) in the abstract is a universally embraced value; hence the sweep of its normativity. We all favor it, though we often disagree with one another about whether a process or condition is in fact inequitable. Perhaps the most important question that faces us—once we have satisfied our most basic needs for the requisites of life (food, clothing, shelter, respect, concern, and so forth)—is whether we are being treated fairly. Most of the conflict in our daily lives, it seems, is over this very question.

That said, what constitutes fair treatment is notoriously and inevitably debatable. Consider some frequent contenders for the fair treatment condition. Perhaps the most common one follows from the norm of equality—that is, the value of equal treatment. Yet the meaning of this ubiquitous norm turns on whether the equal treatment standard is reward based on mere existence, on effort, on productivity, or instead on outcome. The fact that this distinction among these four possibilities (and there could be more) is salient to our moral discourse shows the fundamental importance of line-drawing to our moral judgments. Are workers who are paid different wages being treated unequally? In a descriptive sense, the obvious answer is yes. But in a normative sense, the answer must be: It depends.

An example of both this principle and its exceptions is the Equal Pay Act of 1963. This law requires employers to pay the same wage for the same work regardless of the worker's gender. But this principle applies only when workers labor under the same conditions and when they have the same level of experience, and when their jobs require the same level of skill, effort, and responsibility. The relevance of these discriminating factors (skill, effort, responsibility) should remind us that the notions of equality and fairness are inadequate, indeed hollow ideas unless and until we incorporate into the equality assessment certain other values. In the same way, the Declaration of Independence's proclamation that "all men are created equal" means that—although centuries of blood and toil are far from having fully established it—all humans are entitled at a minimum to equal dignity, respect, and opportunity to lead decent lives.

Important as this equity principle is, however, it leaves most questions about what constitutes equitable treatment—including some of life's most important ones—to be resolved by the development of legal and social norms. And those norms, in turn, instantiate further line-drawing, which can be increasingly fine-tuned. For example, male and female athletes have traditionally competed in separate gender-specific contests, but transgender women athletes are now seeking to compete with cisgender female ones in nominally "women's races" over the protests of the latter. Does equity require the sponsor of such a race to permit transgender women to compete in it? Personally, my answer is no, if the disparity in hormone levels is too large to allow a "level playing field" among the competitors. But this of course raises several questions including what "too large" means. Others may define equity to emphasize that all of the competitors self-identify as women and that this self-identification factor should be the key to drawing an equitable line. No objectively true conception of equity exists here; the definition depends on an extrinsic act of line-drawing that from some perspective can be seen as arbitrary. Invoking the concept of equity cannot resolve such conflicts without resort to some extrinsic value.

Inclusiveness

The third concept that proponents of D, E, and I invoke is inclusiveness. Here, the animating idea is that the organization is open and welcoming to a very wide range of different people. But the attractiveness and character of a group largely depend not only on whom it includes but also on whom it excludes—an insight nicely captured by Groucho Marx's famous drollery that he wouldn't want to join any club that would admit him. This fact is especially true of many of the organizations that proudly proclaim their inclusiveness, particularly universities and those other entities whose prestige (or, as with museums and hospitals, the prestige of their governing boards) consists precisely in their high barriers to entry. These barriers may take a variety of forms, but their essential purpose is to define and preserve the organization's essence through exclusion.

This fact of exclusivity is a source of both self-esteem and enhanced reputation on the part of those on the inside of such organizations. The flip side of this insider pride, however, is often resentment on the part of envious outsiders, particularly if they were previously insiders. A recent example was the decision by the Art Institute of Chicago to fire more than 100 of its volunteer docents—almost all of them relatively wealthy White women knowledgeable about art—for the avowed purpose of enhancing its internal D, E, and I. This was an unusual instance of internal line-drawing becoming public and controversial.

The salient point here is not that many organizations that trumpet their inclusiveness are hypocritical, disingenuous, or as in this case clumsily "woke." Rather, the larger point is that organizations define themselves to a great extent on the basis of their particularism and narrowing exclusivity, and that this carefully cultivated self-definition—indeed their very coherence as organizations—can only be maintained by drawing lines to exclude most of those who might ardently wish to be insiders.

The Morality of Line-Drawing

What does this excursus into the dynamics and interactions of diversity, equity, and inclusiveness in organizational life reveal?

First, it shows how powerful virtue signaling has become as a marker of organizational legitimacy. The spread of virtue signaling in American life is an important development, but one whose complex causes are outside the scope of this essay.

Second, it reminds us that the much-vaunted D, E, and I are not so much moral values in and of themselves as they are placeholders for the far more important and discriminating moral work that occurs when organizations give these three values substantive content through their morally-inflected line-drawing. (Some on the left criticize DEI for privatizing moral responsibilities that instead ought to be assigned to government).

Third, most of an organization's ethical work is now done in the course of implementing D, E, and I. Thus, the sloganeering that surrounds these values raises key questions about what the organization stands for and the terms of its ethical tradeoffs. Its line-drawing is a far more important and revealing measure of its true organizational values than are its abstract professions of D, E, and I.

What I Learned from the Icelandic Ash Cloud*

'Twas the night I was leaving with happiest heart
After three months in Delhi, I would finally depart
Teaching young Indians was all well and good
But New York's my home, so return there I would.

Entering the airport, my soul sang a song
With nonstop in business class, what could go wrong?
My luggage they checked, sent it to the black hole
Like hundreds of others, I ceded control.

---

* *Unpublished.*

Five minutes later, the passengers learned
That no planes would fly while volcanoes churned
Hundreds of travelers heard this information
With gnashing of teeth and much consternation.

What's Iceland to us?, we passengers thought
Halfway 'round the world should affect us naught
If Europe's got problems, well fly the plane east
From traffic control we should be released.

Air India's oracle said not a word
Despite all the protests it certainly heard
Except "go to hotel where you'll stay until
We decide on your fate. Until then be still."

Obedient, we shuffled to heartbreak hotel
For more than two days we've lived travelers' hell
Access to checked luggage, the clothes that we lack?
Access denied: wear what's now on your back.

Of dosas, samosas, I'm sick up to here
I want no more dal, no more rice or paneer
Even hotel A/C won't calm down our spleen
When each day the temp is one-hundred-thirteen.

On TV there's nothing but Bollywood dance
I'd kill for a grade-B Hollywood romance
The guests, many turbaned and salwar chemized
Are losing their tempers, they're highly displeased.

Those without laptops have nothing to do
We chaff at the staff, and shake our fists too
As two days' confinement now stretches to three
I've finished my William Makepeace Thackeray

I've read all the papers, no bookstore is open
The cricket's so boring, to fill time I'm gropin'
The health club is closed, and so is the pool
Oh how could those Icelandic vents be so cruel?

Is this long imprisonment simply bizarre
Or is it just how things today really are?
Are there lessons from this that we moderns can learn
From watching remote Iceland's volcanoes burn?

I now think that such events geological
Can remind us of truth socio-ecological
Chaos doth reign, the small butterfly
Flapping its wings in a glen in Kauai

Transforms the Atlantic currents and climes.
We need reminding, alas, many times
That our earth is small: what happens to thee
Often comes back to influence me.

Part 4

THE MISBEGOTTEN TRUMP PRESIDENCY

Introduction to Part 4

I loathe Donald J. Trump. I not only voted against him twice; I opposed much of what his administration did—or attempted to do—once in office. Needless to say, I thoroughly condemn his conduct after Election Day 2020 (including on January 6, 2001) in the strongest possible terms. (I do applaud his administration's initiation of the Abraham Accords in the Middle East, its championing of school choice, and some other measures).

During the early days of the Trump administration, I published a long limerick, reproduced here, that mocked the President, his character, and some of his actions. I later published some pieces criticizing the Trump administration on a number of policy issues, including its severe limitation on the number of refugees to be admitted and its efforts to implement some of its most controversial policies by declaring national emergencies. I wrote a favorable assessment of the Supreme Court's decision upholding the Trump administration's travel ban, although I opposed the ban as a policy matter. Finally, I published another article excoriating Trump for crudely and cruelly defaming TV commentator Joe Scarborough and a private citizen, Lori Klausutis, whose story had been featured on the "Morning Joe" show.

Limerick[*]

> Let's honor the day we gave birth
> To a nation like none then on earth
> Many would say

---

[*] *Huffington Post*, 7/5/2017, https://www.huffpost.com/entry/trumps-america-limerick_b_595d2b18e4b05c37bb81b507

That's still true today
Though this year has tested our worth.

A brash, boastful brander named Trump
Thought he'd do quite well on the stump
His past he admired:
Pageants, deals and "You're fired"
He'd easily trounce Jeb (lazy lump!)

His campaign excited the masses
Who think that the feds are all asses
He heaped endless scorn
On all foreign-born
While giving bigots fulsome passes.

His passion, as Yeats had foreseen,
Ran to the worst and obscene
McCain, a true hero
To Trump is but zero
Just money, not valor, is green.

His coiffure absurd but well-kempt
His rallies cascades of contempt
With words out of kilter
And tweets without filter
One wishes he felt more verklempt #

Trump saw that his opponent was lame
Her platform just more of the same
Deploring each skeptic
With words narcoleptic
Ne'er was she or her party to blame.

Did Kremlin help out? Can't yet tell
But Manafort's clients sure smell
Spies managed to see
Inside DNC
Which managed a campaign from hell.

Trump somehow won—still a mystery
The least-prepared man in our history

#Yiddish for speechless due to strong emotions

The voters have spoken:
"The system is broken,
It's not run by good folks like me."

Inaugural speech—doom and gloom
The U.S., said Trump, now's a tomb
Firing bile from his cannon
Stoked by Miller and Bannon
Killing pacts he'd never exhume.

Inaugural crowds were "immense"
When photos proved this was nonsense
He blamed doctored pix
And media tricks
To make 44's seem more dense.

The transition, he pledged, would be faster
Turned out to be a disaster
The ethical rules
Written by and for fools
Were swept aside by the new master.

He swiftly attacked our allies
While praising those we should despise
Mining jobs his Grail
Restoring them will fail
They're simply more pies in his skies.

Trump's nominees shucked and they jived
Background they lacked, they contrived
Some beribboned brass
Did have some class
Most others are merit-deprived.

In PR, Trump's one of a kind
Tweets whatever comes into his mind
Rejects logic and facts
Relying on flacks
To clean up the mess left behind.

"Fake news" is his mantra du jour
Only Fox News is honest and pure

Truth is a victim
Of every Trump dictum
For Donald, facts have no allure.

ACA — enemy number one
Yet "repeal and replace" can't get done
Aides' briefings Trump's spurned
"It's complex," he's learned
Reality's not so much fun.

His White House leaks like a sieve
As insiders have truth to give
On Comey and Flynn.
Trump helps Putin win,
Giving hard-won intel the shiv.

Any Mar-a-Lago member or guest
Can hear as the fate of the West
Is discussed over dinner
Trump's pride the sole winner
Boasters don't keep cards close to chest

Awesome power he gives to his kin
No policy chops, but they'll win
In struggles to come
No matter how dumb
As Trump's suck-ups they're in like Flynn.

What honorable person would join
Folks who one's reputation purloin
No wonder top ranks
Are empty—"No thanks
I'd rather earn honesty's coin."

For Trump, the bucks won't stop with him
He's passed it to General Jim
If he has insomnia
He'll just blame Melania
His White House—a narcissist's whim.

Trump's Refugee Limits Betray Past Republican Presidents and the Founders*

Top aides to President Trump, according to White House leaks, are urging him to limit or even eliminate refugee admissions to the United States. The administration has already severely reduced America's refugee program, especially in comparison with the Obama years. In fact, Trump has admitted far fewer refugees than any Republican president in the almost 40 years since the Refugee Act of 1980 was enacted. Further cuts would betray a humanitarian tradition older than the nation. They would also be irrational and self-defeating.

From the arrival of the Pilgrims in 1620, America has been a haven for people fleeing persecution and hopelessness. In 1965, Congress created the modern system of immigration law, ending almost half a century of explicit ethnically discriminatory exclusion, while imposing new limits on most of the western hemisphere. The new law also limited refugee admissions largely to those fleeing communist-dominated countries—a Cold War reflex that ended in 1980 when the much more evenhanded Refugee Act passed (unanimously in the Senate). The act defined refugees as people outside their home countries who would face persecution based on "race, religion, nationality, political opinion, or membership in a particular social group" if they were to return home.

The Refugee Act created two distinct remedies for such persecution—one for those making claims as asylees, the other for refugees proper. The differences are crucial. Asylees, or asylum seekers, are already at our border or inside the country (often illegally) when applying; refugees are abroad when they make their claims and during the vetting process by Homeland Security officials.

Asylees who meet the persecution criteria will almost certainly be admitted without limit—the law sets no numerical limits—if an administrative judge determines their claims are valid. For refugees, a rigid quota caps the number that are admitted annually. The cap is set through a mandated consultation process involving the president and congressional committees. (The consultation for next year's cap has just begun.)

The refugee program's numerical limits and methodical screening of claimants overseas (it often takes years and is aided by organizations such as religious groups) together assure a relatively controlled, rational and

---

* *Los Angeles Times*, 9/23/2019; https://www.latimes.com/opinion/story/2019-09-20/refugee-donald-trump-restrictions-border-crisis

deliberative application process. Asylum decisions, which are initially conducted under severe time and caseload constraints, are much more prone to erroneous inclusion or exclusion. That is especially true now at the border with Mexico, amid mass detentions, legal challenges and political pressures.

These procedural differences explain why reducing refugee quotas, as Trump wants to do, would in no way mitigate the border crisis. That crisis is caused by a huge backlog of asylum applicants, most with weak claims, who are entitled to due process safeguards and must either be detained or released pending their hearings. If released, they may simply melt into the population and never have their claims tested.

The wholly discretionary nature of refugee admissions not only cuts down on errors, it also provides a flexible instrument enabling the U.S. to protect at-risk foreigners who have aided our soldiers, intelligence operations and diplomats abroad, often at grave risk to themselves and their families. These kinds of admissions explain why many top military, national security, and foreign policy leaders (former Defense Secretary James N. Mattis, most recently) express alarm at the administration's eagerness to curtail the program.

Indeed, the reductions Trump has already put in place have taken a huge toll on refugee admissions. As recently as 2016, the United States resettled almost 100,000 refugees. The number admitted fluctuated, but under Presidents Reagan, George H.W. Bush and George W. Bush (except for a time after the Sept. 11 attacks), and Obama, the U.S. has led the world in refugee admissions. Political turbulence abroad and the growing number of anti-democratic regimes taking power in the last few years have pushed the world's refugee numbers to nearly 26 million, the highest levels since World War II, and this doesn't include the 41.3 million internally displaced people and 3.5 million asylum seekers. Yet last year, the U.S. resettled just 23,000 refugees. For the first time, we accepted fewer than Canada, which took in 28,000, despite our population being 10 times larger. This is shameful.

Today's spasm of global displacement and repression demands more, not fewer, refugee admissions. If after the consultation with congressional committees mandated by the Refugee Act, Trump cuts the cap further, Congress should pass a resolution demanding a higher number proportionate to the scale of the current refugee crisis. The president has the upper hand on this issue because of his constitutional powers over foreign affairs and his leading role as spelled out in the Act, but Congress should muster whatever influence it can in this compelling cause.

The Real Problem with Trump's National Emergency Plan*

President Trump has declared a national emergency—purely in order to fund his wall. The courts may—or may not—reject his gambit.

But the fact that he may actually possess the legal authority to require agencies to waste billions of dollars simply to fulfill a foolish campaign promise he thinks won him the election is itself scandalous. The theatrics surrounding his petulant threat to do so obscure a vital question for our democracy going far beyond this (non)crisis, a question to which Congress should immediately turn: Who decides what constitutes a national emergency?

In hundreds of laws, Congress has given the president the power to decide. (The Brennan Center for Justice has compiled an exhaustive list.) But by failing to define crucial terms, legal standards and accountability rules, Congress has handed presidents an all-too-handy tool of tyranny commonly used by autocrats to amass more power, crush dissent and eviscerate democratic institutions. In Mr. Trump's case, it has handed an unguided missile to an ignorant, impetuous man-child.

Congress should have known better. After all, it enacted the National Emergencies Act of 1976, which purported to regulate such declarations, only two years after President Richard Nixon's abuses of power forced his resignation. The Act actually made matters worse in a key respect: It defined a national emergency as "a general declaration of emergency made by the president." This circular definition, of course, is no constraint at all. Or as Humpty Dumpty says to Alice, "it means just what I choose it to mean—neither more nor less."

In the nature of national emergencies, some definitional leeways are unavoidable. But Congress could readily specify certain conditions that must exist before the president can make such a declaration and thus arrogate to himself extraordinary powers—curtailing liberties, seizing property, spending funds appropriated for other purposes and suspending protective laws—that Congress would not otherwise be likely to grant him in advance, or perhaps ever. (Indeed, Congress has the power to override Mr. Trump's declaration and it should in this case—though it probably won't.)

One can easily specify some of the factors in a national emergency condition that any responsible Congress would insist on before allowing such a declaration to take effect: magnitude (the feared incremental harms of the

---

* *New York Times*, 2/14/2019; https://www.nytimes.com/2019/02/14/opinion/trump-national-emergency.html

condition are very large, not just marginal); geographic scope (those harms should be nationwide even if the triggering condition is more localized); extraordinary (the condition should be rare, if not unprecedented); imminence (the anticipated harms should be so close in time that Congress cannot deliberate); and likely effectiveness (the President's action should promise to substantially solve the problem).

Reasonable people may disagree, of course, about precisely how Congress should define and weigh these factors, how they should be applied to the facts on the ground, and whether other factors should be considered. President Trump's wall cannot survive such a rigorous analysis: Even assuming that recent illegal border crossings harm the nation, they are not greater (indeed, they are probably fewer) than in recent decades; Congress has been deliberating (in its fashion) for decades about immigration reform, including border walls; and many Americans believe that the wall would be ineffective and a bad idea. Congress simply disagrees with the President about which border security measures would do the job—an instance of decidedly normal politics.

But my larger claim—that Congress's delegation to presidents of vast, essentially unconstrained power to declare national emergencies has been an irresponsible surrender of its constitutional responsibilities—does not depend on whether my assessment of this particular case is correct. Not since the New Deal has the Supreme Court struck down a statute for this kind of standardless delegation of legislative authority to administrative agencies, but the Roberts Court—activist, conservative and suspicious of broad delegations of power to agencies—recently reached out to review a case, *Gundy v. United States*, that gives it an opportunity to revive the long-dormant and doubtful non-delegation doctrine.

Another way to make the National Emergencies Act more compatible with the rule of law is through a procedure that would broaden participation in all future decisions to declare national emergencies. Under one such reform, the president would have to consult with the leaders of both parties in Congress before issuing a declaration. Even if Congress could not override such a declaration, members would have to take a public position on the facts and reasons invoked as justification by the president. If time were of the essence (not so in this case; Congress has legislated about a wall for more than a decade), their responses would have to be expedited. With such a procedure in place, judicial review of the declaration could be narrow, if at all.

If national emergency declarations are as important as presidents (with Congress's acquiescence) claim them to be, then they are important enough to be subjected to such standards and procedures. In the long run, this is more crucial to the vitality of our democracy than whether President Trump ultimately gets his wall.

The Court Ruled Correctly on the Travel Ban*

In some respects, the Supreme Court's decision on Tuesday rejecting challenges to President Trump's travel ban was highly predictable. Mr. Trump issued his series of executive orders under the authority of a breathtakingly broad statute—specifically, Section 212(f) of the Immigration and Nationality Act—a provision designed to forestall national security threats. And he issued it for two plausible reasons: the proliferation of international terrorism threats against the United States, and the seeming inadequacy of overseas screening ("vetting") of would-be travelers to the United States by some source countries. Given this context, the decision has all the surprise of a Golden State Warriors victory in the N.B.A. finals.

Why, then, did the decision draw four dissenters? Here too the answer is quite straightforward. Mr. Trump is a man who proudly parades his many egregious biases, especially against immigrants in general and Muslims in particular. His campaign was replete with vile stereotypes and schoolyard bullying of minorities of all sorts, conduct that has only worsened since the election. The dissenters took the President at his anti-Muslim word and found support in our long legal tradition, encoded in the First Amendment, protecting religious minorities from overreaching majorities.

The majority justices, no less committed to the Amendment's prohibition against government discrimination against particular religions, nevertheless emphasized the importance of distinguishing between the "statements of a particular President" and the "authority of the Presidency itself"—including Section 212(f).

This distinction—highlighting the principle of deference to the presidency in the foreign affairs and national security areas—provides the key to the court's decision; all nine justices accepted this principle. The question actually dividing them was how much deference Mr. Trump could claim by reason of his foreign-affairs and national-security powers under the Constitution and Section 212(f).

The challengers maintained that the Court could not, and should not, simply accept the almost reflexive presidential claim to deference in this particular area. Instead, they argued, the Court should assess Mr. Trump's action with the skeptical, probing "strict scrutiny" standard traditionally applied to religious discriminations by government.

---

* *New York Times*, 6/26/2018; https://www.nytimes.com/2018/06/26/opinion/the-court-ruled-correctly-on-the-travel-ban.html

The majority emphatically disagreed. Invoking the familiar deference principle commonly applied by the Court when it comes to executive actions in the name of national security, it decided to demand only a "rational basis" for the executive order (indeed, the majority said, it could have applied an even more relaxed "facially legitimate" standard of review). It insisted, rightly in my view, on assessing the order on its face rather than probing Mr. Trump's anti-Muslim motives (as evidenced by his rhetoric) and in trying to parse the relative weight that they played in his decision as compared with his legitimate national security concerns.

With this move, the Court's conclusion was inevitable, resting on the many policy reasons and distinctions adduced in the order. Most of the rest of the Court's opinion was mere window dressing, with a few exceptions.

First, the majority had to deal with another provision of the Immigration and Nationality Act barring religious and other types of discrimination in the issuance of visas. Here, the Court plausibly read this provision to apply only to visas, not to admissions per se—especially (but not only) in light of its broad interpretation of Section 212(f).

The other noteworthy addition—not central to its analysis—was the majority's welcome, justifiably harsh condemnation of the Supreme Court's notorious 1944 *Korematsu* decision, which had upheld the wartime internment of American citizens of Japanese descent. The dissenters used that precedent to try to impugn the majority's reasoning in the present case, indeed the very morality of its decision.

The fact that the Court ruled correctly, however, does not mean that the status quo is acceptable. The most fearful aspect of the Court's decision is already evident in Mr. Trump's immediate, triumphalist response to it. The decision will certainly embolden him in his claims of vast presidential power and indifference to the rule of law, whether on immigration or in other policy areas.

All the more reason, then, for Congress to confront and discipline those claims. It should promptly review Section 212(f) with a view toward prudently constraining any president's power to bar broad classes of aliens whenever he deems it necessary to protect the national interest. At the very least, he should have to make specific factual and national security findings and provide his supporting evidence in as much detail as possible so that the public can assess his actions. Congress should also consider requiring a rigorous, demanding inquiry into the actions and how the administration is implementing them on the ground.

The dangerous temptation of presidents to use their power to overreach and ignore principles of justice is a constant threat to our democracy. This threat is especially grave when the policy objective is praiseworthy, as

President Barack Obama's unilateral, procedurally-deficient Dreamers order was. Although Mr. Trump poses this threat most brazenly and in the extreme, it is by no means confined to him. Indeed, his precedent will embolden his successors.

Trump's "Horrifying Lies" About Lori Klausutis May Cross a Legal Line*

President Trump and his minions relentlessly grind out despicable acts—gratuitous insults to war heroes, over 18,000 (and counting) false or misleading statements, many decisions that courts have ruled illegal. But Mr. Trump's wantonly cruel tweets about the tragic death in 2001 of Lori Klausutis are distinctive: They may constitute intentional torts for which a civil jury could award punitive damages against him.

Here are the key facts. Ms. Klausutis, age 28, died in the Florida district office of a Republican congressman, Joe Scarborough, who was then in Washington. The police found no evidence of foul play and the coroner reported that the cause of death was a hard fall against a hard object precipitated by her floppy mitral valve disease.

That should have been the end of the story, but this month the President tweeted to his 80 million followers that "some people think" that Mr. Scarborough, now a popular MSNBC news host who frequently criticizes Mr. Trump, got "away with murder," and called Mr. Scarborough a "psycho" and a "total nut job."

The President has offered no evidence for this slander because there is none. Last week, Timothy Klausutis, Lori's widower, wrote a remarkably restrained, poignant letter to Jack Dorsey, the head of Twitter, citing the pain that Mr. Trump's "horrifying lies" about his wife's death have caused him and the family, and asking Mr. Dorsey to remove Mr. Trump's tweet. Mr. Dorsey has refused, most likely because the 1996 Communications Decency Act probably protects him from defamation claims for publishing the words of another. However, Twitter added a warning label to the President's false tweets on Tuesday about mail-in ballots, the first time the service has taken such a step.

Mr. Trump's first tort is called intentional infliction of emotional distress, which the courts developed precisely to condemn wanton cruelty to another person who suffers emotionally as a result. This tort, which is sometimes

---

* *New York Times*, 5/28/2020; https://www.nytimes.com/2020/05/28/opinion/twitter-trump-scarborough.html

called "outrage," readily applies to Mr. Trump's tweets about Ms. Klausutis. They were intentional and reckless, and were "extreme and outrageous" without a scintilla of evidence to support them. And they caused severe emotional distress—the protracted, daily-felt grief described in Mr. Klausutis's letter to Mr. Dorsey.

Although the tweets targeted Mr. Scarborough, his own infliction of emotional distress claim may be weaker than Mr. Klausutis's. By shrugging off the tweet as simply political gamesmanship on the President's part, Mr. Scarborough may not have suffered the "severe emotional distress" required for an intentional infliction of emotional distress claim.

Even so, Mr. Scarborough might succeed in a defamation suit against Mr. Trump for reputational harm. After all, the President's innuendo that Mr. Scarborough may have murdered Lori Klausutis—presumably credible to the many Trump Twitter followers who subscribe to conspiracy theories—may seriously harm Mr. Scarborough's reputation with them and others.

Mr. Trump, moreover, often aims his tweets to lead multiple news cycles affecting people well beyond his Twitter followers. The President will surely argue that he has not actually accused anyone of murder and was merely "raising questions." But courts have held that such calculated innuendo can constitute defamation, depending on the facts. This would be for a jury to decide.

Mr. Scarborough, as a public figure in his own right, must satisfy the Supreme Court's demanding test for defamation liability in its landmark *New York Times v. Sullivan* decision. Under this test—designed to free public debate from being unduly constrained by fear of legal liability—Mr. Scarborough must prove that Mr. Trump made his defamatory comment either with actual knowledge that it was false or with "reckless disregard" for whether it was true or false. But the President's tweets about the Klausutis case probably satisfy this test. After all, he has not cited any evidence to support his calumny either before the tweets or in response to the backlash since then. If the jury found for Mr. Scarborough, it could require Mr. Trump to pay substantial punitive damages in addition to compensation for his reputational harm.

Under the court's unanimous 1998 ruling in Paula Jones's sexual harassment suit against President Bill Clinton, both of these lawsuits—by Mr. Klausutis and by Mr. Scarborough—could proceed against the president while he is still in office. Because his tweets reach followers nationwide, the lawsuits could probably be brought in any state. And since the subject of his tweets had nothing to do with his presidential responsibilities, he probably could not hide behind an assertion of executive privilege.

The Klausutis family has suffered enough for almost 20 years without having to endure Mr. Trump's crocodile tears and malicious raking of the coals. Tort law might hold our brutish president to account.

Part 5

CAMPUS FOLLIES

Introduction to Part 5

Higher education institutions are, or should be, a central element of a liberal, discursive, truth-seeking society. The ones that I know best—Yale, where I taught for 35 years, some where I visited to teach, and the many others that I read about as an interested intellectual and observer—proudly proclaim their fidelity and commitment to these values, which are celebrated in the book by my colleague Anthony Kronman that I review here. But the countervailing pressures—political correctness, sheer cowardice, an earnest desire to mollify agitated students, fear of how negative publicity might affect alumni and other attentive constituencies, and other such considerations—coalesce to create conditions that are inimical to straight-up truth-telling.

Several of the pieces that I present here focus on some all-too-representative instances of these moral evasions and compromises. One weighs in on a widely-publicized imbroglio at Yale in which agitated students confronted and harshly denounced the faculty leader of a residential college (traditionally dubbed the "college master" but officially renamed "head of college" in 2016), ostensibly because his wife had circulated a mild suggestion about how students might better respond to Halloween costumes that offended them. Another article asks where the "adults in the room" are when free speech values on campus are under concerted attack, while another criticizes university leaders who cravenly follow student groups' political demands to withdraw invitations to distinguished commencement speakers.

Notwithstanding these administrative and moral failures, however, I explain in another piece why universities are probably better equipped than the federal government to design policies concerning sexual assaults on campuses, while at the same time calling attention to the authoritarian excesses of some university leaders, using Valdosta State University as an example. I present a shorter version of my extended case against race-based affirmative action in colleges and universities—a topic I have studied and written about for more than two decades. (I do favor economic need-based preferences.) The Supreme Court is expected to rule decisively on this issue in June 2023. Finally, both the glories and the follies of campus life are only made possible by massive student loans; an essay explains why the loan system is an impending disaster

What the President of Yale Should Have Said*

On November 10, following the campus thousand-member "March for Resilience" over racial insensitivity, Yale president, Peter Salovey and Yale College Dean Jonathan Holloway emailed those of us in the Yale community affirming "the importance we put on our community's diversity, and the need to increase it, support it, and respect it."

The email embraced "the right of every member of this community to engage in protest," noted that "threats, coercion, and overtly disrespectful acts" are "unacceptable," and praised the "affirming and effective forms of protest" in Monday's march. This can best be read as a well-intentioned effort to assure students, faculty, and alumni that the University administration is on top of the problem.

But what, exactly, is the problem? According to the email, the problem is how to "increase, support, and respect" Yale's "diversity." Just before Halloween, Yale's "intercultural affairs council" emailed students urging them to select their Halloween costumes with sensitivity to the feelings of minorities. Those with a sense of humor will enjoy this earnest email. In response, Erica Christakis, who is associate "master" of Silliman, one of Yale's residential colleges, emailed its students. Combining common sense, respect for students' maturity and moderation, she urged students to decide for themselves on appropriate costumes, and if they found one offensive, either speak about it directly to the offender or ignore it.

This advice, ostensibly, is what unleashed the students' fury as they vilified, traduced, and sought to intimidate the Christakis's, Erica and her husband Nicholas, "master" of Silliman, demanding their resignations. According to a Yale Daily News observer, "This man was surrounded outside his own home by dozens of students, who called him 'f—king disgusting.' They jeered, in clearly implied threat, 'We know where you live.'" Here are some other points that I wish the Salovey-Holloway email had made in the strongest possible terms.

1. The fact that students complain of rampant racism on campus does not mean that it is true. Yale—and virtually every other old institution—countenanced racism and even practiced it, but that period is long gone. Indeed, it is hard to think of an institution that tries harder than Yale does to make students of all backgrounds feel at home, an effort underwritten by a recent $50 million commitment to increase diversity

---

* *Minding the Campus*, 11/15/2015; https://www.mindingthecampus.org/2015/11/15/what-the-president-of-yale-should-have-said-2/

there and by the support of four ethno-specific cultural houses. Much the same is true on other elite campuses. Yes, Yale calls its residential college leaders "masters" and, contrary to student protests, this title is entirely benign, not a vestige of slavery, as some seem to think. (Whether Calhoun College should change its name in light of its eponym's defense of slavery is a more serious question). Historical context—how and why earlier generations saw the world as they did—is part of the moral reasoning process that a university teaches. Condemning what now seems like obvious racism, while entirely appropriate, is the easiest part of such moral reasoning, requiring little insight.

2. The purpose of a great university like ours is not to make students feel comfortable in their views but to unsettle those views with fine teaching and scholarship. Only then can students learn to confront uncomfortable data and ideas and make up their own minds. Mature convictions must be earned through a lifetime of grappling with what is discomfiting and engaging in the kind of reading, listening, and arguing that is a privilege and duty of serious citizenship. A great university must defend itself for what it is and should be—a sanctuary for study and engagement—not a comfortable and comforting cocoon. Students who come with a hypersensitive aversion to conflict and to intellectual diversity (as distinct from the easy, faux diversity of skin color and surname) are in the wrong place.

3. Students state (or shout) many grievances, often in the form of slogans. Some are plausibly justified, others are gross exaggerations or simply false. Some seek genuine dialogue; others seek power grabs and shakedowns meant to foreclose conversation. The university community should demand to know the factual bases for those grievances, examine them on their merits, remedy them if warranted, and reject them if not. Reflexive mea culpae may buy temporary peace and goodwill but only invite more extreme demands. As Yeats warned, passionate intensity can undermine both truth and civility.

4. Mob psychology, whether created by students or others, is a kind of extreme, near-violent form of politics using shouts, threats, and lies as weapons. Honeyed words and apologies cannot mollify it. It thrives when it does not get its way, and failure simply confirms its grievances. The hostility to reason negates the university's very purpose. Salovey, an eminent psychologist, surely knows all this but has not said it. Among this psychology's other tics, it fastens on stupid, hurtful comments by fools and bigots (perhaps not even members of the university community), ascribes these views to many others who in fact condemn them, impugns the university for tolerating racism, and excoriates those on the sidelines as equivocating enemies of the cause. But every community has fools

and bigots and must deal with them in its own way. Yale, a community of trained skeptics, eschews authoritarian solutions to questions of truth, relying instead on open, disciplined discourse to discredit error—even as we know that some of this discourse will itself be false.

5. America's diversity is one of its greatest gifts to the world, and institutions like Yale are right to seek and protect it. But how we define and implement diversity is crucial to its real value in campuses, workplaces, politics, and elsewhere. Getting diversity management right is difficult; good intentions can easily backfire, as I explained in my 2003 book *Diversity in America: Keeping Government at a Safe Distance*.

   Racism, sexism and other odious isms obviously exist, and we should firmly reject them. But combating these isms is especially hard for a university. They are ill-defined and based on subjective intent, so reasonable people disagree about whether they exist in almost any particular case. For the same reason, an accused cannot disprove them. Because many attributes are distributed differently among different groups, and because generalizations are useful, indeed inescapable, it is often unclear—even to the Supreme Court—when a judgment is just a useful generalization or instead reflects invidious bigotry and hostility. This ensures lots of false positives and false negatives. One who feels victimized by an ism resents being told that he is over-reacting and mistaken. His hurt seems like proof enough of intentional harm. On the other side, being falsely accused of an ism today may be equally or more damaging socially than the hurt or indignity felt by the complainant.

6. University officials like us bear some responsibility for the aggressive, obsessive ethnic emphasis practiced on our campus. Through some mixture of cowardice, complaisance, and genuine conviction, we cater to the sensibilities of the most outspoken, politicized students by donning a kind of "kick me" sign. In this identity politics, students have strong incentives to dramatize their wounds as proof of the authenticity of a larger, more heroic social agenda—here, the extirpation of isms.

7. The only way out of this gyre of recrimination and misunderstanding is to cultivate two qualities that are sorely lacking in diversity discourse on campus: candor and thicker skins. On campus, candor should be the easiest virtue, but in fact there is remarkably little of it. Few are willing to concede the deep tensions among diversity, liberty, and equality—and thus the costs to precious values of one position or another. By thicker skins, I mean that we should cultivate a capacity for greater resilience, not greater delicacy. As one commentator put it, the U.S. today has become "a world of endless slights." (Even that comment will elicit anger for suggesting that putative isms are merely slights). This is corrosive in a society

as diverse, interactive, plainspoken, casual, and freewheeling as ours. It chills personal interactions by denying them the lubricating pleasure of spontaneity.

It discourages candid discussion or artistic expression on vital public issues. It enlists formal and informal sanctions in order to reduce what should be robust give-and-take. It invites us to open our wounds, magnify our fears, and parade our sensitivities, to imagine injuries and motivations that do not exist, and to view others, without basis, as enemies. It rewards cant, hyperbole, and reductive rhetoric while penalizing moderation and reason. It encourages us to seek security in groups of people who look, think, or worship like us rather than to venture out in the more diverse public square where our common citizenship is forged. It makes a mockery of rules that are brandished to penalize what is often just ignorance, boorishness, interpretive confusion, ill-considered speech, clumsy provocation, misjudgment, rough or poor humor, and other unfortunate infelicities.

8. We do better to respond to such conduct with constructive engagement, forceful rebuke, pointed rebuttal, and mental shrugging of shoulders and biting of tongues. It is unfair that the people who need the thickest skins are often those who already feel under siege. Two factors, however, can help palliate this unfairness, if not assuage their hurt and indignation. The informal social norms condemning hateful attitudes and conduct are stronger today than ever before. And the alternatives to developing thicker skins are all unappealing, unconstitutional, or unworkable.

9. Our administration pledges to be wiser in the future, though no less committed to lux et veritas. Let our students pledge to do the same.

Free Speech—Where Are the Adults in the Room?*

Almost two years have passed since the Halloween imbroglio at Yale in 2015, which launched the current era of student mobilizations against speech that some students don't want to hear. Whatever their ideological stance, these protests aim to intimidate controversial speakers and those who would invite them to campus, to prevent others from hearing them, and to banish certain ideas and terms from campus discourse.

---

* *Minding the Campus*, 10/23/2017; https://www.mindingthecampus.org/2017/10/23/free-speech-where-are-the-adults-in-the-room/

College leaders invariably denounce violence and affirm their unflagging commitment to robust speech and debate on campus. They invoke the standard tropes of liberal education: to cultivate students' curiosity, knowledge, imagination, and critical thinking by exposing them to diverse ideas about the world. They routinely genuflect before the First Amendment's protection of academic freedom and provocative and unsettling speech. (Private institutions, while not legally bound by the First Amendment, subscribe to the same doxology).

Backing up this free-speech rhetoric is anything but free. Security is very costly. It cost UC Berkeley an estimated $600,000 merely to protect one conservative speaker's visit recently, a drop in the UC system's $7.3 billion budgetary bucket. But at smaller schools, protecting such speakers competes with scarce resources for teaching, financial aid, housing, and other essential functions.

Colleges run other serious risks when campus turbulence threatens to blight the school's reputation with its trustees, major donors, and potential applicants. Presidents who lose control may lose their jobs. Knowing this, they mollify the student groups which threaten to wreak this havoc. Having long ago abandoned the traditional in loco parentis role, their power to shape student conduct is now very limited. Leftist orthodoxy in the classroom is especially prevalent on more elite campuses and in academic departments (the social sciences and humanities, for example) where almost the entire faculty is liberal. (This is evidenced by their campaign contributions, which go almost entirely to Democratic candidates). And even if some professors present a range of perspectives, students probably prefer an unvarnished version of conservatism from true-believer outsiders to liberal professors struggling to appear "balanced."

The fuel for the speech-related disorder is inexhaustible. For many students, especially conservatives, these speakers also help to correct for a perceived leftist orthodoxy in the classroom. Scoring outside anti-establishment speakers with wide name recognition, rhetorical flair, and a taste for provocation revs up student interest and magnifies the organizers' status and recognition on campus, their ideological and militant chops, and their feelings of accomplishment. Some schools even provide student organizations with a budget to support these and other "enrichment" activities. Some politically active outside groups such as the Federalist Society and its counterparts on the left may also subsidize them.

The protesting students can almost always count on some faculty sympathizers with similar motivations as well as a desire to embarrass the equivocating, temporizing administration. At the highest-ranked schools, professors often have great bargaining power due to global reputations and frequent job offers. At lower-ranked schools, many faculties have low status, poor pay, and little job security. Their estrangement encourages solidarity with protesting and disaffected students. And a new study from Brookings suggests that intolerance of unpopular views—and even support for violence to suppress them—is remarkably common among today's college students.

These incentives and conditions help explain why the adults nominally in charge often seem so feckless. More eager to pacify their protesting student and faculty critics than to protect the abstract intellectual values which they claim to revere, they equivocate. As for students, most surely oppose the extremists—but like most silent majorities, they exert less influence than their numbers might warrant.

What is to be done?

1. A counterforce consisting of trustees and major donors—the off-campus people who have invested the most in the institution and care most about its reputation and welfare—should make clear to the administration that their future support of the administration will depend on a clear affirmation that (a) academic values and intellectual diversity are paramount; (b) academic freedom does not protect those who try to stifle other viewpoints; (c) students, faculty and administrators who do not respect these norms do not belong there; and (d) serious sanctions will attend duly-adjudicated violations of those norms—including expulsion or long-term suspension of students, and appropriate measures against even tenured faculty, who actively encouraged those violations. Such interventions by trustees and donors should be reserved for extreme violations of academic values, properly defined, and due process must be assured before sanctions are imposed. The public statement on freedom of expression issued by the University of Chicago in 2012 can serve as a good starting point.

2. More student riots and speech-impeding mobs are likely to end up in court. Several of the most publicized confrontations, such as the intimidation of Professor Bret Weinstein by Evergreen students who wanted him and all other Caucasians off-campus for a whites-free day, ended in settlements—in Weinstein's case for $500,000. Jay Weiser, associate professor of law at Baruch College, points out that the post-Civil-War anti-Ku Klux Klan laws still have power, one of them covering private conspiracies and masked conspirators (the Klan originally and presumably masked Antifa attackers now). Weiser writes: "The statute applies most clearly to racially motivated physical attacks or efforts to exclude persons. Evergreen State is a classic case: After disrupting Mr. Weinstein's

class, students detained the college president and apparently posted photos of themselves brandishing baseball bats on Facebook. Some faculty members demanded disciplinary action against Mr. Weinstein and later assembled with masked Antifa members who attacked counter-protesters." As Weiser notes, Colleges are subject to anti-discrimination statutes such as Section 1981, an anti-KKK act that would cover student and speaker contract rights. If they accept federal funding, they are also subject to Title VI of the Civil Rights Act of 1964, and if the crowd attacked white "supremacy" or "privilege," and if private universities act with deliberate indifference to racially motivated attacks, they may be liable to students or speakers.

While affirming the right to protest peacefully against speakers with whom some disagree, the administration should inform the community about various federal and state law remedies (including reimbursement of attorney fees in some cases) to would-be listeners whose civil rights are violated by speech-impeding or violent protesters, especially those wearing masks or other disguises. Indeed, those in such disguises should not be admitted to such events in the first place.

3. The agencies that accredit universities require them to demonstrate, among other conditions, a commitment to academic freedom, intellectual freedom, and freedom of expression. Defenders of these values on campus can threaten to invoke dis-accreditation remedies for recurrent violations on their campuses.

4. Diversity-talk on today's college campuses is obsessed with gender, race, sexual orientation, and other constructions of identity. In excess, these obsessions degrade intellectual discourse, interpersonal civility, and campus life generally. Colleges now emphasize and promote these often divisive identities rather than fostering the civility, candor, and thicker skins necessary to sustain a robust and competitive diverse society. Colleges' highest educational priority should be intellectual, methodological, and socioeconomic diversity, not a campus peace based on a patronizing co-optation of sullen groups.

Recently, a wealthy donor offered Yale a large matching grant to promote intellectual and viewpoint diversity, especially in faculty hiring. The offer was designed to parallel Yale's $50 million fund for identity diversity, established immediately after the Halloween incident. Yale acknowledged the need, especially in law and certain humanities departments, but declined the gift. Evidently, it has other priorities. Columbia's recently-announced $100 million faculty diversity initiative will likely reinforce its current obsession with ethnic, race, and gender identities rather than augment them with genuinely discordant, conservative voices that might challenge their students' preconceptions.

Opposition to conservative voices is in the DNA of the radical left, inflamed by apocalyptic "Antifa" activists. The radical right's uncompromising contempt for the left is a mirror image. Colleges have a tough job in keeping these clashes on the side of the line that protects speech and promotes genuine viewpoint diversity. These measures would go a long toward holding that precious line.

Assessing Affirmative Action[*]

In affirmative-action cases, the Supreme Court never seems to learn the obvious lesson, or perhaps it is determined to finesse it. The lesson is that universities that are keen to implement race-based affirmative action (and it is hard to find a highly or even moderately selective school that isn't) will figure out a way to do so unless the Court emphatically and clearly prohibits it. The Court's doctrinal fuzziness, which its 2013 decision in *Fisher v. University of Texas* only further obscured, allows these institutions to maintain the preference systems dictated by their political, reputational, and ideological incentives.

In a number of states, the American public has been able to exercise some countervailing influence through the ballot box, and the Supreme Court recently affirmed its right to do so. In a case decided in April, the Court upheld Michigan voters' power to ban affirmative action—indeed, to ban the same affirmative-action program at the University of Michigan that the Supreme Court had upheld in 2003—through a constitutional amendment adopted by voter referendum.

But while Americans consistently voice a firm opposition to affirmative action in university admissions, the public debate surrounding the issue has been clouded by both weakly-reasoned Supreme Court jurisprudence and incoherent factual claims by supporters of race-conscious admissions.

Over the course of 35 years, the Court has upheld race-based affirmative-action programs based solely upon a so-called "diversity rationale." All of the current justices except Antonin Scalia and Clarence Thomas have accepted this rationale. But the premises underlying the diversity rationale for race-based affirmative action are empirically tenuous and theoretically implausible. Policies justified under that rationale thus could not survive if the "strict scrutiny" standard were seriously applied. The Court applies strict scrutiny

---

[*] *National Affairs*, Summer 2014; https://www.nationalaffairs.com/publications/detail/assessing-affirmative-action

when assessing race-based policies like affirmative action, whether in higher education, government hiring, or government contracts. The framers of the 14th Amendment may have countenanced affirmative action favoring former slaves and perhaps their descendants, but they would never have approved of today's affirmative-action programs, in which most of the potential beneficiaries are immigrants or descendants of immigrants. But regardless of whether such programs are constitutional or not, they are undesirable public policy, indeed perverse in practice. Their costs vastly exceed their benefits, and in ways that should cause universities and courts alike to change course.

By considering both the legal architecture of the Court's affirmative-action jurisprudence and the empirical evidence regarding the effects of affirmative action in higher education, we can begin to see the defects of today's affirmative-action regime and the powerful case for change.

Relaxed Scrutiny

The Court's jurisprudence regarding affirmative action in university admissions has taken shape through a series of cases stretching back to Regents of University of California v. *Bakke* in 1978. In that case, the Court allowed a university to consider race in medical-school admissions so long as it was only one of several factors, was used to advance student-body diversity, and there was no specific quota for admission. The Court reaffirmed these three principles a quarter-century later in the 2003 cases of *Grutter v. Bollinger* and *Gratz v. Bollinger*. In *Grutter*, involving the admissions policy of the University of Michigan's law school, the majority ruled that an admissions process giving some advantage to "underrepresented minority students," but also taking into consideration a variety of other factors (applied strictly on an individual basis for each applicant), did not amount to a quota system and so was constitutionally permissible. But in *Gratz*, which looked at that university's undergraduate admissions policy, the Court found that, because it granted a set number of admission points to any racial-minority applicant (rather than considering each applicant individually as the law school did), it amounted to an impermissible quota system.

The Court reaffirmed this standard in the 2013 *Fisher* case, sending the case back to the lower court on the ground that those judges had failed to correctly apply the strict-scrutiny standard. That standard requires "a judicial determination that the burden [the disappointed applicant] is asked to bear" in a system that takes race into account "is precisely tailored to serve a compelling governmental interest."

Strict scrutiny is supposed to be, well, strict. Its purpose is to force reviewing courts to be rigorous, skeptical, and demanding enough to challenge the government's premises, flush out its true motives, and ensure a tight congruence of evidence, legal categories, and policy justifications. Courts apply strict scrutiny when they have strong reasons to think that the state may be playing with fire around highly combustible materials. Racial classifications epitomize this kind of risk.

Many academic advocates of preferences, to be sure, maintain that the Court's strict-scrutiny standard, as elaborated in earlier decisions, was too strict, even Procrustean, and that a "benign" preference adopted by self-abnegating ethnic majorities should be judged less rigorously. There is much to be said for this argument, although benignity is in the eye of the beholder. The large number of people disadvantaged by preferences—all whites; the 48% of Hispanics, similar proportions of Asians, and 80% of Native Americans who self-identify to the Census Bureau as white; anyone else (dark-skinned Middle Easterners, for example) who is not considered part of David Hollinger's "ethno-racial pentagon"; and the more than seven million people (many with black ancestry) who consider themselves multi-racial and wish to be identified as such (if they must be racially identified at all)—are unlikely to think of this disadvantage as benign. But rather than adopting this benign-preference argument, the Court has instead diluted strict scrutiny without actually saying so.

Indeed, the *Grutter* majority did not even come close to applying the strict-scrutiny standard as traditionally understood. As Chief Justice William Rehnquist correctly noted in his dissent, the majority's review of Michigan's preference system was "unprecedented in its deference." The majority failed to explain convincingly why universities that sponsor preferences should receive more such deference than, say, the private employers or municipal procurement agencies whose plans the Court has struck down in the past under strict scrutiny. After all, universities that adopt and structure such programs are responding to the same kind of political, ideological, competitive, social, legal, and institutional pressures that affect employers and government agencies. If anything, the well-documented leftist bias and political correctness of such universities in these matters—on display in their recent backtracking on commencement speakers—should arouse the very suspicion about motives that strict scrutiny is intended to test.

There is no question of good faith. All the university administrators in these cases are clearly doing what they think best advances their institutional values and interests. But the Court has often held, most recently in *Fisher*, that strict scrutiny makes the actors' good faith and the purity of their intentions quite irrelevant as a legal matter.

Justice Sandra Day O'Connor's permissive approach to strict scrutiny in *Grutter* (a laxness that has defined courts' attitudes to affirmative-action programs ever since) deviated radically from her own more rigorous approach to that test in earlier cases. She finessed (or mischaracterized) five crucial questions that bear on affirmative-action policies: the nature of educational diversity; how educational diversity relates to both the "critical mass" idea at the core of Michigan's theory and the ethno-racial stereotypes that the school claimed to abhor; how the majority distinguished between valid and invalid preferences and how Michigan's program fared under that test; the existence of race-neutral alternatives; and the duration of preference policies.

The Court's superficial treatment of these questions reveals the profound weakness of its affirmative-action analysis.

Diversity and Remediation

First, the *Grutter* majority reiterated Justice Lewis Powell's embrace in *Bakke* of student diversity as a compelling state interest sufficient to justify admissions preferences—even as it brushed past the conditions that the *Bakke* plurality had imposed for validating them. Of these conditions, a rigorous, individualized appraisal of an applicant's actual diversity value was the most important.

What the majority did not provide was a coherent account of the meaning of diversity value that went beyond general platitudes. Nor did it explain why the Constitution allowed the law school to define the desired, favored diversity in narrow ethno-racial terms that excluded even most minorities (other than African-Americans, Native Americans, and the Spanish-surnamed) while treating other kinds of diversity as either much less weighty or wholly irrelevant to satisfying the overriding diversity rationale. Indeed, as Justice Thomas pointed out in a footnote in his dissent, the school seemed not to value the additional diversity that black men, who are greatly under-represented relative to black women, would provide.

The only convincing explanation for Michigan's approach had little to do with the goal of educational diversity and everything to do with the desire to remedy the historic injustices suffered by African-Americans and Native Americans. (The moral claims of those with Spanish surnames are more debatable.) This motive, although admirable, is one that the Court has consistently held cannot support the constitutionality of a university's race-based preferences. Any sophisticated observer (surely including all members of the Court) who is not blinded by the rhetorical fog thrown up by the now-obligatory diversity talk, understands that the law school's true purpose was not diversity but remediation.

If Michigan's program were really about educational diversity rather than recompense, it would not have limited the program's benefits to a few favored groups. It would instead have included religion, political ideology, and other demographics that directly represent the different worldviews with which educational diversity is supposedly concerned. Would an evangelical Christian or a conservative Republican create less diversity value for Michigan's students than an applicant whose only special claim to such value was his skin color or surname? The answer, obviously, is no—and this is true whether one defines diversity value in terms of disparate worldviews, interacting with people of unfamiliar backgrounds, encouraging dorm-room chit-chat, or even breaking down traditional stereotypes.

What distinguishes African-American students (at least those descended from American slaves) from these other groups is not their diverse, exotic views but the injustices visited on their ancestors. Those injustices should matter a great deal to our society in general, but the Court has always ruled that they cannot justify race-based university admissions.

Critical Mass

The *Grutter* majority insisted that breaking down ethno-racial stereotypes was crucial to achieving the putative goal of educational diversity, and that the "critical mass" of favored minorities intentionally produced by the school's preferences would help to achieve this goal. But this notion of critical mass is incoherent.

First, critical mass by its very nature must be a matter of the number or proportion of students needed to produce it, yet even the *Grutter* majority had to concede that the Constitution prohibits numerical or proportional quotas and instead requires individualized assessments. Second, the critical-mass criterion is only intelligible if one specifies the level of university activity at which racial assignments are permissible in order to achieve the critical mass. Is the level campus-wide? Program-wide? Each major or only some? Seminars? Lecture courses? Dormitories? Sports teams? *Grutter* didn't say.

Third, the critical-mass goal can be administered only by deferring to the university's judgment on these matters, a level of deference that *Grutter* countenanced but that *Fisher* (as we shall see) emphatically rejects. And finally, the *Grutter* majority saw a very close connection between critical mass and stereotype destruction: "[W]hen a critical mass of underrepresented minority students is present, racial stereotypes lose their force because nonminority students learn that there is no 'minority viewpoint' but rather a variety of viewpoints among minority students." But how can this possibly be? What alchemy enables the law school to prefer students on the basis of skin color or surname—albeit in the name of diversity—without at the same time strengthening the notions of ethno-racial essentialism and viewpoint determinism?

More to the point, what opaque prestidigitation allows the school to admit minority students with academic records that were (whatever the school's metric) substantially weaker than those of their (other minority or majority) competitors without thereby reinforcing stereotypes of academic inferiority? Did the Court majority think that the non-preferred students and faculty were somehow so clueless that they would not notice what was going on and draw the logical and stigmatizing inference that the preferred group's academic performance was inferior? Wouldn't these elite educational institutions by definition attract the most competitive students and faculty? And wouldn't such individuals place a very high (perhaps excessive) value on the coin of their particular realm—academic excellence—partly because they themselves were so well endowed with it?

To recognize the importance that elite schools give to academic factors is emphatically not to say that test scores and GPA are or should be decisive in determining admission. A sensible institution will consider a variety of factors in selecting its student body, although elite schools that hope to maintain their positions will weight academic potential or performance most heavily. But to assert, as admissions officers who defend affirmative action typically do, that people with manifestly inferior academic performance are somehow superior to others with respect to non-academic virtues—leadership, character, community commitments, grappling with obstacles—is to indulge in a patronizing and pernicious stereotype. There is simply no *a priori* reason to believe, for example, that black applicants as a group are more likely to exhibit these "soft" variables than are applicants of other groups. Nor am I aware of any evidence that they in fact do so.

By the same token, a critic of *Grutter* need not deny the obvious fact that preferences of other kinds exist and that some of them may be unfair or otherwise objectionable. Preferences favoring legacies and athletes, for example, are also widespread even at elite schools, and such preferences also engender stereotypes about their academic inferiority (e.g., "dumb jocks"). Why, then, don't preferences based on these variables trigger strict scrutiny, while ethno-racial ones do? Their different legal statuses reflect deep differences in the constitutional and historical meanings of these groups and their experiences. These differences in no way justify admission preferences for athletes and legacies, but they help to explain why their stereotypes are far less corrosive and stigmatizing than those that attach to racial minority preferences.

Invalid Preferences

The majority in *Grutter* defined a theoretically defensible test for the constitutionality of ethno-racial preferences: "[E]ach applicant must be evaluated as an individual and not in a way that makes an applicant's race or ethnicity the defining feature of his or her application," which would place members of all groups on the same admissions track where they would compete "on the same footing." But having announced this test and repeated it in subsequent cases, the majority proceeded to dumb it down so that all could pass it while still insisting on its integrity.

Race and ethnicity, Justice O'Connor wrote in *Grutter*, could be a "'plus' factor" in a system of "individualized assessments" so long as it did not constitute either a "rigid quota" (as in Michigan's undergraduate program) or "racial balancing." But as the dissenting opinions of Chief Justice Rehnquist and Justice Anthony Kennedy showed statistically, the law school weighed the plus factor for race and ethnicity so heavily that it created—in effect though not in name—a two-track system tantamount to racial balancing in its admission offers, and did so in order to achieve its racially-defined "critical mass." The majority, like the law school, wanted to have it both ways: On the one hand, ethno-racial factors must only be a "modest" plus factor in admissions, but on the other hand, few of the favored minorities would have been admitted without them. Again, the majority could only reconcile this inconsistency if—contrary to reason, experience, and egalitarian theory—the favored applicants were so superior to the others on the non-academic criteria that their academic deficits could be ignored.

The truth, as evident from the *Grutter* dissenters' analyses (and indeed from common sense), is that the law school's affirmative-action program could satisfy the majority's constitutional test for only one reason: The program's opacity allowed so much room for subjective, discretionary judgments in the undisclosed weighting of the "soft variables" for individual applicants that rejected students (like Barbara Grutter) could not possibly prove that they were rejected primarily because they were not members of the favored ethno-racial groups. This fact, of course, placed the burden of proof squarely on the shoulders of the individual challenging the preferences—which in turn made the decidedly un-strict nature of the majority's scrutiny that much more pivotal in protecting preferences in such cases.

Race-neutral Alternatives

The *Grutter* majority's abject deference to the university was nowhere more apparent than in how it treated the race-neutral alternatives to which the law school must give "serious, good faith consideration." The Court maintained that the law school had weighed the alternatives but chose to continue using racial criteria because none of the alternatives would have given it the number of preferred minorities that the institution felt it needed to achieve "critical mass." This was true enough, but it was an answer to the wrong question. The right question was: Given a constitutional presumption against ethno-racial preferences—a presumption so strong that strict scrutiny is required to enforce it—how imperfect must a race-neutral alternative be before the Court will allow the state to reject it in favor of a race-conscious (indeed, race-determined) program? There is no clear answer to this question, of course, but the majority did not even ask it, and so it did not consider any alternative approaches.

There are, of course, several alternatives, some of which are essentially race-neutral. None would be perfect, but they would be less problematic than race-conscious admissions. One often-discussed approach, familiar from the many institutional programs that grant need-based tuition assistance, seeks to determine disadvantage or need directly. Extending such programs to schools' initial decisions to admit would be more difficult, of course. Determining economic need directly for a very large number of applicants would be at least as challenging as it has proved to be in the administration of state need-based social-welfare programs. Michael Kinsley, who supports some forms of affirmative action, described the consequences in the *New Yorker*: "Is it worse to be a cleaning lady's son or a coal miner's daughter? Two points if your father didn't go to college, minus one if he finished high school, plus three if you have no father? (or will that reward illegitimacy which we're all trying hard these days not to do?)...Officially sanctioned affirmative action by 'disadvantage' would turn today's festival of competitive victimization into an orgy."

Difficult, surely, but not impossible. Richard Sander, a law professor at the University of California, Los Angeles, and co-author (with Stuart Taylor, Jr.) of the important book Mismatch, reports that he actually devised and implemented a sophisticated system of preferences for UCLA based on economic need, and that the system worked "exceedingly well. Audits against financial aid statements showed little abuse; the preferences substantially changed the social makeup of the class and never, to our knowledge, prompted complaints of unfairness." Such approaches would have to be assessed and attempted more broadly, of course, but they may offer one race-neutral alternative to affirmative action.

Another possible alternative would be a program that automatically admitted students in the upper echelons (say, the top 5% or 10%) of their high-school classes. Texas, Florida, and California have adopted such percentage programs (although Texas, unsatisfied with the number of minorities that its percentage plan yielded, added to it the race-based program challenged in *Fisher*). Percentage programs seem to increase racial diversity on college campuses, though they presumably bring to those campuses many students whose academic preparation is relatively poor (given differences among high schools in different communities).

Another race-neutral alternative would not only increase the number of minority students attending selective institutions but also ameliorate a different, more tractable, and even more socially wasteful kind of problem: A substantial pool of high-school students who are perfectly capable of performing well at selective colleges do not even apply to them, or indeed to any college at all. Caroline Hoxby and her colleagues have shown that applications by these students, many of whom are minorities, can be increased through better information about how to apply, financial-aid opportunities, and other assistance available on campus. Moreover, increasing applications from this group can be accomplished at trivial cost—as little as $6 per student.

Finally, there are ways to reduce the size of ethno-racial preferences without wholly abolishing them. In Mismatch, for instance, Sander and Taylor propose that if ethno-racial preferences are retained, their magnitude should not be permitted to exceed in size the preferences (if any) that the same school uses for socioeconomically disadvantaged students of all races.

Whatever the imperfections in these (or other) race-neutral alternatives may be, they pale before the legal and policy defects of ethno-racial preferences. Most important, the Court has demanded precisely this kind of comparison, most recently and clearly in *Fisher*.

The Duration of Preferences

Much has been made of the *Grutter* majority's expectation that "25 years from now, the use of racial preferences will no longer be necessary." Justice Thomas's recitation, in his dissent, of the grim statistics on comparative academic performance makes such a hope seem unrealistic. And the studies of ethno-racial preferences in other societies provide no support for it either, as the economist Thomas Sowell has shown. To the contrary, they indicate that such preferences, once established, tend to endure and perhaps even expand to new groups and new programmatic benefits.

It is true that six politically diverse states (Arizona, California, Michigan, Nebraska, Oklahoma, and Washington) have banned these preferences by voter referenda, while New Hampshire has done so through statute and Florida through executive order. But California's experience after its voters banned ethno-racial preferences suggests that such bans on affirmative action do not end it; they may simply drive it underground. The California system engaged in a series of stratagems in the early 2000s expressly designed to circumvent the state's ban. Some of the more egregious ones involved channeling minority students to new "critical race studies" programs with lower admissions standards; awarding special admissions credit for foreign-language fluency to minority students who were already native speakers; adopting "percentage" plans that relied for their efficacy on the continuation of segregated schooling patterns; and using unspecified (and unspecifiable) "holistic" criteria as well as winks and nods by admissions officials.

Moreover, the Court's evident desire to end the debate about preferences—by allowing them to continue but insisting that they will not go on forever—is more or less destined to fail. Viewed most charitably, Justice O'Connor's opinion in *Grutter* attempted to craft a kind of compromise that might resolve this bitter debate once and for all, enabling American society to "move on." But if that was her strategy, *Fisher, Schuette,* and other such challenges show that it has failed miserably.

Indeed, O'Connor's hope to use a Court decision to achieve closure—if that was her intention—was probably doomed from the start. Our national experience suggests that divisive public issues in American life, of which affirmative action is certainly one, are not resolved by Court decision or by any official fiat. History has condemned the Court's attempts to settle such issues prematurely, peremptorily, or ex cathedra. *Dred Scott v. Sandford, Plessy v. Ferguson, Lochner v. New York, Roe v. Wade,* and *Bowers v. Hardwick* are among the many decisions that illustrate the point.

In *Fisher,* its most recent decision on the substance of university affirmative-action policies, the Court made a different attempt to foreshorten such policies. The *Fisher* majority (which consisted of seven justices) did not explicitly criticize *Grutter* (or *Bakke*) in any way. Nonetheless, it offered what might fairly be called a stern implicit rebuke. *Fisher* required the states (and reviewing courts) to apply those decisions' precepts and tests more rigorously than the lower court had done when it upheld the Texas program in question.

Specifically, *Fisher* focused attention on the narrow-tailoring prong of the "most rigid" strict-scrutiny standard and on a couple of other requirements that *Grutter* had affirmed. To address strict scrutiny, the decision focused on a few important aspects. First, the desired diversity must be achieved with no more use of race or ethnicity than necessary and only after considering all race-neutral alternatives. Second, even in the higher-education context, the state is entitled to "no deference" on the key factual narrow-tailoring determinations of whether the fit between its programmatic means and its diversity-enhancing end is tight enough, and whether there are workable race-neutral alternatives. And third, the state bears the burden of proof on these issues, proof that will probably require a trial rather than being resolved on summary judgment. Looking beyond strict scrutiny, a school must not use diversity as a pretext for "racial balancing, which is patently unconstitutional," and as a result a program must assess applicants as individuals. Perhaps most telling in *Fisher*'s analysis was the fact that it ignored the idea of "critical mass," a central pillar of *Grutter*'s defense of preferences.

In other words, the Court upheld but seemed to tighten its permissive attitude toward affirmative-action admissions policies. Rather than suggest wistfully that affirmative action might end someday, the majority indicated that it must be constrained. But this warning by the Court about the constitutional infirmities of ethno-racial preferences seems only to have emboldened their advocates, who took the ruling as an unqualified victory. And despite the Court's ruling, very few admissions offices plan to alter their policies.

The Benefits of Diversity, So Defined

Whatever the constitutional status of race-based affirmative action may be, it is even weaker as public policy, for it fails the essential test that any policy must pass: Its diversity-based benefits are lower than its costs.

I shall make no effort here to formally quantify either the benefits or the costs. Instead, my approach is to take the diversity rationale seriously by clarifying the elements that it must entail, and then to show that the social benefits claimed by the programs' proponents are modest at best and plainly swamped by their costs to society and even to many of their supposed beneficiaries.

What, then, are the benefits in terms of diversity that should count in favor of using preferences in university admissions? To answer this essential question, we must address three other closely related ones. What does diversity mean in this context? What is it about any group that accounts for whatever social benefits are conferred by its presence rather than the presence of some other group? And what diversity value is actually generated by the specific groups that affirmative-action programs favor?

Unfortunately, few discussions of diversity and the diversity rationale for affirmative action even address what diversity actually means, much less explain which groups and which kinds of attributes create diversity value. Nevertheless, the ways that affirmative-action programs are designed and defended leave no doubt that program advocates almost always mean ethno-racial diversity. This is true despite the many anomalies, evasions, and confusions that pervade most ethno-racial discourse. For one thing, race is a spurious category. People of different races have married and had children together in America since colonial times, producing a very large number of mixed-race individuals. Furthermore, recent immigrants are included in preference programs. "Hispanic" is a language designation, not a racial one. "Asian" refers to many ethnic, religious, linguistic, and national-origin groups with little or nothing in common with one another, and indeed with histories of deep conflict. The category of Native Americans is equally artificial and absurdly broad.

The preoccupation with race by proponents of the diversity rationale is also misplaced because other attributes are at least as predictive of a person's unique experiences, outlooks, and ideas—and hence at least as relevant to the kind of diversity that universities claim to want. According to a study by Northwestern University's James Lindgren of the demographic correlates of viewpoint differences, political affiliation accounts for the largest cleavages, while religion produces roughly the same cleavages as race. The failure of affirmative-action programs putatively aimed at diversity to base preferences on religion is among the most revealing facts about the programs' true objectives. Indeed, the programs' lack of interest in exploiting our rapidly growing religious heterogeneity for the purpose of campus diversity casts great doubt on the coherence of the diversity rationale as now implemented through these programs. This lack of interest may in turn reflect the remarkably unrepresentative religious composition of university faculties. As University of Texas scholar Sanford Levinson observes: "One sometimes gets the feeling that ostensible defenders of 'diversity' and 'multiculturalism' have no real idea of how truly diverse and multicultural the United States has become, fixated as they are on the 'traditional' racial and ethnic cleavages within this country." A priori (which is how programs selected the groups to be preferred), doesn't the perspective of a Muslim or conservative Christian applicant have at least as much diversity value as that of a middle-class black or Hispanic?

How many African-Americans or members of other preference-favored groups must be present in order to establish the requisite diversity value? Because diversity value surely depends on various factors, any sensible answer must be context-specific. Unfortunately, the law and practice of affirmative-action programs instead offer a wholly reductionist answer to this question. They simply count the number of group members in the relevant community (or their percentage of the community total) and seek proportional representation, at least as a default but often effectively as the final answer.

Defining the relevant community—that which will be used in making the proportionality assessment on which the admission decisions will turn—almost always entails highly controversial judgments, if not arbitrary empirical and normative ones. The relevant baseline for judging proportionality, for example, can only be defined in terms of a number of elusive, hard-to-measure, and internally-competing parameters, including group definition, geography, qualifications, attitudes, applicant pool, and others. Rhetoric aside, the task of actually administering affirmative action requires, ironically, that a program first combine many complex determinations that as a practical matter it can only make through almost comically arbitrary judgments—and then coming up with a bottom-line number that is certain to be breathtaking in its simplicity and lack of context. It would be surprising indeed if institutions that must process thousands of applications for relatively few slots in a very limited period of time did not pursue a spurious or formalistic kind of diversity—one that means color coding and color counting in service of a predetermined color targeting.

How, then, does a favored group in fact confer diversity value on an academic community? This is the second question we must confront when assessing affirmative action. A group can only confer such value if it possesses certain desired qualities as a group. It follows that a group can do this only if those qualities inhere in all members of the group (or else the group should be redefined to exclude those who lack them). But to affirm that a quality inheres in a racial group is to "essentialize" race in a way that utterly contradicts the bulk of our liberal, egalitarian, legal, scientific, and religious values. Together, these values hold that all individuals are unique and formally equal regardless of genetic heritage, and that their race causally determines little or nothing about their character, intelligence, experience, or anything else that is relevant to their diversity value. Indeed, for employers to use racial stereotypes in this way would be flatly illegal—even if the assumptions underlying the stereotypes were true.

The best that can be said of affirmative-action programs' use of diversity in this way is, as David Hollinger has put it, that they have reproduced "the most gross and invidious of popular images of what makes human beings different from one another" for a putatively benign purpose. They are propagating socially inflammatory stereotypes that, even if they were accurate, invite decision-makers to violate people's claim (and constitutional right, according to <u>Bakke</u>, *Grutter*, and *Fisher*) to be judged as individuals, not as members of ascribed groups. By parity of reasoning, legitimating the use of this proxy might equally justify racial profiling by police if it were intended to fight crime and were no less accurate than is the crude stereotyping in affirmative-action programs.

This brings us to the third crucial question about the diversity rationale for affirmative action: What diversity value does a favored group actually confer? Affirmative-action programs attempt to finesse the essentialism difficulty discussed above by assuming certain facts that might make the use of race as a proxy more defensible. They assume, first, that African-American students bring to campus histories and viewpoints that are unique to, and nearly universal among, African-Americans—even though those histories and viewpoints are not racially or genetically hardwired into them. Educational institutions and their African-American members, the programs further assume, should help people of other races to comprehend this experience, and campus diversity can strengthen the foundations of good citizenship in a pluralist democracy. Finally, they assume that race can serve under these circumstances as a rough but serviceable proxy for both diversity value and value diversity.

In their widely discussed 1998 book, *The Shape of the River*, William Bowen and Derek Bok strongly defend these three assumptions. They conclude that race-neutral admissions would substantially reduce the number of interracial social interactions and hence the socialization skills that both white and black students value and contribute to by attending racially diverse institutions.

But this conclusion, which is also supported by a study done to bolster the University of Michigan's defense of its affirmative-action program in the courts, has been challenged from several directions. The first is empirical. A review of survey data shows that most students and faculty place little weight on ethnic diversity as a source of positive educational outcomes, and its regression analysis of peer-group racial-composition effects finds no positive effect on any of the 82 outcome variables used by the American Council on Education.

The second challenge is comparative. Stephan and Abigail Thernstrom, prominent critics of the Bowen-Bok study and authors of an earlier analysis of American race relations that strongly opposed affirmative action, point to a 1997 national survey in which 86% of white adults reported having black friends, and to a 1994 survey in which 73% said that they had "good friends" who were black. To the Thernstroms, the Bowen-Bok study findings justify a different inference: "By these standards, the elite schools are hardly in the proud vanguard of progress. To the contrary, they are lagging woefully behind." Interestingly, both the Bowen-Bok and Thernstrom data on college-age and adult friendships overlook the increasing prevalence of interracial friendships among young Americans even before they reach college, which would suggest that the college experience may be less central to engendering such friendships than either camp supposes.

A third challenge to Bowen-Bok examines how the education process actually works on campuses. Terrance Sandalow, in an important review of *The Shape of the River* in the Michigan Law Review, maintains that any experiential differences between white and black students "are simply irrelevant to most of what students study in the course of their undergraduate careers. The irrelevance of those differences is perhaps most obvious in the study of mathematics and the natural sciences, but it is no less true of most of the humanities and the social sciences." Sandalow goes on to consider the argument, so crucial to the diversity rationale, that African-Americans are likely to advance different ideas unfamiliar to whites:

[E]ven though the subjects I teach deal extensively with racial issues, I cannot recall an instance in which, for example, ideas were expressed by a black student that have not also been expressed by white students. Black students do, at times, call attention to the racial implications of issues that are not facially concerned with race, but white and Asian-American students are in my experience no less likely to do so.

For what it's worth, my 35 years of experience in the classroom confirm this account. Recall, as well, that admissions officers almost never ask applicants about their ideas or viewpoints, much less how salient their race is to them. Outside the classroom, of course, race-based differences might encourage empathy and tolerance, but they might also promote greater conflict. Indeed, the simplistic version of the diversity rationale masks a deeper confusion about the diversity value arising out of social interactions. In this view, diversity demonstrates to people that despite our superficial differences, we are really all alike under the skin. The proposition is clearly true in many respects, but the diversity value that the diversity rationale invokes is supposed to grow out of the decidedly different viewpoints that diverse people are said to bring to these interactions. If we take the rationale seriously, then our similarity under the skin may confer negative, not positive, diversity value. The very logic of this rationale, after all, dictates that we seek differences under the skin, since it is those differences that constitute the payoff to diversity.

These doubts about the "socialization skills" premise of affirmative action are fortified by the dismaying evidence of persistent racial self-isolation on campuses. Orlando Patterson, a leading sociologist of race and an affirmative-action supporter, ruefully notes that "no group of people now seems more committed to segregation than Afro-American students and young professionals."

After carefully interrogating the diversity rationale, then, one is left with serious doubts about its coherence and persuasiveness. There is something to it, surely, but not much. Some advocates, as if recognizing this problem, seek to reconceptualize the diversity rationale into something else. In philosopher Elizabeth Anderson's view, for example, diversity is really "another way of talking about integration," a way that can link diversity to the advocates' "core social justice and democratic concerns." In the same spirit, legal scholar Robert Post sees diversity as the seedbed of "a democratic public culture."

This discursive move, however, is really an effort to change the subject; it defends racial preferences not as a way to enrich the experiences of students and teachers but as a remedy for social inequalities and generalized discrimination. That the Supreme Court has repeatedly prohibited this general remedial justification for racial preferences, of course, is not a conclusive argument against it; the Court, after all, is notoriously fallible. But this diversity rationale, as we have seen, is weak even in its own terms.

The Costs of Affirmative Action

If the diversity benefits of affirmative action are rather dubious, its costs seem very steep indeed. One measure of the costs of affirmative action is the long-standing opposition to it by a substantial majority of Americans. A Gallup poll published in July 2013—after four decades of experience with such programs—found that 67 % of all adults, 59 % of Hispanics, and 44 % of blacks agreed that "applicants should be admitted solely on the basis of merit, even if that results in few minority students being admitted." Only 28 % of all adults, 31 % of Hispanics, and 48 % of blacks agreed that "an applicant's racial and ethnic background should be considered to help promote diversity on college campuses, even if that means admitting some minority students who otherwise would not be admitted."

One leading study of such attitudes found, consistent with other studies, that "the most fundamental factor behind opposition to affirmative action is one of principle." That is, the opponents view preferences, rightly or wrongly, as inconsistent with the ideals of equal opportunity and merit that almost all Americans strongly endorse. Researchers of public attitudes toward affirmative action understand that the phrasing of questions, as well as other contextual factors, can affect survey results and that multiple interpretations of the data are possible. But no researcher in this field doubts that the public remains decidedly and intensely opposed, pretty much regardless of how the questions are framed, the state of the economy, or the age, sex, financial conditions, or general political inclinations of those polled. Indeed, one must presume that if the public actually knew how immense the weighting of ethno-racial preferences in selective college admissions must be in order to implement these programs (as discussed below), its opposition to preferences would be that much greater. The real question about affirmative action, then, is not why so many Americans oppose it but why it has managed to survive and even expand in some cases.

Far more important, however, are the costs borne by affirmative action's own supposed beneficiaries. Sander and Taylor have provided the most exhaustive account of this tragic irony. They conclude that a key "mismatch" between students and schools largely explains "why, even though blacks are more likely to enter college than are whites with similar backgrounds, they will usually get much lower grades, rank toward the bottom of the class, and far more often drop out; why there are so few blacks and Hispanics with science and engineering degrees or with doctorates in any field; and why black law graduates fail bar exams at four times the white rate."

The most disturbing fact about these human costs, Sander and Taylor emphasize, is that they are wholly unnecessary: "[N]early all of these students do have what it takes to succeed" in the absence of affirmative-action preferences; they would just gain this success at the less demanding schools to which they could gain admission without preferences. They continue:

> [T]he main victims of large racial preferences...are not the many whites and Asians who get passed over but rather the many blacks and Hispanics who receive preferences and do badly....Their intellectual confidence has been undermined, their career aspirations have in many cases been derailed, and they must deal with the stigma of being "affirmative-action admits." In the words of liberal scholar Christopher Jencks, "A policy that encourages the nation's future leaders to believe that blacks are slow learners will...do incalculable harm over the long run."

In fact, any declines in minority enrollments in the flagship campuses in state systems subject to bans of affirmative-action admissions tend to be offset by their attendance at less selective schools in the system (or elsewhere)—what Sander and Taylor call a "cascade effect." This outcome is hardly surprising, and a recent econometric study by Georgetown University's Peter Hinrichs and his colleagues confirms it empirically.

Indeed, Sander and Taylor's data show that the academic performance of minority students in the University of California system improved after Proposition 209 banned explicit affirmative-action policies in the state. Their four-year graduation rate rose 55%; the number who earned degrees in STEM fields rose 51%; the number who had GPAs of 3.5 or higher rose by 63%; and the number who earned doctorates and STEM graduate degrees rose by 25%.

Under any reasonable accounting, these immense gains under race-neutral admissions systems vastly outweigh whatever loss of diversity value has occurred at the most selective campuses, Berkeley and UCLA. Indeed, according to Sander, the overall level of integration of both blacks and Hispanics across the eight UC undergraduate campuses increased significantly after Proposition 209; that is, the distribution of both groups more closely approximated the distribution of whites across those campuses. Before the referendum passed, Berkeley and UCLA used racial preferences to attract blacks and Hispanics, and as a result half the blacks in the UC system had been concentrated on those two campuses. After the ban, when those schools could no longer officially employ such policies, this skewing largely disappeared.

A number of prominent scholars have strongly challenged the mismatch hypothesis, particularly as applied to legal education (the focus of Sander's original study), on a variety of methodological grounds. Sander has replied to his critics, and he and Taylor devoted a chapter of their book to reviewing these objections and defending their mismatch claims. It is difficult for a non-specialist to parse these arguments, much less assess them. Certain important facts, however, are perfectly clear even to a non-specialist.

First, the size of the preferences is enormous by any standard. Writing in 2009, Thomas Espenshade and Alexandra Radford reported that the admission "bonus" for being black was equivalent to 310 SAT points relative to whites and even more relative to Asians. The GPA differences are even greater than for SAT scores. Thomas Kane, a researcher in this field, found that black applicants to selective schools "enjoy an advantage equivalent to an increase of two-thirds of a point in [GPA]—on a four point scale—or [the equivalent of] 400 points on the SAT." Second, at every SAT score level, the test, which has long been criticized as being culturally biased against blacks, in fact over-predicts their actual academic performance in college.

In light of these two enduring facts, a substantial mismatch effect is more than a hypothesis. It would be little short of astonishing if no such effect existed.

Affirmative Harm

The public opposition to race-based affirmative-action programs on campus is amply justified. Affirmative action defies—indeed flouts—equal protection and other liberal values. It rests upon a diversity rationale that is theoretically incoherent and in fact produces little if any of the diversity value that alone might justify it (and then only under a dubious rationale). It cannot satisfy the constitutional tests that the Court has laid down and reaffirmed as recently as last year. It has failed to increase its political support in the nation after four decades of energetic advocacy. It fosters corrosive racial stereotypes, poisons race relations, and encourages opacity, dissimulation, and even evasion by its administrators and advocates.

And if that were not enough, affirmative action seems to grievously harm many of its supposed beneficiaries—not to mention the non-preferred groups who are disadvantaged by the practice.

We are far from putting America's history of racial intolerance and injustice behind us, but affirmative action fails to rectify these evils and instead harms both our students and our society as a whole.

Six Reasons Why Student Loans Are a Looming Disaster*

Federal efforts to alleviate the high and rising cost of attending college through student loans have morphed from a policy challenge to a fiscal time bomb threatening to blow up the financial future of tens of millions of Americans and the government's own solvency. Dressed up as a progressive achievement, it is actually a failure—or more accurately, at least five intersecting failures. And the worst part is this: they would all be hard to fix—even in a "normal" political era. (President Biden's current fixes are dubious on both policy and legal grounds.)

The scope of these programs is enormous. More than 44 million Americans (about one in four adults) have student loan debt totaling $1.5 trillion and rising. This debt is incurred (and encouraged) through a handful of U.S. Department of Education (DOE) programs for which public and private institutions constitute a powerful lobbying force. Here, I can discuss only six of the programs' failures: (1) their unsustainable cost trajectory; (2) the immense debt burdens they impose; (3) high college dropout rates; (4) fraud by educational institutions and borrowers; (5) DOE's relative neglect of career and technical education (CTE) which would better serve many of the neediest; and (6) programs' perverse targeting and incentive patterns, which magnify all of these problems.

1. DOE's Unsustainable Cost Trajectory

The loan programs charge borrowers interest and fees, so they should be budget-neutral or even profitable. This feature made them politically popular for many years, but a major Obama-era policy change—the income-based repayment plan (IBRP)—has sharply reversed the budgetary trajectory. The IBRP became available to new borrowers starting in 2014-15. It allows qualified students to cap their monthly loan repayments at an amount geared to their income and family size; Obama further lowered that cap to 10%. A 2017 DOE financial report, analyzed by the *Wall Street Journal*, projected a $36 billion shortfall, up from an $8 billion shortfall just a year earlier. (IBRP's fiscal effect will inevitably grow as more post-2014 borrowers take advantage of it).

Here's the *Journal*'s bad news: "Federal data never before released shows that the default rate [for borrowers who started repaying in 2012] continued

---

* *Minding the Campus*, 9/13/2018; https://www.mindingthecampus.org/2018/09/13/five-reasons-students-loans-are-an-enormous-disaster/

climbing to 16 percent over the next two years, after official tracking ended, meaning more than 841,000 borrowers were in default. Nearly as many were severely delinquent or not repaying their loans (for reasons besides going back to school or being in the military). The share of students facing serious struggles rose to 30 percent overall." This, in a period of (slowly) rising incomes and job growth.

By law, DOE must track default rates for only the first three years, yet this is only the tip of the iceberg: delinquencies increase sharply starting in year 4, and DOE's reports do not include borrowers who are "severely delinquent" or "not repaying the loans." The number of schools experiencing high default rates by that post-2012 group has also increased dramatically, fueled vastly and disproportionately by for-profits. Even these default rates will presumably rise; more schools now urge students to use options that temporarily suspend repayments, accumulating more interest and simply postponing the day of reckoning. Student loans have the highest delinquency rates of any federal credit program, and higher than for private auto, home equity, and mortgage loans. The New York Fed emphasizes that this actually understates the delinquency problem because of students' deferred payment obligations.

2. Borrowers' Debt Burdens

The statistics are scary. Students owe about $1.5 trillion—about $620 billion more than the total U.S. credit-card debt. The debt of the average Class of 2017 graduate was almost $40,000, up 6% from the previous year's cohort. And this burden is greatest for lowest-income students eligible for Pell Grants; their loan debt is higher on average than for higher-income, non-Pell students. As college tuition inexorably rises—for public four-year institutions, more than doubling in constant dollars in the last 30 years, and roughly 5% a year in the last decade—debt burdens will increase accordingly, particularly for lower-income students who attend for-profit colleges such as the immense University of Phoenix (over 160,000 students on 38 campuses). According to the *Hechinger Report*, almost 80% of these students who had dropped out three years earlier had not yet repaid a cent of principal on their federal loans.

3. High College Dropout Rates

These burdens might be sustainable if borrowers were to graduate and then earn at levels reflecting their new credentials. But the reality is altogether worse. Only 57% of college students graduate from any institution within six years of entering. (Another 12% of that cohort are still enrolled after six years). Nearly one-third—disproportionately low-income, first-generation, and minority students—drop out entirely, carrying their student loan debts with them. Importantly, those who later transfer to a 4-year institution are not counted as dropouts. Dropouts are stunningly high at public community colleges (62%) and at 4-year for-profit colleges (64%). Unsurprisingly, dropout rates of 4-year public and private nonprofit institutions are much lower, reflecting the institutions' greater resources and their students' more prosperous families and better prospects.

The much higher dropout rate at for-profit institutions has various causes, including poorly-prepared and lower-income students, many who must simultaneously hold down jobs, and fewer support services for at-risk students. But an important factor is the well-documented fraudulent practices at many of these schools, practices that the DOE recently proposed to protect by easing "gainful employment" disclosure rules.

4. Fraud by Educational Institutions and Borrowers

The student loan programs have long been rife with fraud, which seems only to have increased since the Obama administration took over the programs from the private sector (although private for-profit agencies still do much of the collection and other work). Not all of the documented fraud is perpetrated by private for-profit institutions and collection agencies; some are by student borrowers and even Pell grantees. Indeed, in 2013 the DOE's inspector general reported that this fraud included over 34,000 participants in crime rings. The Obama-spawned IBRPs, which include loan forgiveness options, have surely enabled more fraud. Just since 2015, the DOE has received more than 100,000 fraud complaints; according to a recent review cited by the New York Times, "almost 99% involved for-profit institutions." The Trump DOE, widely criticized for weak enforcement against these schools, which Secretary Betsy DeVos is keen to promote, recently proposed new "Institutional Responsibility" regulations purporting to curb some of this fraud but, according to critics, will actually make fraud harder to combat.

5. Neglect of CTE in Favor of Higher-Status Education

In our cosmopolitan world, one can easily forget that most Americans lack even a community-college diploma. Yet federal (and state and local) student loan programs largely neglect CTE and other intensive work-focused vocational programs, instead emphasizing higher-level, campus-based institutions. The economic returns of a college diploma are certainly large, and unemployment risks are lower: a 2015 Georgetown study found that workers with a bachelor's degree earn $1 million more over their lifetimes than those with only a high-school diploma, even though the latter have a four-year head start. (This is on average; field of major matters a lot). But many of the student loans go to art, music, and design students who carry a disproportionate debt load while facing limited future income prospects.

College is not the best choice for everyone, especially when one considers its high cost (including the opportunity costs during those four years), the substantial probability of dropping out along the way, and the consequent waste of much of the money expended (depending on the value of the foreshortened college experience), the interest paid on the loans, and the debts' limiting effect on their future ability to obtain loans and thus life choices. Importantly, Oren Cass points out, "A college degree is neither necessary nor sufficient for reaching the middle class. The wage and salary distributions for college graduates and high-school graduates overlap significantly; high-earning high-school graduates in a wide variety of fields that require no college degree earn substantially more than low-earning college graduates."

Yet, despite the strong arguments to enlarge CTE opportunities for those who reject or drop out of college, all levels of government fail to support this alternative path significantly. Washington spent only $1 billion on CTE in 2016, compared with more than $70 billion subsidizing college attendance; much the same is true of state and local governments. CTE programs vary in their effectiveness, of course, but we have seen that the same is true of higher education institutions and the loan programs that support, and in many cases, sustain them, including the worst ones.

6. *Perverse Targeting and Incentives*

Federal student loan programs are a classic example of distributive politics: coalitions designed to concentrate benefits while widely dispersing costs. Typically, relatively few of the subsidies go to low-income families; instead, they tend to go to the better off. Nor is it clear that this taxpayer-provided subsidy actually affects educational attainments in general. Those who receive them would likely have attended college even without them; the IBRP tends to benefit high-earning people who can carry high debt, which is one reason that politicians across the political spectrum use the loan programs to appeal to middle- and upper-class voters. And as the *Wall Street Journal* editorialized in 2013, IBRPs increase moral hazard, incentivizing delinquency: "Take out a big loan, work 10 years for the government repaying as little as possible, and then have your debt entirely forgiven. . . .Borrowers who enroll in [such] plans owe on average three times more than those who opt for the standard 10-year amortization schedule. They thus present the greatest risk to taxpayers."

Consider several other perverse incentives of these programs. They encourage schools to raise tuition and fees—they nearly tripled over the last 20 years (rising much faster than wages)—thus reducing access. They also encourage institutions to substitute federal money for their own financial assistance, thus reducing the programs' net effect. Also, the programs (along with other federal and state rules) may have contributed to the doubling of the administrative staff-student ratio since 1975, during which the faculty-student ratio has changed very little.

Program redesign could reduce some of these perverse incentives. Remarkably, however, little rigorous policy assessment of the loan programs' effectiveness and tradeoffs has been done—perhaps because of the powerful constituencies that support the status quo, favoring only changes that expand initial access to programs, regardless of the dire longer-term effects on so many students. Secretary DeVos's mission to further weaken already negligible enforcement against the for-profit sector is only the most recent example.

As more prosperous Americans pull further away from those seeking a chance to educate themselves or their children into the middle class, the federal government must fundamentally reform student loans so that they reduce disadvantage instead of multiplying it.

The Garden of College Excellence Is Growing Weeds*

Anthony Kronman, my long-time Yale Law School colleague and perhaps the most eloquent individual I know personally, has written a brave, high-minded, and often persuasive argument about the values and choices that should animate our greatest colleges and universities but no longer do. His book, *Education's End: Why Our Colleges and Universities Have Given Up on the Meaning of Life*, is also quixotic in the manner of King Canute who ordered the sea to retreat, knowing that as a mere mortal, he would fail. Unlike Canute, Kronman utterly believes what he says, yet the stars, alas, are aligned against him.

This book could not be more timely. The cascade of campus contretemps over academic values and due process in recent years seems relentless. A partial list would include student protests over right-wing speakers on campus and demands for trigger warnings and other protections from unwelcome (i.e., conservative) provocations by faculty, administrators, and other sources; curricular disputes; admissions and financial aid policies; regulation of students' sexual relations; demands for an army of diversity specialists; and other

---

* *Minding the Campus*, 9/12/2019; https://www.mindingthecampus.org/2019/09/12/the-garden-of-college-excellence-is-growing-weeds/

offenses against political correctness creatively ginned up by hypersensitive, politically "woke" members of the community. When the pending lawsuit by Asian-descent students to Harvard's ethnic admission program is decided, the war will surely intensify.

These specific disputes are manifestations of competing conceptions of the academy's role in American life today—a larger challenge that Kronman passionately engages. Its framing argument is easily stated. (It is also obsessively repeated, an authorial tic redeemed by his graceful writing and his subject's vital importance). Two norms clash on today's campuses. The first is what he calls the "aristocratic" spirit—a provocative label that will surely invite misunderstanding, even caricature: "Many people," he notes, "have an allergy to the word 'aristocracy.' To them, it implies unearned privilege and exploitative domination. In the original sense, though, the word simply means the rule of the best." Kronman is clear that higher education is an inherently aristocratic activity which should be organized, conducted, and defended as such. His "best" are the faculty who profess and execute aristocratic ideals. Only they possess the hard-won knowledge and authority to frame the compelling intellectual questions to be debated in the classroom and to judge whether the debaters have enacted those ideals.

Kronman believes that our academic mandarins consistently betray this sacred trust by capitulating to a conflicting norm: a "democratic" ethos defined by egalitarian and majoritarian values which have an inexorably leveling effect. Kronman wants to confine this democratic norm to its proper realm—politics, broadly defined—where he personally favors "progressive positions on the whole." Alas, he laments, the democratic norm has bled into many of the campus policies that aristocratic norms should govern. His scrupulous exploration and defense of this distinction are, well, masterful (a term to which I'll return).

To justify his aristocratic conception of higher education—a "community of conversation"—Kronman draws deeply from the writings of Plato, John Adams, Alexis de Tocqueville, Immanuel Kant, Oliver Wendell Holmes, Jr., Irving Babbitt, H.L. Mencken, and others. Each in his own way decried the inevitable leveling effects of majoritarianism in a liberal polity, and each saw exalting education as a leading tool to control them. Even Thomas Jefferson, while excoriating inherited rank and privilege, favored a natural aristocracy populated through superior character and learning. Tocqueville admired America's commitment to equality and popular sovereignty but feared its vulnerability to a "tyranny of the majority," which would breed materialism and mediocrity and suppress the aristocratic values of excellence and distinction. To these lofty educational goals, Holmes added the pursuit of "spiritual things," even of the "infinite."

Some of these seekers for larger meanings placed hope in genuine religious uplift (not the flim-flam tent preaching memorably mocked by Mencken). Babbitt, a tough-minded Harvard humanities scholar, called for a disciplined curriculum dedicated to high intellectual standards, not "sentimental humanitarianism." The common normative thread among these visionaries was "the importance of studying the great works of the past; the belief that education is a moral enterprise; and, above all the value of independent-mindedness" in the face of majoritarian leveling and mediocrity.

But serpents dwell in this glorious garden of excellence—threats to this aristocratic vision of conversation, learning and disciplined self-mastery. One threat, Kronman warns, is universities' pursuit of "the vocational ideal": the belief that we are fulfilled mainly by our work rather than our leisure, and the concomitant calibration of our imputed status according to what we do rather than who we are. Who we are, he claims, depends on our "character and competence in the art of living." Yet higher education today is "in thrall" to this vocational ideal, adopting "the egalitarian morality of our democratic culture" rather than promoting "what is rare and fine among human works and human beings." (Precisely what he means by all of these empyrean concepts, so central to his argument, remains opaque despite his efforts to define them—a point to which I shall return).

The central element of Kronman's aristocratic culture is the "conversational ideal." Although academic leaders duly invoke it at campus ceremonies, they are incapable of instantiating it. "They fail to grasp that the distinctiveness of a college or university is a function of its devotion to a conversational ideal that has no place in political life (a mistake their civil libertarian opponents make too). They do not appreciate that the pursuit of this ideal is a calling that demands even less deference to the feelings of others than one reasonably expects in many non-academic settings. And they fail to see that the spirit of inclusion it fosters is one that gathers teachers and students for the sake of discovering the truth—a uniquely difficult and demanding inquiry in which all are welcome, but some get further than others and grow into fuller possession of the liberating power of thought." Clarifying this point, he distinguishes the community of conversation on his idealized campus from family dinner table conversation ("where love rules and feelings matter") and from a public Speaker's Corner ("where citizens compete as sellers and buyers but have no duty to converse" or even remain).

Kronman, the erstwhile progressive, eagerly acknowledges what egalitarians decry: the multiplication of advantage in American life that engenders "a self-perpetuating socioeconomic elite" that dominates our campuses—a condition recently underscored by efforts of wealthy parents and complicit universities to corrupt the admissions process. But he maintains—wishfully but implausibly—that these unearned advantages will shake out in merit-based differences in grades and rankings once on campus. Egalitarians' efforts, he claims, should be "for the sake of having a fair chance to show that one is really and truly unequal to other, less gifted and less industrious students." (emphases original)

But if equality of access and opportunity are essential to the desired inequality of outcomes, as Kronman contends, isn't this an argument for affirmative action, which he opposes? Here he waffles. He first asserts that diversity's value, properly understood, is gravely distorted by affirmative action, which "represents the intrusion into the academy of an egalitarian ideal of fairness that has an unimpeachable authority outside the walls of our colleges and universities but less or none within them." Yet he later asserts that "some affirmative action in the admissions process is morally justified, even required" as the university decides who may "participate in its selective and privileged milieu." He neither reconciles this with his lodestar, academic "excellence," nor discusses affirmative action's actual perverse consequences (which I have emphasized in two decades of writings on the subject).

Kronman's final chapter applies his critique of political correctness to disputes about changing college names and removing statues that honor historical figures who advanced now-dubious ideas. He rightly insists that students learn by both precept and example to tolerate the moral complexity, ambiguity, and tensions of historical judgments, and to avoid the acontextual "presentism" that historians wisely decry. He particularizes this view in an extended critique of Yale's decision to rename Calhoun College (named for a distinguished statesman and Vice President who fiercely defended slavery), and the title of residential college "masters." To drive his point home, he quotes Charles Davis, Calhoun College's beloved black master who opposed the name change and urged Yalies to: "be strong enough to face the past and fight it, which those who forget, by chance or by will, lose the power to do." Kronman concludes this analysis by urging universities to resist political pressures, which belong to "a different order of values and expectations; [universities'] first responsibility is to themselves and their undemocratic way of life."

The chaste conception of intellectual life on a Kronmanian campus ultimately rests on his notion of character, which is "difficult to define but hardly unintelligible." His aristocratic campus ethos, in sharp contrast with the now-regnant vocational ideal, imparts to students "a love of those things for which a person of fine character should care" and "is distinguished by the confident belief that men and women can be ranked according to the success in the general work of being human." His other formulations of character are likewise opaque, stressing "greatness in the work of being human" as opposed to "mediocrity and failure." Nor does he say how our universities can somehow maintain this ideal while also conducting its many other desirable activities—extramural research, athletics, community relations, programs in countries that don't share American ideals, much less Kronman's—in concert with people and institutions that neither share not understand it.

Perhaps most important, he fails to distinguish between the Yales and Harvards of this world with their vast endowments of money and intellectual students committed to the conversational ideal, and the great majority of institutions that have neither and thus will inevitably pursue the vocational idea at which he sneers.

This brilliant, bracing book would have done better to rest its argument for educational excellence less on vague and controversial notions of what character and "being human" entail, and more on the vital need to educate students on what they often miss: the elusiveness of contested empirical facts, the centrality of these facts to moral discourse and decision-making, and the importance of teaching the privileged few how to detect cant and expose imposture in this truth- and candor-deprived society. These more functional lessons are as essential to clear thinking and excellent citizenship as aristocratic character-building is, and wholly consistent with it.

The Commencement Disinvitation Season[*]

On our elite campuses, the venerable, august Commencement exercise has taken on a new significance. Until very recently, it was a photogenic occasion, a pleasant rite of passage, in which new graduates and their families were treated (or subjected) to forgettable speeches and predictable advice-giving by eminent windbags of various stripes.

Today, the Commencement season features a succession of embarrassed announcements either that the colleges and universities have rescinded their invitations to certain speakers, or that the invited speakers themselves have decided not to appear for the occasion. (Consult the Foundation for Individual Rights in Education for a full report on this trend over the past 15 years). In the former case, the institution alludes (with admirable delicacy) to the controversy that has arisen over the speaker's past pronouncements or affiliations. In the latter case, the once-invited speakers explain (with conspicuous graciousness) that they are declining the honor because they do not wish to divert the audience's attention from what should be the occasion's focus: the celebration of the graduating students' stellar achievements in having

---

[*] *Huffington Post*, 5/30/2014; https://www.huffpost.com/entry/the-commencement-disinvit_b_5417184

survived the rigors of their undergraduate years. Both the institutions and the speakers evince great respect for the wishes of the students.

These now-ritualistic volte-faces would be comical in their faux politeness were it not for the sheer hypocrisy, inconsistency, and illogic that they only thinly conceal. The institutions justify their reversals on the ground that the students should ultimately decide who will speak to them. This approach to speaker selection is plausible but hardly convincing. After all, the institution decides which courses students are required to take, which books and articles they must read in those courses, and many other features of students' academic experience on campus. Many of the finest institutions (Yale and Princeton, for example) do not have commencement speakers at all.

The institutions that do recruit commencement speakers but then either disinvite them—or in effect allow a rump of students to do so—claim to be honoring the feelings of their students. But note that this deference to the delicate sensibilities of the students applies only to the views of some of their students—and likely a small minority of them at that. The silent majority, whose wishes the institution presumably had in mind when it invited the speaker, is suddenly rendered irrelevant. What has prevailed is not the will of the majority or of the thoughtful; what carries the day is the will of the noisiest, most aggressive partisans. And make no mistake; this prevailing minority is partisan. If there is an instance of conservative students at an elite institution preventing a liberal speaker from delivering a commencement address, I am not aware of it.

Most dismaying about these disinvitations, however, is what they reveal about the values that these institutions instantiate in some of their actual practices—as distinguished from the values that they proclaim in their encomia to themselves, and their pitches to their donors and the public. The issue is certainly not freedom of speech; the institutions are entitled to decide for themselves who will speak to them, and no one has a right to speak at commencement.

Instead, the central issue is how some of our leading institutions of higher education conceive of their pedagogical responsibilities. The epithet of political correctness fails to capture the extent of their abdication in these cases; in truth, they have abandoned some of the most elementary aspects of the precious academic mission that we have entrusted to them. Here are just three ways in which they have dishonored this mission.

First, an invitation to deliver a commencement address supposedly exemplifies the institution's wish to honor the distinction and achievement that the speaker has gained in the larger world that their new graduates will soon enter, achievements to which they might aspire. An invitation should not signal the institution's, much less some students,' agreement with the speaker's point of view on particular issues. Consider several of the most recent spate of disinvitations. Aayan Hirsi Ali, rejected by Brandeis, could tell students a remarkable life story of courage and triumph over immense obstacles, only some of them religious. She should be a beacon to students who claim to cherish women's rights enough to question some of Islam's misogynistic practices. But taking controversial positions, as Hirsi Ali and Condoleeza Rice (rejected by Rutgers) have, is not necessary for institutions to capitulate to some students' ire. Smith College rejected Christine Lagarde, one of the most accomplished women in the world, not because of anything she said or did but because of policies that some parts of her large organization have adopted in the developing world. The meticulousness of some students' moral posturing is what these institutions seem to honor most.

Second, some of the institutions invoke as justification the discomfort that their students will feel at having to listen to speakers with whom they strongly disagree. But on complex issues—and all of those with which the speakers are involved are very complex—discomfort is not a vice but rather the beginning of wisdom. It is precisely the easy certitudes and unearned self-assurance about such issues that educators should always strive to unsettle and dispel.

Third, the institutions' actions only serve to reinforce their students' existing tendencies to fly to familiar, conventional moralisms rather than forcing them to struggle with the stubborn, often elusive facts and competing values and moralities that tough problems always entail. (I sometimes tell my students that such easy posturing is the classroom equivalent of premature ejaculation; they are quick and feel good but are otherwise not fruitful). This struggle—presided over by conscientious, knowledgeable teachers willing to play the skeptic, agnostic, and Devil's advocate at the risk of unpopularity—that constitutes a true education. Only such a struggle can enable students to unpack moral ideals such as fairness, racial justice, equality, the proper roles of markets and government, and so forth—and to think rigorously about them before arriving at a normative position.

The only encouraging feature of these disinvitations is the virtual unanimity with which pundits across the ideological spectrum—not just the conservative traditionalists—have condemned them, chastising and mocking the institutions, the militant protesters, or both. The good news is that the academic values of truth-seeking and impartiality are indeed alive and well. The bad news is that it is up to those outside the academy to demand the protection of these values.

On Sexual Assault Policy, Trust Colleges Not Uncle Sam*

Sexual harassment and sexual violence complaints are surging on campuses. The Obama administration pressured colleges and universities to assure

---

* *Los Angeles Times,* 5/14/2014; https://www.latimes.com/nation/la-oe-0515-schuck-sexual-assault-campus-obama-20140515-story.html more confidentiality for accusers, conduct anonymous student surveys, and train bystanders to intervene. It named scores of institutions that it believed weren't doing these things—I taught at two of them, Yale and UC Berkeley—and asked Congress to impose stiff penalties on institutions that do not comply. The Trump administration eased some of these requirements to afford greater procedural protections to the accused, but the Biden administration re-installed Obama's educational civil right chief who has sought to reinstate the earlier procedures.

But what is the proper role of the federal government in this situation? Few want to raise this question; after all, the complainants want help wherever they can get it, and the institutions fear that questioning federal intervention will make them seem like latter-day "Bull" Connors, shielding injustice by denouncing "outside agitators."

In truth, the federal government should prod institutions to find their own campus-specific remedies for sexual assaults on students rather than forcing them to conform to Washington's dictates. Here's why advice is better than mandates:

First, the problem of campus violence defies simple solutions. Many institutions that are deeply concerned about campus rape, that are neither misogynist nor indifferent, have yet to come up with a full solution. This strongly suggests that the problem is inherently difficult to remedy, not that the schools aren't trying hard enough.

Most assault is related to alcohol and drug abuse among new drinkers, both male and female, who like to take risks but sometimes go too far. College students, suddenly free from parental supervision, live in an aggressive popular culture fueled by peer pressure. The boundaries separating normal libido, unwelcome sex, and repellent violence can be blurry, especially if students are in a drunken stupor. If some of the most earnest, best-educated people in America have not yet figured out how to control this, federal officials probably cannot do better.

Second, institutions already have powerful incentives to protect their students, even if they are not yet fully effective. Their failure to prevent campus assaults threatens their most basic economic and reputational interests, as well as their moral standing. Media reports and student protests about sexual victimization infuriate tuition-paying parents and alumni, reduce the loyalty and generosity of donors, and impair the institutions' ability to compete for applicants and resources. Serious legal risks abound. More students are suing and winning large damage awards against their colleges. Information about sexual assaults and other crimes on campus, which institutions must publicize under federal law, may spawn still more lawsuits. State legislators investigate.

Prosecutors may even seek criminal sanctions. For the institutions, taking this problem lightly is simply not an option.

Third, individual colleges and universities have far more experience and knowledge than the government about what will and won't work in reshaping the conduct and mores of their students. Indeed, the federal government brings to the table no particular problem-solving expertise or methodology; its tools are indignation, of which there is already plenty, and its mailed fist, which the institutions are already feeling. Also militating against a federal solution is the enormous diversity among institutions. They vary by religious orientation, single-gender or coed campuses, rural or urban, large or small, student housing arrangements, and a host of other differences. Any effective remedy for sexual assaults will be campus-specific and achieved only after experimenting with various approaches.

Finally, fair and accurate procedures for handling sexual assault claims are very hard to design, as we know from the continuing, centuries-old controversies over what constitutes due process of law. School officials are not trained as interrogators, mediators or judges. Seldom are there other direct witnesses to the encounter, and the pivotal but often ambiguous issue of consent usually turns on "he said / she said" evidence. Complainants often want the investigation, adjudication and remedy to be strictly confidential, yet a secret process may well prejudice the fundamental constitutional right of the accused to confront his accuser and defend himself. Confidentiality also makes it harder for an institution to keep the accuser and the accused from encountering each other, thus inflaming their conflict. Lastly, the institutions have fewer and weaker sanctions to impose than courts do.

Finding the appropriate balance among these competing values, deciding on the appropriate roles of the institutions and the formal criminal justice system, and resolving countless procedural issues are formidable challenges. It will require a flexible learning process tailored to diverse institutions and conditions, not the kind of national, one-size-fits-all mandate that the administration seems to be promoting.

The federal government is essential for many important things: protecting voting, equal opportunity and other civil rights of vulnerable minorities; correcting for many market failures; mobilizing incentives; and more. But understanding, regulating and fine-tuning intimate, tension-filled relationships between young people in the shadow of criminal law—the context in which sexual assault often occurs—is not its metier.

No one knows how to do this perfectly, and educational institutions must do much more to figure out and implement a solution, but they are far more likely than federal bureaucrats to come up with fair and effective solutions.

Valdosta and the Future of the Authoritarian Campus*

A federal jury in Georgia has held Ronald Zaccari, the former president of Valdosta State University, liable for damages in a lawsuit by a former student, Hayden Barnes, whom Zaccari expelled in 2007 without according him a due process hearing. Zaccari did so after Barnes had conducted a passionate, energetic, unrelenting campaign on campus against the administration's plan to construct a new parking deck at an estimated cost of $30 million, which Barnes argued would be better spent on almost 3000 full scholarships for needy university students. The breaking point for Zaccari apparently occurred when Barnes referred to the project as a "memorial" garage, which Zaccari took to be a personal threat to his safety, justifying a summary expulsion.

Such outrageous violations by college administrators of their students' and teachers' peaceful exercise of First Amendment rights are all too common. The legal challenges are usually based on 42 U.S.C. Section 1983, a civil rights law dating back to 1871 that provides a remedy (money damages, injunctions, or both) in federal (and state) courts against state and local officials who violate a right secured by the U.S. Constitution, federal statutes, or other sources of federal law. (States themselves can be sued only under narrow circumstances because of the Eleventh Amendment).

Two Kinds of Immunity

Because state university administrators are state officials, they will usually defend not only on the facts but on the legal ground that Section 1983 principles confer immunity from being sued, especially for money damages. There are two types of immunity that they may claim: absolute or qualified. Defendant officials whose actions against the plaintiff were judicial, prosecutorial, or legislative in nature are absolutely immune regardless of how illegal their conduct was. End of case.

But when university officials act in an administrative capacity, as in expelling students, they can claim only qualified immunity, not absolute. This means that the immunity can be overcome if the plaintiff shows that the officials did not act in good faith in the sense that the right claimed by the plaintiff—here, a right to a due process hearing before expulsion—was "clearly established" by the legal precedents when the officials acted. Valdosta's immunity defense failed because Barnes was able to show that his right to a

---

* *Minding the Campus*, 2/21/2013, http://www.mindingthecampus.com/originals/2013/02/valdosta_and_the_future of the authoritarian campus

hearing before being expelled for protected activity was indeed "clearly established." In certain situations, plaintiffs who prevail in their Sec. 1983 actions can recover their legal fees as well, which Barnes will try to do.

Verdicts like these should certainly capture the attention of university presidents. What is less clear is whether Barnes' victory will cause them to be more respectful of campus dissenters' First Amendment rights. Here are five reasons to doubt that public universities will change their self-protective ways. First, the Valdosta decision was hardly the first successful challenge to suppressions of campus dissent, yet earlier victories seem not to have caused universities to be more tolerant of it. Second, the $50,000 jury award seems like a small amount—a slap on Zaccari's wrist—given the flagrant violation of Barnes' constitutional rights and the presumed interruption of his education (though I have not examined the damages evidence presented to the jury).This liability would hardly rate a footnote in most university budgets.

Boards Don't Like to Undercut Presidents

Third, university presidents are powerful people on campus and, like many powerful people in all walks of life, can become authoritarian when they feel threatened. This is particularly true when the university trustees support them, which is usually the case. The governing boards of public institutions set broad policy, hire the top officials, determine their salaries, and thus can call the shots on many important issues. They will be reluctant to undercut the president with whom they are closely identified. They also tend to have strong political connections—this is probably why they were selected in the first place—and are responsive to state legislators and governors who may also want to suppress student or faculty criticism of the university, which often reflects on themselves.

A fourth reason to doubt that the Valdosta case will induce universities to strongly protect authority-threatening dissent is that the universities often win in court. Barnes' case may be unusual in that it was particularly strong on both the facts and the law. His actions, after all, were peaceful and clearly protected by the First Amendment, and Vaccari expelled him without a constitutionally-required hearing. In many other cases, however, plaintiffs may lose, perhaps because the university can offer some other, ostensibly legitimate reason for its action.

Consider the protracted Ward Churchill case in which the University of Colorado's Board of Regents terminated Churchill, a tenured professor, on the ground that he had plagiarized and engaged in other professional misconduct. This September, five years after Churchill sued the Board for violating his First Amendment rights, the Colorado Supreme Court held that the

Board was immune because the right that Churchill invoked was not "clearly established."(Some facts in the case suggest that the Board may have used his professional misconduct as a kind of pretext for the real, original reason for terminating him—that he had compared some 9/11 victims to Nazi Adolf Eichmann). The outcomes of such cases are hard to predict because the line between protected academic freedom and legitimate administrative prerogatives is not well-defined.

But the most worrisome reason why some universities violate the First Amendment rights of dissenters is that so many of them marinate their campuses in political correctness and group-think, most of it predictable left-wing orthodoxy. While paying lip service to academic freedom and diversity, academic institutions often seem willing to sacrifice those precious values in favor of collegiality, convention, and campus peace. Public universities are particularly eager to propitiate the powers that be—the public officials who govern them, the taxpayers and trustees who fund them, and the media through whom they reach the voters—while private universities have their own sacred cows to protect. Alas, we can look forward to more Valdosta cases in the future.

Part 6

IMMIGRANTS, CITIZENS, AND REFUGEES

Introduction to Part 6

I have long been deeply interested in the history, sociology, economics, and policy surrounding immigration. More than perhaps any other nation, the U.S. has been shaped by it. But the cliché that we are a nation of immigrants conceals the deep divisions and bitter struggles that Americans have experienced from the very beginning over questions of who may join our society and under what conditions. In my writings, I have always been very pro-immigration, including endorsing larger legal immigration quotas, expanding refugee admissions, designing generous legalization programs for many of the undocumented, and securing our borders as a necessary condition for such reforms.

In this Part, I include three articles that shed light on these most fundamental questions about the nature of the American polity. The first is a very recent analysis of certain aspects of immigration policy that are shaping partisan conflicts over illegal migration. It focuses on what the Biden administration and Democrats in Congress can do to advance an agenda that could possibly loosen the policy logjam. The second piece is about birthright citizenship—the legal rule that anyone born on U.S. soil, even if the parents lack legal status here, is nevertheless automatically a U.S. citizen. In a highly controversial book on the subject published by me and Professor Rogers Smith back in 1985, we argued that this rule violates the consensual principle underlying the Citizenship Clause of the 14th Amendment. The American version of birthright citizenship is more absolute than that of probably any other country today and has long been criticized, most recently by President Trump, but even he did not seriously challenge it—although many other liberal democracies with birthright citizenship are narrowing its scope to address the challenges presented by large-scale illegal migration. My article establishes the context of this controversy and proposes a novel solution.

The final article – the longest in this collection – presents an innovative proposal that I advanced many years ago designed to resolve, or at least ameliorate, the tragically chronic and steadily growing refugee flows throughout the world. The problem has only grown worse since 2015 when I updated the article. At the end of 2022, the World Refugee Survey reported over 100 million refugees, which does not include the millions displaced since then by the war in Ukraine.

Democrats' Vulnerability and Opportunity on Immigration Policy*

President Biden and the Democrats face severe headwinds in the upcoming 2024 elections. Among the gusts blowing are surging inflation, the Covid pandemic, politicized federal deficits, the abortion wars, the indelible images of a botched Afghanistan withdrawal, Republicans' gerrymandered advantages in many key states, and a large number of Senate seats to defend. Meanwhile some new problems have arisen—including public weariness of the growing fiscal cost of a Ukraine rescue mission despite admiration for the extraordinary, inspiring Ukrainian resistance.

But the Democrats face another, more familiar challenge: their own leaders' position on undocumented immigration, especially at the southern border. While the number of undocumented persons seeking to cross the border has long been high, it is historically higher than ever and will rise even more during the warm weather months. With the undocumented routinely asserting asylum claims—most know this is a crucial part of the migration game—hearing requirements for those who can credibly allege fear back home are soaring. To make matters worse, the Biden Administration has tied itself in knots over whether and how to pursue "Title 42" enforcement that authorizes prompt removal for public health (here, Covid) reasons and thus avoids time- and resource-consuming legal requirements for an asylum hearing at the border.

The Title 42 imbroglio is just one of many legal disputes that have arisen over the southern border. Others include the conditions in which would-be border-crossers are detained, reunification of families, the education and care of children, and prompt notification of child welfare agencies operating at the border. This forces federal judges in Texas and nearby states to play an ill-defined (sometimes ill-informed) but nonetheless central role in developing and implementing immigration policy on the ground. Because the line

---

* *American Purpose*, 6/30/22, https://www.americanpurpose.com/articles/time-to-stop-digging/

between Biden administration policy and the often skeptical or downright hostile decisions by the courts is blurred, it is often unclear who is responsible for calling the shots. This pattern of shared responsibility and uncertain deference tends to produce great confusion and dodging of responsibility. In theory, the courts have the last word, but the realistic constraints of administering conditions around the border leave most of the blame for the chaos on the Administration.

On June 10, 2022, President Biden, with twenty leaders of other regional countries, signed a Los Angeles Declaration on Migration and Protection designed to regularize pressure on the American border by tripling the number of refugees the United States will admit from Latin America during the next two years; tripling the number currently admitted from the region; and issuing 11,500 more seasonal worker visas from Central America and Haiti. In return, Mexico, Canada, Spain, and some other related countries agreed to increase their intake and curb human trafficking.

Notably, however, El Salvador, Venezuela, and Honduras—major contributors to the northward flow—did not participate in the Los Angeles Declaration, and serious doubts about its limited impact and implementation continue. Indeed, only a few days later, the *New York Times* reported on a huge caravan of over 6,000 migrants, most from Mexico and Venezuela, occupying entire highways on their way to the U.S. border. With the LA Declaration addressing a mere drop in the migration bucket, the Administration has clearly signaled its reluctance to adopt the harsher enforcement measures demanded by Republicans on the congressional and presidential campaign trails.

The focus on illegal border-crossing largely ignores the roughly half of the undocumented population who previously entered on legal visas but who then overstayed or violated other visa conditions. Biden has plenty of company in this weak interior enforcement. No administration of either party, including Trump's, has seriously pursued it: Factory raids are politically disruptive and sanctions imposed on employers are rare and low. Without pressure from Washington, including an overhaul of the E-Verify system that is key to interior enforcement, enforcement will remain casual and feckless.

In truth, enforcement problems would plague any administration beset by these conditions and limitations: Immigration enforcement that is both humane and effective is mostly a contradiction in terms. But the Biden administration faces an additional burden that Republicans don't: the Democratic Left, including Vice-President Kamala Harris. In a June 2020 Democratic presidential debate, then-Senator Harris answered a question about deporting people who are in the U.S. illegally but who have committed no other offense. Harris, who clearly welcomed the question, immediately and vehemently responded: "Absolutely not, they should not be deported." Neither Biden nor any other candidate contradicted her, yet a different answer—"Yes, they should be deported unless they have a valid asylum claim or some other special legal claim to remain"—should have been a no-brainer.

Harris's unequivocal response ignores perhaps the key fact about U.S. immigration politics and policy: Most Americans will accept more legal immigrants only if they believe we can effectively limit illegal ones. This is why "secure borders" is a mantra of all immigration politics: It is an essential feature of nationhood and one to which Democratic leaders have always purported to subscribe—until Harris's response. Ignoring what voters demand on this issue is a huge political gift to Republican candidates, one that will keep on giving as they press their Democratic opponents to defend the indefensible words of their vice president and her debate colleagues.

But this is not all. Democrats' proudly progressive leaders have enthusiastically advocated not only non-enforcement of our borders but other extreme and unpopular measures. A forthcoming monograph by Jack Citrin and Berkeley colleagues about Americans' attitudes toward immigration confirms how low the public support is for many measures recently endorsed by some Democratic leaders:

> Examples include abolishing ICE [the main border enforcement agency], decriminalizing illegal border crossings, sanctuary cities, extending government benefits such as health insurance to illegal immigrants, and preserving (let alone expanding) the "diversity" visa lottery. All are deeply unpopular. For example, a Harvard-Harris poll from early 2017 found 80% of the public opposed to a standard conception of sanctuary cities. Americans opposed the diversity lottery in a Reuters poll by 60-25. A PBS News Hour-Marist poll from December 2019 found 66% thought decriminalizing illegal border crossings a "bad idea," to 27% who thought it a good one, while in the same poll 62% thought "a national health insurance program available for immigrants who are in the U.S. illegally" a bad idea and only 33% a good idea.

These Democrats don't seem to realize that the same American voters who demand enforcement-secured borders also favor immigration—so long as it is legal and at levels they view as moderate. More than any other nation (Canada perhaps excepted), Americans admire legal immigrants, especially those they know personally. This is hardly surprising; the vast majority of legal immigrants are law-abiding, patriotic, and progressing toward English fluency. Many of them marry Americans, have remarkable personal stories (like Americans' own ancestors), and quickly identify with their new country.

Moreover, the Citrin study reveals that Americans' insistence on border security is more nuanced than one might think. Two examples illustrate this point. First, public demands for secure borders do not extend to support for building a wall. Second, their universal demand for border security coexists with a flexibility about the undocumented who are already here and already integrating into our society. Indeed, lopsided majorities favor a path to citizenship for this population.

How much comfort should the Democratic Left take on immigration policy issues from Biden's election victory? Not much. Trump was perhaps the most anti-immigration candidate since the Know-Nothings of the 1850s, making it relatively easy for Democrats to gain broad voter support on immigration issues. Even so, the Electoral College vote was too close for comfort. The Democratic Left should also be troubled that Trump and Republicans more generally attracted an unexpected number of Latino voters. Indeed, growing Latino and Asian support for Republicans may be a longer-term political shift.

Another danger for the Democratic Left—or opportunity, as some may see it—is the possibility that Biden will not run for a second term; after all, he would be eighty-two on Inauguration Day, far older than any other President, and his approval ratings are dismal. Kamala Harris, a singularly weak candidate already in addition to her extreme views on immigration enforcement, will have an inside track. This all suggests that the Biden administration is endangering Democrats' electoral prospects by being identified with a feckless set of immigration enforcement policies.

The good news for Democrats is that much valuable immigration reform can be advanced before 2024. The bad news is that much of it will be politically difficult, with the Republicans being unlikely to cooperate if it means handing Biden a victory. Still, the Democrats can make a strong meritorious case on a number of measures which include some that Republicans may have to support or even sponsor. After all, Republicans are likely to gain seats, more governing responsibility, and perhaps even control of one or both chambers in the next Congress.

Their first reform should be to invest the necessary resources in stronger immigration enforcement, both at the borders and in the interior. This is an obvious measure, of course, and all administrations, Biden's included, promise to do so. But the measures taken are never adequate to meet the ever-greater challenge. Last year, a record number (more than 1.7 million) of apparently undocumented would-be border crossers were taken into custody, at least briefly—vastly exceeding the Border Patrol's detention capacity. Neither the Biden administration nor any of its predecessors has invested the fiscal and human resources necessary to make a significant reduction in this human tsunami. It will require a quantum leap in all sorts of resources: line and supervisory officers, detention space, immigration judges, attorneys, translators, transport, diplomatic arrangements, detection technology, and facilities for health, child care, and other human needs. A grand bargain with congressional Republicans would have to include a serious commitment to interior enforcement—with all of the disruption and cost that it entails—and a willingness to share blame and credit equally.

Obviously, the undocumented immigration challenge also includes those already here. For a decade, the Deferred Action for Childhood Arrivals (DACA) program has authorized temporary relief from removal for almost two million "Dreamers" (minors who entered the United States illegally with their parents). Roughly 800,000 have actually received it. The program, however, was invalidated (again) last summer by a federal district judge in Texas and is not taking new applications. The Biden administration can aid these families only by slow-walking their removals, an evasive tactic that inevitably undermines the credibility of the nation's larger immigration-enforcement effort. A permanent resolution is essential. Relatedly, the number of "mixed-status" families—those headed by unauthorized adults but that also includes U.S. citizens under eighteen—likely exceeds six million and is steadily growing. ICE can't simply remove these adults without causing immense harm—not only to their unauthorized family members but also to their U.S. citizen (or noncitizen) children and communities. Policy ought to be realistic about this.

Relative to the estimated eleven million illegal immigrants residing in the United States, the nation's removal capacity is in fact severely limited. If past is prologue, ICE will formally remove relatively few—far fewer than 1 percent—of them: 55,000 in 2021; less than a third of the 185,000 in 2020; itself a large decline from 2019. (These low numbers don't count the informal removals effectuated during the pandemic under Title 42). Here is where a neglected keystone of immigration enforcement comes into play—the systems of immigration courts and detention through which virtually every contested removal case must pass. Despite a large recent increase in immigration judges, their backlog of cases is at a record level of almost 1.6 million cases. And while detention facilities for those awaiting court hearings have also been expanded, they are still so limited that the vast majority of detainees must be released pending their long-delayed hearings. This inevitably results in much absconding, illegal work in the United States, and a sense of futility on the part of ICE, the judges, and the public. Sharply increasing the number of immigration judges would reduce the case backlog and shorten periods of detention.

Legalizing the millions of otherwise law-abiding undocumented people who are long-settled in the country would be a relatively easy form of amnesty. The Migration Policy Institute reports that almost two-thirds of this population have lived here for more than a decade, and 22 percent for more than twenty years. Federal law recognizes the difficulty of removing such long-settled illegal residents. Congress long ago enacted a "registry" provision legalizing those undocumented residents who had lived here with "good moral character" for at least fifteen years. Applying the same logic and time frame now, Congress should extend the same relief to otherwise law-abiding undocumented residents settled here since, say, 2007. This would better focus ICE enforcement resources, recognize that assimilation occurs over time, and relieve the deportation anxiety of millions of families.

Amnesty for more recently arrived immigrants is more complicated, however; it must be much more carefully designed to minimize moral anomalies, administrative glitches, and perverse incentives.

Finally, there is the policy option of candid realism. Both political parties might conclude that if Congress would enact some new, generous version of DACA, an updated registry, the kind of broad legalization enacted in 1986, more robust levels of border enforcement (including a more tailored version of Title 42) and employer sanctions, this package might be deemed a satisfactory, realistic policy mix, all things considered. If political ownership of this agenda were shared between the parties and if the public were educated about its pragmatic merits—big ifs, to be sure—genuine progress on one of our most enduring but potentially manageable problems is possible.

Birthright of a Nation[*]

Despite persistent calls for comprehensive immigration reform, the hot debate today is about an old issue: birthright citizenship.

The citizenship clause of the 14th Amendment, adopted in 1868, provides that "all persons born or naturalized in the United States, and subject to the jurisdiction thereof, are citizens of the United States..." This language has traditionally been interpreted to give automatic citizenship to anyone born on American soil, even to the children of illegal immigrants.

Congress plans to hold hearings this fall on a constitutional amendment to change that language, something even moderate Republican senators like South Carolina's Lindsey Graham support. With a new study showing that undocumented mothers account for a disproportionate number of births,

---

[*] *New York Times*, 8/13/2010; https://www.nytimes.com/2010/08/14/opinion/14schuck.html

even some Democrats might find it hard to stand opposed to altering the citizenship clause.

Fortunately, the history of the clause suggests an effective, pragmatic solution that should appeal to both parties. The clause's purpose was to guarantee citizenship for former slaves—a right Congress had enacted in 1866—and to overrule the infamous *Dred Scott* decision, which had denied blacks citizenship and helped precipitate the Civil War. But the clause also excluded from birthright citizenship people who were not "subject to the jurisdiction thereof." This exclusion was primarily aimed at the American-born children of American Indians and foreign diplomats and soldiers, categories governed by other sovereign entities.

The citizenship clause reflected a new American approach to political membership. Under common law dating back to the early 17th century, national allegiance had been perpetual, not consensual. Our country contested this assumption during the War of 1812 after the British impressed Americans into the Royal Navy, insisting that they remained the king's subjects.

By 1868, Congress had come to view citizenship as a mutual relationship to which both the nation and the individual must consent. This explains why it passed—one day before the citizenship clause was ratified—the Expatriation Act, allowing Americans to shed their American or foreign citizenship.

Particularly relevant to today's controversy was the floor debate on the citizenship clause. It suggested that the American-born children of resident aliens would indeed be citizens, a suggestion confirmed in an 1898 Supreme Court decision involving the son of a resident Chinese couple.

Congress did not, however, discuss the status of children of illegal immigrants. In 1868, federal law didn't limit immigration, so no parents were here illegally.

Nevertheless, it is hard to believe that Congress would have surrendered the power to regulate citizenship for such a group, much less grant it automatically to people whom it might someday bar from the country. The Supreme Court has never squarely held otherwise, although it did assume, without explanation, in a brief 1982 footnote that the American-born children of illegal immigrants were constitutional citizens. This history suggests that Congress can act on birthright citizenship without a constitutional amendment.

Fast-forward to today to an America with 11 million illegal immigrants. If the Constitution permits Congress to regulate their children's citizenship by statute, what should that statute provide?

This question is much harder than the zealots on both sides suggest. The argument against any birthright citizenship is that these children are here as a result of an illegal act and thus have no claim to membership in a country built on the ideal of mutual consent.

In the extreme case of "anchor babies"—children born after a mother briefly crosses the border to give birth—the notion of automatic citizenship for the child strikes most people as not only anomalous but also offensive. No other developed country except Canada, which has relatively few illegal immigrants, has rules that would allow it.

At the same time, we rightly resist punishing children for their parents' wrongs. Without birthright citizenship, they could be legally stranded, perhaps even stateless, in a country where they were born and may spend their lives. And because more than a third of undocumented parents have at least one American child, ending birthright citizenship would greatly increase the number of undocumented people in the country.

Fortunately, these strongly competing values, combined with the notion of mutual-consent citizenship, suggest a solution: condition the citizenship of such children on having what international law terms a "genuine connection" to American society.

This is already a practice in some European countries, where laws requiring blood ties to existing citizens have been relaxed to give birthright citizenship to children of illegal immigrants who have lived in the country for some time—Britain, for example, requires 10 years and no long absences from the country.

Congress should do likewise, perhaps conditioning birthright citizenship on a certain number of years of education in American schools; such children could apply for citizenship at, say, age 10. The children would become citizens retroactively, regardless of their parents' status.

Other aspects of the larger immigration debate would continue, of course. But such a principled yet pragmatic solution to the birthright citizenship question could point the way toward common ground on immigration reform.

Refugee Burden-Sharing: A Modest Proposal*

The world is teeming with refugees. The World Refugee Survey in 2022 estimated a total of 30 million individuals living outside of their countries and in need of international protection and assistance. This immense population increases with the proliferation of conditions that generate refugees and facilitate migration: political repression, armed conflict, civil strife, environmental disaster, famine, social and economic disintegration, wretched governmental policies, and improvements in communications and

---

* *Yale Journal of International Law*, 1997; Vol 22: 243-297, supplemented in 2015 before the European refugee crisis in that year.

transportation opportunities. Refugee emergencies are so endemic that the rhetoric of crisis today is as likely to numb as it is to energize.

In 1997, I published a proposal in the *Yale Journal of International Law* designed to help deal with this problem in a way that would increase the amount of refugee protection afforded by the United States and other states. My proposal would create regional trading systems in refugee protection obligations that would be mandated by treaty commitments among potential receiving countries. Not surprisingly, the proposal was controversial—and remains so. Harvard professor Michael Sandel, among others, criticized it for seeming to "commodify" human relationships and obligations that should be based instead on principles of justice—an argument I address in part 5 below.

In what follows, I present the essential elements of my analysis and proposal in an abbreviated version; footnotes are available in the published article, cited at the beginning of this piece.

The current legal and political arrangements for managing refugee flows were established to manage European cross-border refugee flows during the post-World War II era. The causes of these flows became much more varied as time went on, their locus shifted during the 1960s, 1970s, and 1980s to other regions (notably Africa, southern and southeast Asia, the Middle East, and the Caribbean), and internally displaced individuals became more numerous than border-crossing refugees. By the 1980s, Europe had come to think of the refugee burden as more of a problem for the Third World and the United States than for itself. Protected from large-scale refugee movements by an impregnable Iron Curtain in the east, Europe seemed relatively immune to the threat.

But with the dissolution of the Soviet Union, Germany's reunification, the militarization of bitter ethnic conflicts in the Balkans, and the failure of many former European colonies to establish viable political and economic systems, refugees poured into the very heart of Europe. Moreover, new migration routes, facilitated by cheap transportation and intricate social networks, brought migrants to Europe (and thence to the United States) from Asia, Africa, and the Pacific archipelago. Although only a relatively small percentage of these migrants are likely to meet the legal qualifications for refugee status defined in the 1951 Convention Relating to the Status of Refugees, many of them nevertheless seek some form of temporary or permanent protection and must be processed in one or another receiving state until their status can be determined—with the attendant fiscal, social, and political burdens on the receiving state that such processing ordinarily entails.

Virtually all discussions of refugee law and policy focus on the acute vulnerability of refugees. These commentaries seek ways to alleviate the sufferings of refugees, either by fulfilling or extending the protections to which they are entitled or by eliminating the political conditions that impel them to flee from their homelands. The reason for this focus on the refugees themselves is as obvious as it is sound and humane: Refugees present egregious cases of injustice and compelling claims for some form of international protection. Their claims are compelling not so much because they often live in conditions of poverty, unemployment, rude shelter, and mistreatment. After all, these are the conditions of daily life for most other humans unfortunate enough to have been born into the wrong social class in the wrong place at the wrong time. These conditions are also those in which most refugees lived before their flight made them objects of international law's concern. Instead, what marks refugees off for particular solicitude is their radical, enforced dislocation and isolation and their uncertain legal status as aliens. They are of special humanitarian concern because they were compelled to abandon the only protections and solaces that can render the harsh vicissitudes of life endurable: the assistance (however minimal) of their own governments and the social supports of their customary communities.

My perspective here, however, is quite different. Rather than focus on the suffering that refugees endure or the root causes of their flight, I take these tragic facts as given. I emphasize instead the burdens that the sudden, massive refugee flows that are now endemic impose on states. I do so not because these burdens are more than the international order, as a whole, can or should bear (they are not), but because I am convinced of the following three propositions.

First, the emerging state responses to these burdens are seriously jeopardizing the viability of any meaningful regime of international human rights protection. Second, any realistic solution to this problem must somehow forestall these responses by easing these burdens in exchange for a set of obligations that states are more willing to accept and implement. Third, this can only be accomplished by distributing obligations more widely and fairly among states over time.

Doubtless, my effort to salvage a meaningful human rights regime from the carcass of state sovereignty will seem rather odd to many well-informed commentators on refugee law and policy in the academy and in the field. They often maintain that state sovereignty constitutes perhaps the chief threat and impediment to the fulfillment of human rights goals. To them, state sovereignty is the problem, not the solution. This view is certainly plausible. After all, nation-states are today the principal designers and executors of human rights violations. They also encourage, abet, condone, or at least fail to prevent many human rights violations committed by ostensibly private groups. Finally, the principle of state sovereignty often delegitimates and stymies proposed interventions by states and supranational groups into the offending state's territory—interventions that might prevent or rectify violations occurring entirely within national borders. In each of these ways, the nation-state has indeed impeded and confounded human rights goals, just as its critics suggest.

This line of argument is true as far as it goes, but it does not go nearly far enough. For it is also true that for the foreseeable future, genuine human rights protections—particularly the protection of refugees—can only be enforced and implemented by sovereign states or by other entities such as supranational agencies and nongovernmental organizations (NGOs) working with their assistance or sufferance. This is a brutal reality of which any practicable, meaningful reform proposal must take full account. To ignore or deny it is to engage in a dangerous fatuity.

But the link between sovereignty and protection is more than a regrettable necessity. While malefactors have committed great crimes in the name of state sovereignty, the nation-state has also been an essential, powerful force for justice. The mature nation-state is a unique formation conceived through communal imagination, cemented by history, fueled by political ideology, and equilibrated by institutions. Its combination of scale, power, predictability, and normativity enables it to generate levels of self-sacrifice and coordinated action in the common interest that other groupings, whether larger or smaller, seem incapable of generating.

However one appraises the overall relationship between nation-states and human rights, the analysis and proposal that follow are constructed on a premise that few knowledgeable observers of the current refugee regime can seriously dispute. My premise is that the current refugee regime is broken—in the limited but important sense that it fails to afford adequate protection to the enormous and growing number of people fleeing from what seem to be, and often are, intolerable conditions—and that it needs fixing. This is not to deny the many important and often heroic responses that the international community has mounted to address human rights emergencies. Indeed, in the next section I describe one such response, the Comprehensive Plan of Action and Orderly Departure Program in Southeast Asia (CPA), in some detail. In 2015, amid the Syrian refugee crisis, Germany orchestrated another large refugee rescue in Europe. It is simply to say that much more needs to be done as these emergencies continue to proliferate.

This paper proceeds in several parts. In Part 1, I discuss some of the inadequacies of the current refugee protection regime. In Part 2, I summarize the CPA experience, a vitally important large-scale example of a negotiated refugee burden-sharing arrangement, which suggests both the value of international burden-sharing quotas and the need to create a more reliable, effective structure for prescribing and administering them. In Part 3, I consider four broad strategies for improving refugee protection. In the order of their abstract desirability, they are: (A) eliminating the root causes of refugee flows; (B) prompt repatriation of refugees; (C) temporary protection of refugees; and (D) permanent resettlement of refugees in third countries. I conclude (with virtually all other commentators) that each of these is problematic and that the practical realities of refugee crises and international refugee politics often require resort to the temporary protection and permanent resettlement strategies because the more desirable ones are simply not available.

Part 4 describes my proposal, which is intended to ameliorate some, but certainly not all, of the most important inadequacies in the current system. Details aside, the proposal consists of two main elements. First, a group of states would agree to observe a strong norm of proportional burden-sharing for refugees, would seek to induce other states to join the group, and would arrange for an existing or newly-established international agency to assign to each participating state a refugee protection quota. A state's quota would commit it to assure temporary protection or permanent resettlement for a certain number of refugees over a certain period of time. Second, the participating states would then be permitted to trade their quotas by paying others to fulfill their obligations. As noted immediately below, states would participate in the quota-cum-market system voluntarily, albeit under the influence of their more powerful neighbors. Accordingly, the system should require only limited regulation by the agency whose chief responsibilities would be to administer the system, including the quotas and the flow of information about refugees, and to ascertain whether the requisite protection is actually being delivered. I propose that this scheme be entirely consensual on the part of the participating states and that it be established on a regional or even a sub-regional basis, rather than on a global one. These states would define the refugees who might look to them for protection according to agreed-upon criteria. For example, the criteria might prefer refugees from countries of origin located in the region, refugees in first-asylum states located there, or refugees from countries with historical ties to participating states.

A regionally structured system would possess several important advantages over a more global one. It could exploit a tradition of regional responsibility for localized refugee flows and solutions, the greater commonality of interests and values that regions tend to share, and the more intense patterns of interaction that they exhibit. It would minimize the psychological, fiscal, and other costs of having to relocate refugees over long distances and of locating them farther from their homes. Its limited size and consensual character would also make it administratively more manageable. As with other groups seeking gains from trade, however, participating states would have an incentive to expand the membership over time if the scheme proved successful.

I also discuss in Part 4 why this unusual burden-sharing scheme might actually be politically acceptable and practically workable. Such a happy outcome, however, is far from assured. Under the existing regime, after all, states that are not states of origin or of first asylum are entirely free to join in, or refrain from, refugee protection efforts, as their interests dictate. Why, then, would they choose to surrender that freedom of action and accept a burden-sharing obligation that is likely to be costly, risk domestic political tensions, and probably ratchet upwards over time? Some states will probably reject such an obligation out of hand; they will point out that they neither generate refugee flows nor are likely to receive them. They may also point to the fact that the kind of massive refugee flows that occurred in Rwanda, the former Yugoslavia, and Syria are the exception, not the rule. The larger, wealthier, and more stable states can often absorb smaller, more gradual refugee movements without resorting to extraordinary measures. Even these states, however, might be attracted to burden-sharing for the same reason that many individuals are attracted to catastrophic health insurance: States may rationally prefer to incur a small and predictable protection burden now in order to avoid bearing large, sudden, unpredictable, unwanted, and unstoppable refugee inflows in the future. They might prefer a system that creates strong incentives for more states to support temporary protection of refugees, largely in the Third World, over the current one, which generates strong pressures for an even more dreaded (from their perspective) form of relief: permanent resettlement.

As the world grows smaller and more interconnected, and as an increasing number of refugees can more easily reach more places and claim protection there, such "refugee crisis insurance" might well be a "good buy"—perhaps even for relatively insular states. By introducing a market in quota obligations, the scheme would permit even greater flexibility. For many states, then, this burden-sharing scheme would be fairer and more rational than the status quo—especially if, as I propose, it were established on a regional basis. So, at least, I argue. Part 4 concludes by discussing how such a scheme would be enforced. Briefly, I suggest that while the scheme would be administered and to some extent enforced by an international agency, it is the states with the greatest interest in a better refugee protection system—those in North America and Western Europe—that would have the strongest incentives to deploy the various carrots and sticks of international diplomacy at their disposal (trade benefits, other forms of assistance, security guarantees, etc.) in order to secure both initial agreement and subsequent compliance.

Because the proposal will certainly be controversial in the refugee-policy community, Part 5 defends it against a variety of anticipated objections, particularly to its market element, which is bound to arouse the most opposition. At the outset, however, I wish to emphasize a point that should inform one's reaction to the entire analysis. Although the proposal entails many problems, virtually all of those problems already exist, sometimes to an even greater degree, in the current system. For this reason, I urge readers to keep the "compared to what" question firmly in mind as they ponder these problems.

1. The Current Regime for Protecting Refugees

The existing system of refugee protection is almost universally criticized by the individuals and organizations most committed to human rights goals, and by the governments that are affected by how this system functions. The bills of particulars in the various indictments converge in many respects. All commentators recognize that the system was designed in the post-World War II era to deal with a predominantly European displaced population facing prospects quite different from those confronting today's refugees. Modern globalization of the world economy, the revolutions in transportation and communications, and the dissolution of colonial empires into a plethora of weak and often oppressive states—developments so consequential for the magnitude and character of contemporary refugee flows—all lay in the future. The system that developed is one in which each state of first asylum must determine the status of the claimant—in particular, whether the person qualifies as a refugee under the 1951 Convention Relating to the Status of Refugees. If so, the claimant may be entitled as a matter of international, and perhaps domestic, law to the panoply of rights that the Convention accords refugees. From the perspective of refugees seeking protection, this system suffers from a number of serious flaws. Since all of these flaws have already received much attention and extensive critical analysis from refugee advocates, international organizations, and scholars of international human rights law, I will discuss them only briefly.

The core legal concepts embedded in the refugee definition—persecution on account of race, religion, national origin, political opinion, or membership in a particular social group—are expansive and ambiguous enough to have engendered enormous uncertainties when applied to particular cases. On the other hand, these concepts are quite narrow relative to the diverse circumstances and motives that may prompt individuals to leave their countries in haste and in a vulnerable condition. The refugee protection system, however, has less to do with the legal niceties of the Refugee Convention than with the political prerogatives of sovereign states. Each state judges for itself whether a particular migrant or group of migrants who reaches its territory or seeks resettlement there will receive that, or any, relief. Each state, moreover, possesses powerful disincentives to provide relief, especially on its own territory. Such relief is costly to provide; at a minimum, it includes food, clothing, shelter, and information. If the state does not allow the migrants to come and go as they please, it must keep them in custody or under close surveillance. If they remain in custody in close quarters and enforced idleness, the risks of violence, crime, and other social pathologies are correspondingly great. Although refugees are often kept in the most squalid conditions, those conditions may nevertheless be superior to those in which most citizens of the receiving state live. In any event, the admission and maintenance of even small numbers of refugees over long periods of time are almost certain to occasion bitter political opposition within the receiving state, especially if the refugees are permitted to compete for scarce jobs. The presence of refugee populations can create serious foreign policy embarrassments. In sufficient numbers and under certain conditions, the mere presence of refugees can constitute a genuine national security threat to the receiving state. They may prompt domestic rioting, ethnic violence, and the destabilization of the regime—and perhaps even its overthrow. In this sense, refugee protection is not simply a human rights issue; it can also be a matter of geopolitical significance affecting the security of the international order.

Nor are these risks equally distributed across the globe. On the contrary, this distribution is decidedly lumpy. Until the demise of the former Soviet Union and the outbreak of hostilities in the former Yugoslavia, Europe had generated and received relatively few refugees for decades. Even today, most refugee flows occur in Africa and southern Asia, and the brunt of refugee burdens is predominantly borne by neighboring states in those regions, as with the current refugee crises in the states bordering Syria.

A state inclined to comply with only the letter of the Refugee Convention is not obliged to afford much protection to the migrant. The duty of "nonrefoulement"—the obligation not to return a refugee to conditions of persecution—is clear enough, but most of the other rights-defining provisions of the Convention contain qualifying phrases and other limitations designed to protect the interests and prerogatives of the receiving state. For many states, free-riding appears to be the rational strategy in the area of refugee protection. This means accepting as few refugees as possible in the hope that others will assume the burdens of resettling or otherwise dealing with them. The pursuit of a free-rider strategy is constrained only by whatever pressures can be exerted by domestic refugee advocates, international human rights organizations, and other states that can deploy a variety of carrots or sticks.

The primary institutional advocates for refugees within the system, and the most insistent voices calling for state compliance with its norms, are the United Nations High Commissioner for Refugees (UNHCR) and the many secular and religious NGOs working in the refugee field. Yet both UNHCR and the NGOs are chronically underfunded relative to their growing protection responsibilities and are vulnerable to political attack by the receiving states, on whom they must rely for their operating authority, budget, cooperation, and legitimacy. In reality, the receiving states compromise these institutional advocates at every turn. Under the exceedingly difficult circumstances in which UNHCR and the NGOs must usually work, the wonder is that they perform as effectively as they do.

For these and other reasons, refugee protection has proven to be woefully inadequate—a conclusion to which countless human victims bear grim and silent witness. This inadequacy is especially apparent during refugee emergencies such as those in southeastern Asia during the 1970s and 1980s, and in Africa and the former Yugoslavia in the 1990s. Here, however, I wish to emphasize one systemic, institutional failure that I believe contributes substantially to all of the others: the failure of refugee burden-sharing among states. If meaningful reform of the refugee protection system is to occur, burden-sharing must be at its center.

The problem is simpler to state than to solve. Although the entire international community ought to shoulder the burdens of dealing with massive refugee flows, only a relatively small number of nations and regions actually do so. Some of those least capable of bearing these burdens have in fact carried a disproportionately large share of them. This is most strikingly true of some African states that often serve as countries of first asylum for many of the most wretched refugees. Conversely, some of the states that are most capable of incurring refugee burdens have stood on the sidelines watching. No strong norm of refugee burden-sharing currently exists in international law or practice. This is not to say that the appeal of such a norm has gone unremarked. In recent years, a number of commentators have called upon the international community to create or recognize a norm of equitable burden-sharing. Some have inferred a principle of international solidarity from more abstract principles of justice or have discerned such a principle from existing international instruments, from which the norm of equitable burden-sharing of refugees might be derived as a logical and normatively desirable corollary. Such inferences, however, are more in the nature of moral exhortation and prudential argument than expositions of authoritative legal principles. In practice, there have been very few instances of large-scale burden-sharing arrangements designed to expand rather than restrict refugee protection. The most important example is the CPA.

2. *The Comprehensive Plan of Action*

The CPA resettlement program provides a useful study of the conditions under which burden-sharing can succeed. The program was developed and refined over an extended period of time, and involved intensive bilateral and multilateral negotiations conducted in a crisis atmosphere in which national self-interest was the main driving force and jerry-built, practical solutions were the principal desiderata. After the sweep of Communist victories in Southeast Asia in 1975, well over two million people fled Vietnam, Cambodia, and Laos for "first asylum" in neighboring countries. Before 1979, these people received relatively little international assistance, and refugee camps were poorly organized. A coordinated international response began in July 1979, when the United Nations convened an international conference in Geneva to seek solutions to the burgeoning refugee crisis. Conference participants were attentive to the differing abilities of countries to assist the refugees. In its report on the conference, UNHCR noted: "Since the countries of first asylum were developing countries confronted with serious economic and social constraints, it was essential that countries outside the area assumed the principal responsibility for resettlement." The sixty-five governments attending the Geneva conference agreed to three principal commitments: (1) countries in the region would provide at least temporary asylum; (2) the international community would offer resettlement places for those who had already fled; and (3) the countries of origin would discourage hazardous departures and would cooperate with the United Nations and other countries to promote direct outflows through an Orderly Departure Program (ODP). The 1979 accord reflected the national self-interest of the conference participants. Resettlement countries wanted to preserve the precarious temporary refuge policies of first-asylum countries, which were not signatories to the 1951 Refugee Convention or to its 1967 Protocol. The United States in particular was committed to protecting its wartime allies and to providing "a non-Communist alternative to the peoples of Indochina." In addition to providing humanitarian assistance, the US interest was served by a system that accorded presumptive refugee status to all those fleeing the Southeast Asian Communist regimes. The resettlement program also supported the conventional immigration policy goals of resettlement countries. First-asylum countries in Southeast Asia, burdened by the expense and political difficulties of providing refuge, hoped to stem the tide of refugees and spread the costs of assistance. As one observer noted, these countries were persuaded to provide first asylum by the "assurance that the international community will effectively take care of the refugees, and the smooth operation of a resettlement programme aiming at an equitable sharing of the burden imposed on the southeast Asian countries." The cooperation of the first asylum countries was also bolstered by Vietnam's agreement to reduce the outflows by resuming its dubious policy of prohibiting illegal departures and by creating an in-country ODP. Finally, the costs to first-asylum countries were reduced by agreements to place some first-asylum camps under UNHCR auspices and to have UNHCR cover the direct costs of their operation.

The Geneva conference produced immediate results. In 1979, thirty-eight countries accepted Indochinese refugees for resettlement. Vietnam clamped down on smuggling operations, causing an immediate decline in refugee outflows. Resettlement rates increased, causing the population of boat people in the region to decline from 205,000 in mid-1979 to 40,000 three years later. From 1979 until 1989, over 1.7 million Indochinese refugees were resettled under the framework laid out at the 1979 conference, and over 150,000 left through the ODP.

In addition to the confluence of national self-interests, the Indochinese resettlement program demonstrates three points about burden-sharing. First, full-scale international cooperation was implemented under the leadership of the United States and UNHCR. UNHCR coordinated international discussions, established refugee camps and holding centers, channeled funds to care for the refugees, and monitored the implementation of the resettlement programs. The United States, the largest resettlement country, shouldered a significant share of the costs. The sheer number of cooperating countries reflected, at least in part, US leadership. Had the United States and UNHCR not borne the brunt of the resettlement and organizational burdens, the international consensus might have unraveled. Second, the program's success depended upon the full cooperation of all countries involved; any one country's shirking its responsibilities could upset the precarious international balance. Several incidents illustrate this point. In May 1989, Malaysia instituted a policy of turning back boatloads of Vietnamese refugees and migrants, likely causing some neighboring countries to experience a drastic increase in boat arrivals. In Indonesia, for instance, 3,787 Vietnamese arrived in May alone—the highest figure since the beginning of the outflow. Another such example occurred in 1986, when Vietnam suspended interviews of ODP applicants for US departures. As a result, illegal departures from Vietnam surged, along with the number of arrivals in first asylum countries. The neighboring countries responded by refusing asylum to the new arrivals. Thailand, for example, began sending back boats and denied those migrants who were admitted an opportunity to seek resettlement.

Similar reactions occurred in Indonesia and Hong Kong. In sum, one country's defection triggered exclusionary reactions in others; interlocking interests contributed not only to the implementation of burden-sharing programs, but also to their effective maintenance.

Third, effective burden-sharing requires efforts to reduce the burdens on all countries and spread them over time. As the Indochinese resettlement program progressed, countries began worrying that it caused a "pull effect" by encouraging people to flee their countries in search of resettlement in the West. As the number of boat arrivals increased and the average stay in the refugee camps lengthened in the late 1980s, first-asylum countries began taking unilateral and sometimes inhumane measures to deter further arrivals and to reduce camp populations. In response to these concerns, the resettlement program was refined in 1989 at a second Geneva conference on Indochinese refugees. The conference participants adopted a new program, the CPA, to address the Vietnamese and Lao refugee problems.

The CPA, which was scheduled to expire on June 30, 1996, preserved the basic framework of the earlier resettlement program, with one modification. Under the CPA, refugee status was no longer conferred automatically on all those who arrived in first-asylum countries; instead, arrivals were subject to refugee screening by local immigration officials. Those screened in were eligible to seek resettlement in a third country, while those screened out remained in holding centers and faced eventual repatriation. To balance concerns over national sovereignty and human rights, conference participants agreed to establish a "region-wide refugee status-determination process . . .in accordance with national legislation and internationally accepted practice," including UNHCR training and oversight. To secure the support of first-asylum countries, resettlement countries committed to expedited resettlement of all refugees who arrived prior to the cut-off date set by the CPA.

The CPA also called for additional countries to join the resettlement effort: At the time of the sixth follow-up meeting of the Steering Committee of the International Conference on Indochinese Refugees in March 1995, there remained 36,339 screened-out Vietnamese and 2,048 with refugee status in first-asylum countries. Although the Steering Committee called for the completion of all repatriation and resettlement by the end of 1995, the process was delayed both because a number of screened-out Vietnamese refused to be repatriated at all costs, and because the United States proposed to offer screened-out boat people a second chance to apply for refugee status according to U.S. refugee criteria rather than CPA criteria. Word of the U.S. proposal sparked "violent anti-repatriation protests" in the camps and impeded the repatriation and resettlement under the CPA. In early 1996, the Vietnamese government and the United States agreed to procedures whereby "potential returnees would register for a US interview before departing the camps. Upon return to Vietnam, they would go back to their areas of origin to await their interview. Those accepted would be processed for US resettlement." UNHCR announced that the CPA would formally end on June 30, 1996.

3. Four Remedial Strategies

Broadly speaking, the problem of massive refugee flows can be addressed in only four ways. I will call these the root cause, repatriation, temporary protection, and permanent resettlement strategies. Each has its own distinctive advantages and disadvantages. In Part 4 of this article, I describe, and in Part 5 defend, a novel version of the temporary protection and permanent resettlement strategies, which together I call proportional burden-sharing.

It is essential to emphasize at the outset (and I will repeat this point later on) that although I focus on temporary protection and resettlement through proportional burden-sharing, they are actually the least attractive of the four strategies *in principle*, and sometimes even in practice. In short, they are—particularly resettlement—strategies of last resort, but all too often they are the *only* resorts. The grim reality is that the root cause and repatriation strategies are often either unavailable or implemented in ways that fail to protect refugees as effectively as even an imperfect system of proportional burden-sharing might.

One may argue that the end of the Cold War meant the cessation of long, remorseless wars of national liberation fueled by Soviet-sponsored regimes implacably hostile to returning refugees. With the spread of democratic governance (so the argument runs), the refugee flows of today and tomorrow are more environmentally than politically or ideologically driven; hence refugees can readily return once the environmental crisis is over. This cheerier scenario may come to pass, but there is as yet little evidence to support it and, in fact, some that tends to contradict it. Although the sources of refugee flows are indeed changing, the violence and the distribution of weaponry per conflict are increasing, making refugee repatriation more difficult. The current situations in Libya, Syria, Mali, and other war-torn areas suggest that this is likely to continue.

Nevertheless, my argument in favor of a burden-sharing system does not rest on any strong claim about the particular level of protection that future crises may require. To support my argument, it is enough that significant protection is likely to become a compelling need sometime within the political time horizon of the major receiving states; that the uncertainties about the timing, magnitude, duration, and resolution of the precipitating refugee crises are seriously problematic for these states (not to mention for the refugees); and that these states view as unsatisfactory the ad hoc improvisations that have been used to handle this problem in the past.

My argument for a formal system of proportional burden-sharing, then, is a decidedly qualified one. It proposes that in situations in which the root causes of a refugee crisis can be prevented or eliminated, or in which repatriation can be safely accomplished, those strategies are preferable to proportional burden-sharing and should be pursued. Only in situations in which these conditions cannot be satisfied does a system of proportional burden-sharing, implemented through either temporary protection or, in the last resort, permanent resettlement, become salient.

A. *The Root Cause Strategy*

Eliminating or preventing the political, economic, environmental, and cultural conditions that prompt refugees to flee their homes and countries in the first place is the most attractive approach by far. Obviously, this strategy, if effective, precludes the necessity for flight and hence forestalls the suffering that attends it.

The difficulty with a root cause strategy, of course, is that it is extremely difficult to execute. One must be able to accurately identify the conditions ultimately prompting flight and then be able to rectify those conditions. Both identification and rectification are daunting obstacles. The easiest case for identifying root causes should be the environmental disaster. Yet even here, causal patterns are often complex and elusive, as when environmental conditions interact with underlying economic and social practices to produce a catastrophe that would not have occurred otherwise. As for persecution-induced flight, even a readily identified malefactor or regime, such as Syria's Assad, may not be the root cause. As in the environmental case, the brutal regime's hegemony could be epiphenomenal, with the true causes embedded in underlying political or cultural traditions—habituation to authoritarianism, for example—that would probably survive the regime.

An even more serious obstacle to a successful root cause strategy, however, is the problem of rectification. Even those root causes that can be accurately identified are often impossible to change—at least in the short run and with the limited policy instruments available even to states willing (within limits) to act to prevent human rights abuses. The fecklessness of the United Nations in dealing with refugee-producing atrocities committed by local satrapies in the former Yugoslavia is a particularly telling and grim example. In part, this impotence reflects the constraints on intervention posed by the strong norm of national sovereignty in international law and politics. Despite several instances in which this norm has been overridden in the name of human rights, it continues to be a formidable limitation on our ability to mount and deploy a root cause strategy in other states. Even if the norm against intervention did not exist, the underlying social realities are notoriously hard to reform—even in one's own country, not to mention in other societies whose workings we understand far less. In such circumstances, the law of unintended consequences operates with a particularly remorseless logic.

Not surprisingly, the most common and uncontroversial means through which states seek to prevent the flow of refugees and other migrants from source countries are the consensual policies of trade, investment, development assistance, and other forms of foreign aid. Along with border controls, such policies—culminating in NAFTA—have been the cornerstone of U.S. efforts to reduce the flow of undocumented workers and their families from Mexico.

But while these policies may be mutually beneficial and highly desirable on their own terms, their potential for strengthening the source country's economy, polity, and society in ways that will reduce refugee and immigrant flows—at least in the short run—is relatively limited. Indeed, economic development in the source country may actually have the opposite effect. By increasing the education and mobility levels of potential migrants, improving their information about conditions and opportunities in destination countries, and raising their expectations, economic development can encourage those with the greatest energy, courage, and determination to try their luck elsewhere. Development also tends to create a middle class that demands political liberalization from undemocratic regimes, which may respond with the kinds of repressive measures that often generate refugee flows. Again, the capacity of economic and political development to ameliorate human rights abuses and stem refugee and immigrant flows cannot seriously be questioned. However, the course and pace of such development and its effects on migration patterns are poorly understood and notoriously unpredictable. Root cause strategies that are premised on the easy cultivation and rapid success of development are likely to be disappointing.

B. *The Repatriation Strategy*

If, as is usually the case, the root causes of refugee flows cannot be prevented or eliminated, it follows that refugees will flee. In that event, the paramount goal of a human-rights strategy must be to restore the normalcy of refugees' lives by returning them to their homes and families as soon as possible. This approach is more practicable than the root cause strategy and is likely to be far less expensive than the temporary protection or permanent resettlement strategies, as it does not require (indeed, it hopes to prevent) refugees from establishing new roots in the country of refuge. In fact, many refugees are eventually repatriated, some within a relatively short period of time after their initial flight. For the others, however, "eventually" can be a very long time indeed. In principle, repatriation should not occur until conditions in the source country have stabilized enough for the refugees to return safely. If the regime that persecuted them remains in power, such a return may be dangerous. Their homes and businesses may have been seized, occupied, or formally expropriated by the regime or private marauders, leaving them little to which they can return. They also may have reason to fear death or other reprisals at home should they return. For these reasons, voluntary repatriation may not be possible for years, even for those refugees who ardently wish to return to their homelands, while forcible repatriation may be resisted even to the point of violence or suicide.

The "endgame" of the CPA presented a variation on the same theme. With more than one million Indochinese refugees resettled since 1975, mostly in the United States, approximately 33,000 boat people, whose claims to refugee status had been repeatedly rejected, remained in southeast Asian camps.

Under the CPA, these people were to be repatriated—by force, if necessary. In the United States, Senator Jesse Helms, Congressman Christopher Smith, and other elected officials opposed repatriation, insisting that these refugees would face persecution if returned to Vietnam and that they should instead be permitted to resettle in the United States. This, in turn, emboldened the remaining boat people to resist repatriation to the point of rioting, destroying camp buildings, taking hostages, and in many cases escaping. The United States, unwilling to face the prospect of effectuating a forcible repatriation that might require it to spill the blood of innocents who had already suffered for years in the camps, reached an eleventh-hour agreement with Vietnam for a repatriation that for many of the returnees might only be brief. Under the agreement, they would be returned to Vietnam, where they would be permitted to file yet another claim for refugee status and apply once again for resettlement in the United States. It was expected that thousands of these claims would succeed. In this way, the United States adopted a new substrategy—what might be called "temporary repatriation."

C. *The Temporary Protection Strategy*

If conditions in the source country make immediate repatriation (whether temporary or permanent) impossible, one must adopt an interim approach until the refugees can be safely returned. This, of course, is the purpose of granting political asylum; it is a temporary protected status that may, but does not necessarily, lead to a right of permanent residence. Indeed, if the conditions in the source country change so that the threat of persecution no longer exists, asylum may be properly rescinded. But although traditional refugee law is preoccupied with questions of asylum eligibility, determination, and rights, the number of individuals granted asylum is but a tiny fraction of those who actually receive protection and an even smaller fraction of those who genuinely need protection. Most countries of first asylum have concluded that the fiscal and political costs of adjudicating mass asylum claims, granting employment and residence rights while those claims are pending, and permanently integrating asylees into their societies are simply unacceptable. As a result, asylum law has become less and less relevant to the protection problem in mass influx situations. Other solutions are desperately needed.

Instead of granting asylum, the more common response of states faced with large refugee influxes—even those with highly developed asylum determination systems and absorptive capacity—has been to provide some form of temporary protection in the protecting state. Properly and humanely deployed, it can be a flexible, practicable regime of protection in mass influx situations so long as states observe certain safeguards—decent living standards, access to a fair asylum determination process, and genuine non-refoulement. If these conditions are met, there should be no objection to a protecting state "renting space" outside of its territory to provide temporary safe haven.

Indeed, temporary protection has the great virtue that it can usually be effectuated in or near the first-asylum state, which tends to be near the refugee's country of origin. It therefore minimizes the psychological and economic costs of moving the refugee again; it safely maintains refugees in their present location and close to their past and hopefully future home.

Moreover, because grants of asylum or permanent resettlement are relatively rare, and safe repatriation may be impossible, the refugee's options are likely to be temporary protection or nothing.

Temporary protection is also a desirable strategy from the perspective of industrialized states' narrow self-interest. It is a way to keep refugees safely (in both senses) in the Third World from which most of them come, thereby alleviating the pressures to grant them permanent resettlement in the First World. Any refugee protection scheme that does not promise to accomplish these goals is unlikely to attract the necessary political support by industrialized states. It is for this reason that a meaningful system of refugee protection must rest on the foundation of a viable temporary refuge option. Even so, temporary protection can impose serious costs on industrialized states. If temporary protection is to succeed in deterring migration to their territories, these states must ensure that the migrants are protected under conditions of detention, isolation, and privation with little hope of gaining legal status, while also providing levels of safety and hygiene demanded by their domestic standards of decency, if not by the vague common-denominator norms of international refugee law. This is an exceedingly difficult balance to strike, and even such minimal levels of amenity can be very costly for the government to maintain, especially over a long period of time. Time, then, is of the essence. The protecting state may find that "temporary" safe haven is something of an illusion, if not an oxymoron—that what was justified as short-term relief has a way of becoming, in effect, permanent resettlement. This development is of the utmost importance for the future of refugee protection. If potential protecting states come to believe that refuge granted on a nominally "temporary" basis is likely to become permanent, they will be more reluctant to offer it.

This is increasingly the case in the United States, where temporary protection either on or near American soil has recently been ratcheted upward into more or less permanent residence. The most important example of this is the Salvadorans who entered the United States illegally during the 1980s and who, after having successfully avoided deportation, were granted temporary protected status under the special provisions of the Immigration Act of 1990. The Immigration Act authorized such relief on the understanding that the Salvadorans would return to El Salvador once conditions there stabilized.

During the early 1990s, the administration and Congress extended the departure dates several times and when the program finally expired in December 1994, the government granted nine more months for the Salvadorans to file for asylum or seek legal status. This concession reflected the fact that the government had massively violated Salvadorans' legal rights in processing and rejecting their asylum claims during the 1980s. Approximately 150,000 of them reapplied. Most experts predicted that few of the almost 200,000 original TPS Salvadorans would ever have to leave. As many skeptics had predicted, TPS turned out in the Salvadoran case to be "a slow way of saying yes." The Salvadoran experience makes it doubtful that the US government will grant temporary protection quite as readily in the future as it did to them—although TPS has remained an essential remedy.

Even when the United States moved its temporary protection program offshore by placing Cuban migrants on Guantánamo and in Panama, most of them ended up receiving permanent residence, despite the frequent insistence by the president and attorney general that these Cubans would never be permitted to enter the United States. The Cubans managed to convert temporary protection into permanent status not because the United States deemed them refugees—quite the contrary—but because the government, for a combination of political and fiscal reasons, was not prepared to return them to Cuba or to continue their temporary protection status in the Guantánamo and Panama camps.

Several other forms of temporary protection have been attempted. In some cases, military action or UN fiat has established putatively safe enclaves in the countries of origin, as in northern Iraq, Libya, and the former Yugoslavia. The conditions necessary to create and maintain such enclaves, however, are quite limited. In other cases, the destination state has negotiated bilateral or multilateral "readmission agreements" with third countries (usually countries of transit) to admit (or readmit) certain categories of migrants and to provide them with certain services and protections until they can be repatriated or their status otherwise regularized. Germany has concluded these agreements with a number of its neighbors. The principal purpose of such agreements, of course, is not humanitarian but more effective border control by enlisting the cooperation of neighboring states through which the migrants pass. From the perspective of the destination state, however, this assistance by the transit states may be costly to procure. Such arrangements, moreover, also risk human rights violations by the transit states, whose citizens are likely to be hostile to the migrants' presence. This hostility can be expected to increase as time goes on.

Temporary refuge is the keystone of the refugee protection structure. If past is prologue, states will always confine their grants of asylum and permanent resettlement to a relatively small number of refugees; for most refugees, the best that they can hope for is temporary protection. Unless the system can credibly assure states that the temporary protection they grant will indeed be temporary, its availability to refugees is likely to be undermined, with tragic effects. Thus, an important test of the value of any reform is whether it can maintain that credibility. I hope to demonstrate in Part 4 that proportional burden-sharing through marketable quotas would create the incentives to satisfy that test.

D. Permanent Resettlement

As I noted earlier, resettlement must be the protective strategy of last resort, employed only when the root causes of flight cannot be prevented or eliminated, and safe repatriation to the country of origin or to another site of temporary protection within a reasonable period of time cannot be effectuated. Resettlement in a third country is costly to the refugee, who must be uprooted once again and then reestablished in a society that is likely to be alien in culture, language, and other respects. It is also costly to the receiving country, which must either assist the refugees to assimilate successfully or run the social risks of their failure to do so. These costs are likely to be much higher than temporary protection, which can lead to repatriation in the not-too-distant future.

As we have just seen, however, repatriation in the short term is impossible in a tragically large number of cases. This is especially true when the migration flow has been fueled by policies of uncompromising and perhaps permanent ethnic or religious persecution carried out by the regime in power in the country of origin. For persecuted minorities who have fled, the alternative to resettlement is to languish for many years in what amounts to a prison, isolated from normal social intercourse and economic activity and without the amenities of family life. In such cases, resettlement—problematic as it is—may be the "least bad" remedy.

* * *

4. The Proposal: Proportional Burden-Sharing

What, then, is to be done? My proposal seeks a refugee protection system that can simultaneously achieve four major objectives: (1) maximization of protection resources; (2) observance of human rights principles; (3) respect for political constraints; and (4) administrative simplicity. Before explaining the proposal, I will briefly discuss each of these goals.

<u>Maximization of Resources Available for Protection.</u> I view this as the paramount objective; its primacy justifies compromising, where necessary, other important but less central goals. Protection resources can be maximized in two ways: by drawing new resources into the system and by better utilizing whatever resources exist. Thus, as many states as possible should participate in the protective system, not just those that possess a particular resource (such as cash, space, or ethnic diversity) or that happen to border a refugee producing area. In addition, the system should create incentives to use those resources most effectively. Specifically, it should encourage each state to allocate whatever resources it possesses or can mobilize to the refugee protection strategy or strategies—root cause, temporary protection-cum-repatriation, and resettlement—that can be most widely implemented at the least cost.

<u>Observance of Human Rights Principles.</u> The system should ensure that refugees actually receive the protection to which international human rights law already entitles them. Failing that—and recognizing that the current system often falls far short on this score—their treatment should at least be no worse than it is now.

<u>Respect for Political Constraints</u>. The system should acknowledge the important political constraints that will inevitably continue to shape any meaningful international regime of refugee protection, and its institutions and practices should take due account of them. These constraints are quite formidable, and I do not wish to minimize them. Some of them might seem inimical to more expansive refugee protection; they appear to be decidedly unpromising materials for policy reform. Yet as I explain below, we can hope to turn three of these constraining conditions—the abiding forces of state sovereignty and self-interest, the growing vulnerability of all states to unwanted refugee influxes, and the diversity of states' traditions and resources for dealing with refugee flows—to some advantage. Indeed, any reform must come

to terms with these conditions. A market-oriented approach is particularly capable of exploiting them.

Administrative Simplicity. Consistent with its other goals, the system should adopt a decentralized decision-making structure, leaving as much initiative as possible to individual states. It should seek to minimize the informational requirements and other transaction costs of the system's decision-makers.

The proposal consists of five main structural elements:

(A) agreement by states in a region on a strong norm that all ought to bear a share in responding to needs of temporary protection and permanent resettlement, proportional to their burden-bearing capacity; (B) a process for determining the number of those who need such protection; (C) a set of criteria for allocating this burden among states in the form of quotas; (D) a market in which states can purchase and sell quota compliance obligations; and (E) an international authority to administer the quota system and regulate this market. I will discuss each of these elements and then identify some of the implementation and enforcement issues that would need to be resolved for the system to work.

In noting these implementation issues, I wish to emphasize what will be obvious to any well-informed reader: many additional details must be addressed before the scheme can be fully realized. I recognize, of course, that the devil is often in the details. Nevertheless, I think that I am justified in assuming that should agreement be reached on the main outlines of the five structural elements discussed immediately below, the rest can, through negotiation, be worked out. Accordingly, I do not dwell on the details here.

A. The Principle of Burden-Sharing

As noted in Part 1, international practice in the area of refugee protection reveals the existence of what might be called a weak norm of burden-sharing. A number of international instruments and scholarly analyses proclaim the importance of such a norm and exhort states to observe it. On the more mundane level of international practice, refugee-receiving states have entered into a number of arrangements in recent decades to share the burdens of major refugee crises, notably the CPA in Indochina, and the 1989 Conference on Central American Refugees.

This burden-sharing norm, however, is manifestly weak. In the international instruments in which it can be discerned, the burden-sharing imperative is essentially precatory and hortatory; even its most energetic scholarly exponents like Guy Goodwin-Gill seem to view it more as a moral aspiration than as a legally-binding duty on all states. No effort has been mounted to enforce the norm against the numerous states that ignore it. Even in the war in the former Yugoslavia, which was waged with appalling ferocity in the very heart of Europe, the burden of protecting refugees was shared only to a very limited extent, with Croatia, Slovenia, and Germany bearing the brunt of it.

Nevertheless, the moral and prudential foundations for imposing such a duty seem sturdy enough to establish a more robust burden-sharing regime. Joanne Thorburn advances three arguments for this norm, based on human rights, states' self-interest, and the non-refoulement principle. Another justification for the burden-sharing norm is based on the adventitious character of most refugee crises. Refugee flows usually occur with a suddenness, violence, and magnitude that can swiftly overwhelm the resources of a first asylum state that may only be linked to the flow by an accident of nature—its coincidental proximity to the source country. In this respect, refugee emergencies resemble natural disasters like earthquakes and tornadoes, and the norm of international solidarity and burden-sharing is relatively strong vis-à-vis such calamities.

The relationship of first-asylum states to refugee flows, of course, does not always possess this random, adventitious character. In some cases, the first asylum state, far from being an innocent bystander, bears some causal and hence moral responsibility for refugee flows; it may even have fanned or instigated the unrest that unleashed the crisis. The first-asylum state may hope to use the refugees' flight to discredit or destabilize the source country regime (for example, American policy towards Castro's Cuba), or it may have revanchist designs on the source country (for example, Indian and Pakistani policies in Kashmir). Like some societies plagued by certain natural disasters, first asylum states sometimes bring refugee crises on themselves.

The possibility that some first-asylum states are complicit in refugee flows should surely be taken into account in designing and administering a reformed system of refugee protection. Indeed, imposing a binding obligation to bear some of the burdens that such a state causes might reduce its propensity to instigate refugee crises in the first place. Even so, the more compelling fact is that first-asylum states ordinarily are not in any morally meaningful sense responsible for their plight. Recognition of this is an important building block in the necessary structure of justification and political support for a norm of universal burden-sharing.

If the innocent helplessness of most first-asylum states is a morally constructive support for this norm, another fact—that different states face somewhat different risks of becoming a first-asylum country—tends to undermine political support for the norm. This risk differential makes it difficult to secure agreement on, much less compliance with, the norm because it reinforces the incentives of relatively insular and hence low-risk states to avoid burden-sharing by free-riding on the self-interested efforts of the higher-risk states, leaving the latter to bear all of the burdens. This process of defection by low-risk states undermines the viability of any system, like the current one, that relies on voluntary burden-sharing and generates very weak incentives to cooperate. The analogy to the problem of adverse selection in the insurance context—in which those presenting relatively low risks will not participate in insurance pools that charge them average-risk premiums—is apt.

No burden-sharing scheme, including the "refugee crisis insurance" approach proposed here, can be effective unless this problem of differential risks is squarely addressed. Generally speaking, there are only two possible solutions to this problem. The first is to increase the estimates by traditionally insular states of their risk of becoming a first-asylum country. The second is to strengthen the other non-risk-related incentives of all states, but especially of those at low risk of refugee flows, to participate in burden-sharing efforts. Both approaches are difficult to implement. Nevertheless, recent developments have rendered them, especially the first, somewhat more promising.

The risk that any state will become a first-asylum country is growing. The economic, spatial, and geopolitical barriers that until recently inhibited mass refugee flows are falling. Virtually all states realize that their territories are potential targets of sudden and possibly large refugee movements, with all of the attendant risks, political and otherwise, that such movements pose to the regime in power. Today, no state is immune; even island nations like Japan and Australia are vulnerable to spasmodic in-migration from the mainland. In addition, global warming is increasing the risk of migration from island and low-lying countries, such as the Maldives, to more elevated neighbors.

Ironically, this reality, which is certainly regrettable from the insular states' perspective, presents an opportunity to increase the acceptance of burden-sharing. The change in risk has been most dramatic in Germany and Japan. The Basic Law of Germany expressly provides that it is not a country of immigration, and the nation's history prior to 1989 was consistent with this tenet. Beginning in 1989, however, a huge influx of asylum-seekers into Germany dramatically challenged this tradition. Immigration and refugee policy has become a central issue in German politics. Like Germany, Japan has only recently begun to seriously consider the need to fashion an immigration and refugee policy. Although it still receives few refugee claims, they are increasing—as is the number of foreigners, legal and illegal, living in Japan. Perhaps more important, Japan is experiencing growing concerns about potential political convulsions in China, Hong Kong, and North Korea that could quickly send millions of refugees streaming across the short distance that separates Japan from mainland east Asia.

For states like Germany, previously protected by the Iron Curtain but now a country of first asylum on a massive scale, and Japan, no longer protected by its geography from becoming a first-asylum state, the strategic implications of their new vulnerability are immense. No longer can they simply free ride on other states' policies of refugee control and management to protect them from major influxes into their own territories. Indeed, the new interdependence of states goes beyond this; historically insular states are now more likely to face refugee flows resulting from the restrictive practices of other states. Thus, states previously at low risk of becoming first-asylum countries may now find a cooperative strategy far more attractive than they would have only a few years ago.

Under this refugee-crisis insurance approach, all states arrange to bear some refugee protection burdens so that none will be saddled with a refugee crisis that it must bear alone. The German and Japanese experiences can serve as vivid lessons for other states that have resisted burden-sharing in the belief that they are still immune from large refugee flows. The incentives for burden-sharing based on motives other than fear of becoming a first-asylum state remain weak in most regions. The traditional willingness of many sub-Saharan African states, with UNHCR assistance, to offer temporary protection to refugees from neighboring countries is the greatest exception. Pakistan's protection of millions of Afghani refugees during the 1980s is another, although pressure and aid from the United States were instrumental in eliciting this response. Once we move beyond temporary protection to permanent resettlement, as noted above, only Scandinavia, the United States, Canada, and a few other states offer it to a significant number of refugees.

Precisely because the altruistic motives for burden-sharing are so weak, these powerful states have strong reasons to induce others to cooperate by manipulating the formidable carrots and sticks that the powerful states control. In the past, these states, actuated by a combination of humanitarian and deeply self-interested motives, have managed to persuade recalcitrant first-asylum states like Thailand, Hong Kong, and Pakistan to temporarily protect refugees on their territories (although the period of temporary protection often proved to be quite protracted). As international economic developments improve industrialized states' leverage over first-asylum states with respect to trade concessions, technical assistance, and access to financial and other support, this approach, which entails the tactical use of political pressure, negotiation, and resource transfers, may bear additional fruit.

The success of a proportional burden-sharing system depends critically on the relatively powerful states' ability to use this leverage more skillfully and forcefully to induce broader participation in the system as refugee flows increase. This is likely to be most practicable in a regionally-organized system. In any event, one should recall that the current system of protection is equally dependent on the more powerful states exercising leverage and transferring resources to persuade the weaker first-asylum states to harbor refugees. A proportional burden-sharing system can only improve the chances that such influence would be effectively deployed. This examination of the structure of incentives for refugee burden-sharing does not at all minimize the political obstacles that would impede its implementation, but it provides some hope that the prospects for gaining broader agreement on a more robust burden-sharing norm could improve in the future.

The next question is: What should be the actual content of that norm? The norm should express a principle of fairness in the distribution of refugee protection burdens. Specifically, it should satisfy three criteria of fairness: consent, broad participation, and proportionality. Consent is essential. No state should be obliged to participate in the burden-sharing scheme unless it voluntarily undertakes to do so. This is a concession not only to practical politics but also to a concern that states both feel a genuine commitment to the enterprise and take responsibility for its success or failure. As the discussion immediately above suggests, a state may consent for a variety of reasons. Its consent is not ordinarily vitiated by the fact that it feels constrained to participate because of pressures exerted by other, more powerful states. States in the international system routinely deploy carrots and sticks in order to influence the decisions of other states and actors; only in the most extreme case would such inducements amount to duress that negates consent.

Broad participation in a proportional burden-sharing scheme by consenting states is justified on the basis of each state's membership in an international community, which entails certain minimal rights and obligations defined by international law, including the duty to protect refugees. If the scheme is carried out on a regional basis, as I propose, participation is likely to be widespread, if not universal, within that region because of the more firmly-entrenched patterns of intraregional influence and the relative homogeneity of wealth and values within regions. A broadly participatory arrangement has several advantages: it minimizes each state's burden by distributing it among many states, and it overcomes the free rider and adverse selection problems by making it very difficult for states to opt out. Consequently, it eliminates the demoralization that participants experience when they perceive that they have been "suckered" by the defection of others.

The proportionality principle is both a norm of fairness and a constraint dictated by political prudence. It demands that a state's share of the burden be limited to its burden-bearing capacity relative to that of all other states in the international community. Rough proportionality is probably essential to both consent and broad participation. Taken together, these three criteria imply a norm that all states in a region must shoulder some of the burden, but that none must shoulder a burden that it cannot in fairness bear.

B. The Needs Assessment Process

In order to allocate the burden of refugee protection, we must first consider how the overall burden is to be defined, determined, and used as the basis for assigning quotas. The overall burden is defined as the number of refugees who need to be offered protection—either temporary refuge or permanent resettlement—during a given time period. This number would be calculated by an international agency to be described below, and would be adjusted as unanticipated refugee emergencies occur. Suffice it to say that the agency must be equipped to conduct the necessary investigations, make the requisite factual findings, administer and enforce the quotas, and regulate the quota market with due regard to changing circumstances.

Two difficult, inevitably controversial issues are embedded in this definition: the number of people seeking protection who are to be treated as refugees, and the number of those refugees who need either temporary protection or permanent resettlement (rather than immediate repatriation). Both issues, however, already arise under the current system and can be resolved, as they are now, through a combination of factual analysis, calculated conceptual ambiguity, and old-fashioned negotiation. As a formal matter, the first issue—refugee status—is a legal one requiring application of the refugee definition under the Refugee Convention or its domestic law equivalent. To varying extents in different states, asylum adjudications exhibit such formalism. In contrast, decisions about which individuals are to be temporarily or permanently protected are relatively ad hoc; they focus less on the legal refugee definition than on the number of people that the protecting state can handle and, in the case of resettlement, on the putative refugee's social and political acceptability to the receiving state. Accordingly, many of those selected for temporary or permanent protection would probably fail to qualify as refugees in the more legalistic setting of asylum adjudication. This practice suggests that the international agency can resolve the issue of refugee status for purposes of this scheme through the relatively informal, low-cost modalities that UNHCR, the first-asylum states, and other states (often with NGO assistance) now use to make protection decisions.

The agency must then calculate a world-wide total of refugees who need temporary protection and a total of those who need permanent resettlement, and then allocate those totals among participating states by assigning a quota to each. The notion of "need" that must inform such a calculation is bound to be controversial. To some extent, need is in the eye of the beholder, as evidenced by the frequent disagreements that now arise over this issue between (and within) UNHCR, potential protecting states, and NGOs. Under the current system, UNHCR determines how many slots are needed and proceeds to solicit offers from states that it thinks can be persuaded to offer protection. In resisting these entreaties, states may dispute UNHCR's assessment of need, as well as assert their inability to accept more refugees. If further negotiations ensue, the parties may articulate competing conceptions of need; hopefully, some agreement on numbers (if not on the underlying conceptions) may be reached.

Under the proposal, the agency would proceed in a similar fashion. The stakes in its needs assessments, however, would be much higher than they are now because the assessments would generate the overall numbers to determine each state's binding quota. For this reason, it would be essential for the agency to render its needs assessments more transparent and to establish procedures enabling states to contest the findings on which their shares would be premised. Both needs assessments and procedures for challenging them are common in many areas of social policy and administrative law. Their design in the protection context should pose no special difficulties, other than the political ones owing to the weaker enforcement mechanisms in the international realm and the delays that such challenges might entail. The current system elides enforcement problems, of course, but only because it relies entirely on voluntary protection offers extended by a relatively small number of states. The agency's determination as to how many people need only temporary protection and how many instead need resettlement is, of course, a very difficult one, requiring much information that is hard to obtain and even harder to verify, as well as predictions that may be little more than educated guesses. For the same reason, the line between temporary and permanent refuge is not easily maintained; as with the TPS Salvadorans, many refugees cannot be repatriated by the protecting state despite its energetic efforts to do so.

Again, it is important to recognize that the current system must make the same kinds of difficult determinations so that UNHCR can plan the allocation of its limited resources and negotiate with potential protecting states. An additional advantage of a burden-sharing system, however, is that those states—fearing that erroneous predictions and determinations could leave them with more (or more permanent) refugees than they initially bargained for—would have strong incentives to ensure that the determinations are accurate, that other participating states bear their fair shares and minimize the necessity for permanent resettlement, and, most importantly, that temporary protection does not become permanent without the state's genuine consent.

C. *The Criteria for Allocating the Protection Burden*

In order to implement the proportionality principle discussed earlier, the quota should be based exclusively on what I call the protection criterion, which is designed to measure the capacity of the state in question to provide refugees with the most minimal safeguards and amenities to which they are entitled under the Refugee Convention. They primarily include food, clothing, shelter, and physical security. In the kind of regional, consensual burden-sharing scheme that I propose, the participating states would of course be free to adopt whatever protection criterion (or criteria) they prefer. Nevertheless, national wealth is a compelling index. Protective capacity is largely, though not exclusively, a function of national wealth. Human rights law aspires to assure refugees the most basic necessities of life and personal security, and a state's wealth is the single best surrogate for those factors that actually determine its ability to provide these necessities, directly or indirectly. National wealth is also readily quantifiable, albeit not without some controversy around the edges, and it is a factor so closely related to national prestige that states are unlikely to succeed in minimizing it in a strategic effort to reduce their share of refugee burdens.

Other plausible criteria lack the administrative advantages of a wealth criterion. Consider the example of assimilative capacity. One might want states' quotas to reflect their different propensities to assimilate refugees and other foreigners. The notion of assimilation, however, is notoriously hard to define or gauge objectively. Indeed, the scholars who study it disagree strenuously about why, how, and when it occurs. There are also normative objections to an assimilation criterion. Although it is highly desirable for states to facilitate affirmatively the integration of foreigners to whom they offer permanent resettlement, states are under no international legal duty to assure them full integration; states are only obligated to provide basic safeguards such as the right to work and to be free from discrimination. Full assimilation, moreover, is fundamentally incompatible with a regime of temporary protection—relief that states will only provide if they believe that it will terminate within a reasonably short period of time and thus before full integration occurs. As noted in Part 4, maintaining the credibility of temporary protection is essential to the viability of the protection system as a whole.

Finally, a criterion that would enlarge states' quotas if they succeed in assimilating foreigners would perversely punish states for their openness and generosity.

The attractiveness of national wealth as the sole criterion for assigning refugee protection quotas is especially great in a system like the one I propose here, which would allow a state to pay other states to provide those protection services that it cannot or will not provide on its own territory. For this reason, a state's wealth should probably trump other objective factors such as population density and land mass. Although these factors may well affect the ease with which a state can protect or resettle refugees on its own territory, these factors are probably best taken into account as they are reflected in the prices that states are willing to pay to transfer their burden to other states. For example, Malaysia and Singapore are countries of relatively great wealth but with high population densities, small land mass, and severe ethnic tensions that refugees might further inflame. These countries would be assigned large quotas but would probably offer a high price to shift the protection burden elsewhere.

Two exemptions from the quota system should be provided, and neither is likely to be controversial in practice. First, no quota should be assigned to a state that engages in systematic violations of human rights, nor should such states be permitted to purchase other states' quotas. Although the reason for this principle is obvious, some objections to it are also obvious. Applying the criterion in a world in which the number of repressive states remains tragically large would require some elusive and morally dubious distinctions. A few relatively easy cases exist (Syria and North Korea, for example), but the gradations of brutality between these and many other regimes are subtle, and line-drawing will surely be both difficult and controversial. Furthermore, if states view participation in the protection quota system as a burden rather than a benefit, this creates a perverse incentive: the exemption, by relieving states of a burden, could seem to reward human rights violations and hence encourage them. Although a state could only qualify for the exemption by being labeled as a human rights violator, this obloquy, which already attaches to such states, has manifestly failed to reform their odious conduct and is even less likely to do so when asserted as part of a refugee protection scheme. In the context of the regional, consensual arrangement that I propose, this perverse incentive would be irrelevant. In such a scheme, the regional powers would have to agree on which states would participate and under what conditions. The regional leaders would surely be under great internal and external pressure to exclude the worst human rights violators. Dissenting states need not join, and the rogue states themselves would hardly complain about being exempted from burden-sharing obligations.

The second exception should be for states whose wealth falls below some minimal level, as determined by international agencies. Again, the justification is obvious: If such states cannot assure basic sustenance to their own people, they can hardly provide effective protection to strangers. This second exemption can overlap with the first, as demonstrated by the example of Haiti, which is both destitute and a persistent human rights violator.

Apart from these two exemptions, temporary adjustments to a country's wealth-driven quota may be the best that the system can manage by way of further refining the criterion. Certain exigent conditions substantially impairing a state's ability to accept or pay for refugee protection—for example, a state of war or natural disaster—might justify a temporary quota reduction or even a suspension. For similar reasons, the system should reduce a state's quota to reflect the number of refugees who are already on its territory and to whom it offers either asylum or temporary protection of a specified duration. Such a credit, and the incentives that it creates for the receiving state, would also minimize the emotional and economic costs of moving refugees, who have already suffered at least one dislocation, from an asylum state to another state.

If such temporary quota adjustments were permitted, of course, states would press hard to obtain relief under them. Each adjustment, moreover, would entail vexing definitional and measurement problems. Refinement of the quota system through adjustments of this kind, then, would inevitably increase the administrative complexity of the system.

D. A Market in Refugee Protection Quotas

Would states be interested in paying others to protect refugees? The short answer is that they already are doing so. In some refugee crises like Rwanda, some relatively wealthy states contribute funds to the first-asylum state to support its protection efforts in situ. Although these delegations of protection resources and responsibilities are certainly better than nothing, they suffer from a number of limitations. The delegation transactions are inevitably ad hoc, with each transaction having to be organized and coordinated by UNHCR, a dedicated but sluggish and highly politicized bureaucracy. They invite strategic behavior by states with conflicting interests hoping to free-ride on the efforts of others.

A market system cannot eliminate these conditions, but it can hope to leverage certain constraints on refugee protection into an improved system. Just as the increasing refugee flows, which expose even traditionally insular states to the risk of sudden influxes, might encourage such states to participate in the system of refugee protection, a market system might transform two other real-world constraints into important refugee policy virtues. First, state actors are motivated largely by their perceptions of national self-interest, broadly defined; they are unlikely to adopt humanitarian policies that are inconsistent with those perceptions. Second, states vary enormously in both the attitudes and the resources that they bring to refugee policy. A few states willingly devote substantial resources to refugee protection while other states do little but pass the buck. Although reformers cannot count on changing either the motivations or heterogeneity of states, they can devise mechanisms to guide states' self-interest into channels conducive to humanitarian goals. These mechanisms can encourage states to exploit their heterogeneity through exchanges that serve both their self-interest and the public interest in refugee protection. A properly regulated market in refugee protection quotas promises to accomplish both of these ends.

Once a state receives its quota, it must decide whether it will discharge it by offering protection to refugees (either temporary safe haven or permanent resettlement) on its own territory and, if so, which form of protection it will provide. It must then identify the particular refugees whom it will protect. In addition to domestic political considerations, this selection process now entails a number of interactions—interviews, investigations, consultations, and negotiations—with UNHCR, other potential receiving states, the first asylum state, NGOs, and of course the particular refugees who are seeking protection.

Under my proposal, the state would have an additional option. Rather than protect the quota refugees itself (presumably, but not necessarily, on its own territory), it could transfer part or all of its quota obligation to another state in a voluntary, public transaction. In effect, the transferor state would pay the transferee state, which might not be a member of the regional burden-sharing system. The transferor state would be purchasing a discharge of its obligation from the transferee. The payment presumably would take the form of cash, but it could, in principle, be any resources that the transferee values enough to accept: credit, commodities, development assistance, technical advice, weapons, political support, or some combination of these assets.

At first blush, it might seem preferable simply to create a centrally administered refugee protection fund into which each state would be obliged to pay a sum equal to its share under the protection criterion. The central authority would then contract with individual states for protection services. This approach, however, entails at least two important disadvantages. First, it would restrict the acceptable currency of trade to cash, thereby limiting the number and flexibility of possible transactions. The proposed system, in contrast, would permit a transferee state to accept not only cash but also any other resources, including political support and other hard-to-monetize assets, that it values more than cash. Second, a centralized system would be more complex and involve higher transaction costs than a more decentralized system in which state-to-state negotiations and transactions would predominate. For these reasons, states are more likely to accept the burden-sharing norm if it is effectuated through a market system.

Why might states enter into such transactions? As in any voluntary exchange, the parties will only do so if the exchange makes each of them better off, and it is entirely possible that no deals would in fact be struck. Even in this case, refugee protection would still be better off than under the existing system because of the quota state's commitment to its initial quota. Here, the transferor can only induce the transferee to accept the transferor's obligation by paying the transferee enough to compensate it for the additional burden of accepting the transferor's quota. This is precisely why interstate heterogeneity, with respect to both their attitudes toward refugees and their resources for dealing with a refugee burden, can be a policy virtue.

Consider the example of Japan. Any regional system that included Japan would certainly assign it a large quota; after all, its people are among the wealthiest per capita in the world and remain the wealthiest in Asia. With a remarkably homogeneous population and no tradition of refugee protection, immigration, or assimilation of foreigners, Japan would presumably be eager to purchase a discharge of its large protection obligation from another country—perhaps Australia, New Zealand, or another Pacific Rim state—and at a high price, reflecting both its high cost of living and its determination to maintain its ethnic homogeneity. (Growing concerns about population decline may alter Japan's position on this).

Ethnically homogeneous, densely populated, and somewhat xenophobic states like Japan are not the only ones that might be willing to pay to be relieved of their burdens. The United States in effect did this in response to the 1994 exodus from Cuba when it persuaded Panama and several islands in the region to accept about 9,000 refugees, albeit only on a temporary basis.

Canada, Australia, New Zealand, Scandinavia, many European Union nations, Brazil, and other high-quota states with low population densities and a tradition of receiving and assimilating refugees and other immigrants would also be competing in regional or larger markets. Like all other immigrant-receiving societies, these states are now facing strong public pressures to admit fewer refugees and immigrants. A quota market would offer them a flexible solution to this political dilemma. It would enable them to respond to these restrictionist pressures not by reducing the level of refugee protection that their humanitarian traditions demand but by actually increasing it. This is because the high-quota states that would likely be purchasers of quota discharges also have high prices for most commodities, products, and services that refugees need. The costs per refugee are bound to be much higher in these states than almost anywhere else in the world. Refugees are entitled only to basic protection from persecution, not residence in the society of their choice. Human rights policy should seek neither more nor less than this.

By facilitating voluntary trades, moreover, the quota market could reduce the overall cost of the refugee protection system, giving it more "bang for the buck." First, it would tend to move protection programs from higher-cost states to lower-cost ones, enabling more refugees to be protected for any given resource level than under the existing system. Second, by increasing the number of states in a region that participate in the refugee protection system (as either buyers or sellers of discharge quotas), the system would reflect in the quota's market price the costs of shifting refugees from the state of first asylum to another place; hence, those costs would be minimized. In this way, high-quota states would seek to discharge their quotas by paying states of first asylum or neighbors of such states to protect those refugees where they are already located. Third, the quota price would reflect the risk that protection, initially meant to be temporary, will evolve into the more costly situations of long-term custody and permanent resettlement. Thus, transferor states, wishing to minimize the price they must pay to induce transferees to assume their burden, would have an interest in maintaining the integrity of temporary protection, which in turn is essential to the viability of any voluntary refugee protection system, including the current one.

The other side of the market—potential transferee states—should be reasonably crowded. All states want, and most desperately need, the hard currency that the high-quota states would presumably use to pay for their quota discharges, although transferee states might also value other forms of payment. Some potential transferee states have not been notably receptive to refugees but already have ethnically diverse populations and may have vast empty spaces (and residential controls) for temporary protection or resettlement. Russia and Brazil are examples. Even a wealthy state with a sizable quota of its own might nevertheless be willing to accept some additional refugees, especially if its costs of doing so are fully, or perhaps even more than fully, covered by a transferor's payment. The state's motive might be humanitarian, ideological, ethnic, or geopolitical, rather than, or in addition to, the mercenary pursuit of hard currency.

A potential source of uncertainty in a quota market is the identity of the particular refugees who comprise a state's tradable quota. Ordinarily, states do not accept refugees for temporary protection or resettlement until they have interviewed them and compiled a more or less particularized dossier. Under the proposed system, this information might be even more valuable; several states, not just one, would want it in order to decide whether and at what price to trade. States considering whether to buy or sell quotas would seek to use such information to predict the economic, social, and political effects of such a trade.

Just as states under the current system usually give careful consideration to precisely which individuals or groups they are being asked to protect, states under the proposal would pay particular attention to whether they have historical ties to certain refugees based on language, ethnicity, or other relationships to the receiving state. They will value whatever data on the refugees' social class, level of education, ethnicity, age, religion, family status, and any other demographic variables that may help them predict how quickly those refugees will assimilate, how productive they will be, which public services they will consume, and so forth. If states value such information but cannot obtain it, the costs and risks of trading will increase.

Amassing the information should not be too costly. First-asylum states already gather enough data to determine refugee status or otherwise decide what to do with the individual. Moreover, no state will seek information that is not worth the cost of gathering and assessing it. Refugees may want to limit uncontrolled access to personal information about themselves, fearing not only loss of privacy but also reprisals by their state of origin. These concerns can probably be met through confidentiality requirements.

Another problem—that such information lends itself to discriminatory group judgments by receiving states—seems inescapable. Certainly, it exists under the current system. A state's willingness to accept refugees depends in part on how it evaluates the refugees' prospects for early return or, if resettlement is necessary, for assimilation and productivity in the receiving state. These evaluations turn on the states' assessments of the demographic characteristics of different racial and ethnic groups and on the states' historical ties to those groups. Although such assessments invite prejudicial and discriminatory judgments that would be odious in any other context, it is hard to see how they can be avoided here. Virtually every state that admits immigrants discriminates on the basis of national origin (source country), social class (skill or educational level), and ethnicity (family, linguistic, or cultural ties). The relatively few states that agree to protect refugees engage in a discriminatory selection process in which they choose how many refugees, and which ones, they will accept. The haggling is particularly intense where permanent resettlement, with its higher stakes, is proposed.

The political reality is that states would be even more reluctant to accept refugees for protection if they could not pick and choose in this fashion. Perhaps they could be induced to agree on a "blind" allocation process behind a Rawlsian veil of ignorance. Would this be preferable? It seems doubtful. The fact is that certain affinities—religious, linguistic, ethnic, and occupational—between a receiving state and refugees tend to facilitate larger quotas, more generous treatment (in the case of temporary protection), and more rapid assimilation (in the case of resettlement). The proposed burden-sharing system seeks to make a virtue of this necessity by using a quota market, in which such affinities would be reflected in quota prices, to attract more states and more resources into the vital work of refugee protection.

This issue probably cannot be resolved without further analysis and experience. The most important empirical question is how specific the information about the refugees in the quota must be in order to meet the demands of potential trading states. The answer depends largely on the relative costs and benefits of obtaining more specific information. Some states might be satisfied with broad demographic data on group composition; others might insist on the kind of refugee-specific identifying information that raises confidentiality and safety concerns. Such preferences probably vary from state to state. A state's demand for refugee-specific information will also be affected by whether it offers only temporary protection, in which case particularized information is less important, or permanent resettlement, in which case the state will usually require it.

The problem of discriminatory refugee selection is not a new one, and the proposed burden-sharing scheme should not be faulted for failing to offer a neat solution that earlier efforts could not manage to devise. The CPA, the most comprehensive burden-sharing program yet established, allocated refugees through a process of intensive negotiation among the participating states in which certain demographic affinities were informally recognized as legitimate bases for assigning particular groups of refugees to one state rather than to another. Although all states would prefer that "their" refugees possess such affinities, some states were more insistent on them than others. In the end, the United States was perhaps the least insistent, accepting many refugees whom other states would not take.

E. An International Authority

The proposal entails certain tasks that only an agency can perform. The agency must gather information about refugee protection needs, assign quotas to the states, develop policies to facilitate the market in quotas, disseminate information about market transactions, and deploy whatever authority the states grant it (or it can muster informally) to ensure that refugees' rights under international law are fully protected.

Although the states that would establish burden-sharing schemes might wish to assign these tasks to a new or existing regional agency, UNHCR is an obvious candidate to carry them out. UNHCR does not now assign quotas or supervise a market, but it already performs other functions that have allowed it to amass enormous expertise in refugee protection. There are good reasons, then, to entrust the quota and market responsibilities to UNHCR and to provide it with the resources and authority necessary to execute them. There are also reasons to expect that UNHCR's effectiveness would improve under the proposed scheme, as the participating states would have strong incentives to strengthen UNHCR's capacity by providing it with adequate resources and political support.

The agency should disseminate information about market transactions, but it need not otherwise devote much attention to policing them. Sovereign states should be presumed to be fully capable of protecting their own transactional interests in this market. What states cannot be relied upon to protect, however, are the interests of the refugees who enter their territory, which to some degree conflict with the states' interests in minimizing the burdens of refugee admissions. Although the states must retain the primary responsibility for the welfare of those refugees, the agency has crucial roles of advocacy and perhaps enforcement in pressing the states to observe international legal principles governing the treatment of refugees.

Precisely how the agency plays these roles depends in part on the formal authority that the agency receives from the states and the informal leverage that it can generate. In addition, the agency must help to resolve certain policy issues surrounding the structure and performance of the quota market. Two such issues—applications for temporary quota adjustments, and the specificity of the information about refugees—have already been discussed. Other policy issues are certain to arise. The transactions themselves, however, should be negotiated and effectuated state-to-state, not through the agency as an intermediary.

A Response to (Anticipated) Critics

A number of objections to a market in refugee-protection quotas can be readily anticipated. Here, I respond to the three most likely ones: (1) unworkability; (2) quality of protection; and (3) commodification. Each of these objections raises legitimate concerns. Most of them can be met in the design of the proposed system. For a few, doubts do remain. Again, however, these doubts apply at least as strongly to the existing system.

(1) The Unworkability Objection

The first objection proceeds from the argument that the scheme is politically unacceptable and thus practically unworkable. Agreement among states is necessary to establish the system, yet states, so the argument goes, have no incentive to conclude such an agreement because a quota system would limit the freedom of action they now enjoy and impose additional burdens on them. If states actually had the desire to create such a system, they would already have done so. Furthermore, a system of quotas would be complex and difficult to administer. Finally, it would be impossible to enforce such a system in the absence of a central entity possessing the requisite legal authority and coercive power. No such entity exists in the international sphere.

This unworkability objection really consists of three somewhat distinct points concerning incentives, administrability, and enforceability. I have already discussed these to some extent. I will consider them now in greater detail.

Incentives. The logic of the claim about incentives is contingent on the circumstances specified by the observer. Any structure of incentives is inevitably contextual, a function of the conditions and choices that confront the decision maker at a particular point in time. I have shown that the refugee context is indeed changing in ways that are altering the objective risks that states face, their likely perceptions about such risks, and their policy choices.

The key change is the apparently permanent refugee crisis. No state is wholly immune to this crisis, which is already affecting how states perceive their risks of becoming a country of first asylum. These new perceptions, I suggest, should make states more receptive than they have previously been to a form of burden-sharing, a strategy that I have termed refugee crisis insurance. Today, even (or perhaps especially) a traditionally insular state might rationally prefer to agree in advance to accept a limited number of refugees in exchange for an assurance that other states will relieve it of any additional burden in the event of a refugee emergency that suddenly transforms it into a first-asylum country. Finally, as discussed below, the states with the greatest stakes in a broader distribution of refugee protection burdens are precisely the ones that possess the largest stock of carrots and sticks.

Thus, the incentives to support such a burden-sharing strategy are now in place. Whether states will in fact act on them, of course, is an entirely different question; one must never underestimate the durability of old perceptions and policies. Nevertheless, the refugee pressures that have been building on some traditionally insular states like Germany, Japan, Australia, and New Zealand, and the growing sense of urgency—even crisis—among some of these states indicate that the new incentives are affecting state behavior. The rise of at least embryonic regional refugee burden-sharing (and burden-avoiding) arrangements in Europe and North America provides additional evidence of such a transformation.

Administrability. It is certainly true that quota systems can be difficult to operate. They require an administrative agency to resolve a number of methodological, empirical, and normative questions, to implement the system in the face of many practical and political obstacles, and to make adjustments to accommodate constantly changing conditions. If the scheme is consensual at its inception—with states participating only if it serves their interests—this would reduce, but not eliminate, these obstacles. The best evidence of such a system's administrability would be the operation of analogous schemes in other areas of public policy. During the last decade, many proposals have been made in which a regulatory authority would permit regulated entities to trade entitlements or obligations as a way to improve the regulated activity's allocative efficiency. A few of these proposals would necessitate international agreements. My proposal for tradeable refugee-protection quotas draws on this approach. Two market-oriented schemes of this general kind in the US—New Jersey's "fair share" affordable housing program, and emissions trading under the Clean Air Act—are of some interest to refugee-policy reformers because they rely on assigned quotas, allow trading of those quotas, and have already been implemented to some extent.

It is hard to know precisely what lessons, if any, refugee-policy reformers should draw from the experiences of the domestic housing and emissions control programs and the emerging international environmental accords. These programs are similar to a refugee-quota scheme in a few respects but different in many others. All of these market-based schemes impose obligations and then permit the obligors to trade those obligations to others. Each is designed to derive greater social benefit (affordable housing, pollution control, refugee protection) from a given level of resources. Each seeks to take account of the heterogeneity among the obligors (communities, polluters, and countries) and to turn it to social advantage. Both the New Jersey program and my refugee quota proposal are based on still-controversial norms of equitable burden-sharing, although they concern radically different goods (housing and protection from persecution) that are allocated in altogether different ways. In the housing program, both quota allocation and compliance measurement are plagued by definitional problems. These problems, however, might not hobble a refugee-quota scheme in which strict legal definitions of "refugee" are of less practical importance. Such a scheme, moreover, may not require the kind of complex technocratic knowledge that pollution control agencies must possess in order to administer an emissions-trading system effectively.

Enforceability. Once states agree to participate in a refugee-quota scheme, monitoring compliance should not be particularly difficult, as UNHCR can readily count refugees, verify their destinations, and record transactions among states. Enforcement, however, would be far more problematic. Subscribing states would presumably have the same mixed motives to comply as they do in the case of other treaty obligations. These motives balance a desire to sustain a scheme of international cooperation to which they have agreed and that they believe furthers their national interest, and a desire to win or retain the approbation of actual or potential trading partners and politico-military allies, against a desire to free ride and retain their autonomy.

As with other international agreements, enforceability will depend largely on the degree to which powerful states wish to see the system implemented and are prepared to press other states to comply. I have argued that in this case, those with the greatest stakes in the scheme's success are the states that now feel obliged to accept refugees for permanent resettlement, as well as certain other non-resettlement states like Japan that might value refugee crisis insurance nonetheless. Happily, these are also the states that possess the most powerful levers for securing compliance with the quotas. Whether they would in fact use their influence for this purpose, of course, is a separate question. Once again, however, it is worth emphasizing that international cooperation is no less essential to the effectiveness of the current system.

I have proposed that the burden-sharing system initially be established on a regional basis. Participation by more states would of course be desirable and should be a goal for the future, but a scheme developed by a small number of powerful states in a region would, as noted earlier, have distinct advantages. These states could establish whatever conditions and criteria they deem necessary to protect their vital national interests. These interests would surely include their desire to discourage free-rider behavior by other, non-participating states by penalizing their recalcitrance and rewarding their cooperation. If the scheme were successful—if it managed to diffuse refugee crises and to distribute protection burdens more broadly and fairly—other states might wish to join this market or to form markets of their own, thereby gradually enlarging the pool of burden-sharing states. I have also proposed that the new system of refugee protection be consensual, a feature of the current system and indeed of almost all collaborations in the international sphere. Today, states decide to protect refugees if and to the extent that they wish, for their own reasons, to do so. This is not to say, of course, that they enjoy complete freedom of action. Receiving states decide to protect refugees only after balancing a variety of considerations, including the seriousness with which they regard their obligations under the Refugee Convention. Some of their reasons are humanitarian; others are not. Some states may conclude that they have little choice but to acquiesce in other states' requests to participate, backed by positive or negative inducements. The proposed system would be no different. Indeed, I have just suggested that its viability depends on the willingness of powerful receiving states to deploy these inducements, if necessary, in order to enforce the quotas.

(2) The Quality-of-Protection Objection

A more serious question relates not to the number of refugees who would be protected under the proposed system but to the quality of protection that would be provided in the receiving states. Under the current voluntary system, receiving states may fail to provide refugees with the full protections to which international law entitles them. Such failures, of course, are far more common with respect to the protection of those who claim asylum or other forms of temporary protection than with respect to resettled refugees, who usually become eligible for permanent legal status in short order. Even so, it would not be surprising if states that have traditionally volunteered to protect refugees tended to treat them better than states that agree to do so for the first time and in exchange for compensation.

This is a genuine risk, but it is not peculiar to the quota-market proposal. Indeed, the risk attaches to any move towards more universal burden-sharing that brings previously non-participating states into the refugee-protection system. There are several techniques for minimizing this risk; they cannot wholly eliminate it. First, states that pay others to fulfill their quotas cannot thereby divest themselves of the duty to ensure that the rights of their quota refugees are fully protected. They should be under an independent, continuing legal responsibility to see that the states with which they deal also protect those rights. They could enforce this responsibility through contractual provisions, liens on receiving states' assets, and diplomatic remedies.

Second, the payments to the receiving state should not be made through an initial lump-sum transfer. Instead, the pressure for continuing compliance with human rights and other obligations can be maximized by making payments on a periodic basis. Again, the problem of ensuring that resources that the donor provides for refugee protection are in fact used for that purpose, rather than being drained off by corruption or inefficient administration, is a ubiquitous one, especially in the impoverished regions in which many refugee crises arise. It is not at all peculiar to the proposed burden-sharing scheme.

Third, the administering agency, whether it be UNHCR or another, should be given wide-ranging authority to monitor and publicize the treatment of resettled refugees in light of humanitarian standards. Paying states must ensure that the agency receives the resources it needs to carry out its essential monitoring and reporting functions. By drawing more states into the protection system and by imposing on transferors as well as transferees a continuing responsibility for the proper expenditure of protection funds, the proposed system should increase support for the agency's activities.

The proposed expansion of the refugee-protection system beyond the traditional receiving states raises a related quality problem. The quota transfers permitted under a market system increase the probability that refugees will end up being offered protection in a state in which they simply do not want to be. The states that the market newly draws into the system are likely to be poorer, more geographically isolated, ethnically dissimilar, and have different social policies than the traditional receiving states. Refugees offered protection by a relatively unattractive state are placed in an unenviable position. They may have few options, all of them undesirable. They can reject the offer and remain where they are, in perhaps indefinite limbo, hoping that something better comes along. They can try to return home, which may be dangerous or even suicidal. Or they can accept the offer and receive protection in a country in which they expect to be unhappy.

Under the current system, however, refugees confront essentially the same options, with the difference being that there is a higher ex ante probability that the offering state will be an attractive one in which to live, temporarily or permanently. The refugees' options are limited because their rights under international law are limited. They are entitled only to non-refoulement and the other basic protections accorded by the Refugee Convention. They have no right to receive those protections in any particular state. Many refugees struggle, against great odds, to move from the state that initially offered them protection to one in which they prefer to live. Many succeed in doing so. Refugees, however, have no rights *qua* refugees to be protected in one state rather than in another. To create such a right would certainly reduce the willingness of states to grant protection, and it is almost inconceivable that the international community would ever do so.

A system of quotas (marketable or not) is designed to draw more states into the refugee-protection system and to increase the number of refugees receiving protection, but the quality of this protection may be reduced if the newly participating states are permitted to be less hospitable to refugees. This tension between the total amount of protection (in the sense of the number receiving it) and the quality of protection enjoyed by those who receive it transcends the marketable quota proposal; it applies, *mutatis mutandis*, to any reform that seeks to broaden refugee burden-sharing.

As stated earlier, I believe that the paramount goal for refugee policy should be to maximize the number of individuals receiving basic protection against threats to their lives and freedoms. Maximizing the quality of life enjoyed by those who receive that basic protection is highly desirable, of course, but it remains secondary to this primary purpose. Those who hold different normative priorities will view the proposal less favorably, but they will be hard pressed, I think, to devise a better one.

(3) *The Commodification Objection*

A final objection is directed not at the idea of quotas per se but at the moral implications of a system of marketable refugee quotas. This objection holds that such a market would allow and encourage states to traffic in human beings—and desperately vulnerable human beings at that—and that this offends common morality.

The political philosopher Michael Sandel has criticized my proposal on this ground. To Sandel, there is something distasteful about a market in refugees, even if it leads to more refugees finding asylum. But what exactly is objectionable about it? It has something to do with the fact that a market in refugees changes our view of who refugees are and how they should be treated. It encourages the participants—the buyers, the sellers, and also those whose asylum is being haggled over—to think of refugees as burdens to be unloaded or as revenue or labor sources, rather than as human beings in peril. One might acknowledge the degrading effect of a market in refugees and still conclude that the scheme does more good than harm.

But what the example illustrates is that markets are not mere mechanisms. They embody certain norms. They presuppose—and promote—certain ways of valuing the goods being exchanged.

For four reasons, my response to this objection is brief. First, the objection is a familiar one that society has often rejected, for good reason. It is made whenever the market is used to allocate scarce goods or activities—organ transplants, education, environmental controls, communications spectra, childbearing, and low-cost housing, to name a few examples—that have traditionally been allocated, at least ostensibly, through administrative or other "non-market" mechanisms. In each of these cases, money changes hands as an inducement in ways that promote socially desirable outcomes—without any obvious devaluation of human life in the process. Quite the contrary; human values are thereby enhanced.

Second, the commodification objection implies that the relevant comparison is between a callous market-based system that would arbitrarily allocate refugees to diverse places and fates, and a more rational system that allocates them according to some exalted principle of justice. In reality, of course, the existing refugee system does not even pretend to approach such an ideal.

Rather, it is a system that—in common practice, if not in law—allows states of first asylum to decide whether and how to protect the individuals who manage to reach them, and allows a handful of other states to select the small number of refugees they will accept for resettlement, usually based on their judgments about the refugees' prospects for assimilation. This system leaves the majority of refugees to languish indefinitely in dehumanizing, squalid camps or to be repatriated to conditions of possible persecution and almost certain suffering. Given the harsh reality of a dehumanizing status quo, a commodification objection to my proposal reform seems quite beside the point.

Third, the proposed system is perfectly compatible with whatever regulatory protections and market constraints are thought conducive to securing overriding public values. This is not to say, however, that any such constraint could be imposed without sacrificing other goals, including the willingness of states to participate in the burden-sharing system. Here as elsewhere, the market exacts its price; there is no free lunch. But it is to say that we can and should seek an optimal mix of the conflicting values.

Finally, the commodification objection would fail even on its own terms if the market-based system actually succeeded in protecting more refugees, with a quality of protection no worse, and at a lower cost, than in the current system. Although new schemes seldom work exactly as planned, and prudence thus dictates caution on the part of reformers (including confining the proposal to a regional, consensual demonstration), I have adduced strong reasons to believe that the proposed scheme could indeed produce each of these advantages.

Conclusion

The need for improved refugee protection is both manifest and growing. The existing system, jerry-built to address conditions that have changed dramatically since its inception, exhibits a number of major flaws. At the most general level, the two most important flaws include a failure to furnish at least temporary protection to a large number of refugees who desperately need it, and an unfair distribution of burdens among states able to provide protection. The maintenance of even this unsatisfactory system ultimately depends on the willingness of the relatively powerful industrial nations to use their leverage—their array of carrots and sticks—to induce the first-asylum states to offer temporary protection and, where permanent protection is necessary, to arrange for a limited number of resettlement slots in their own countries.

Equitable burden-sharing among states is a noble vision but not a new one. What is required to instantiate it is a system of norms, incentives, and institutions that can mobilize the necessary protection resources from states that will always be reluctant to commit them, especially if they believe that the protection will be permanent, not temporary. No system can eliminate this reluctance; it is endemic to states' narrow conceptions of their national self-interest. But the refugee burden-sharing scheme—by proposing a regionally based, consensual arrangement combining a quota system that distributes refugee burdens among the wealthier states with a market option that can redistribute protection resources to other states that can more effectively use them to harbor more refugees—promises to increase the overall level and quality of protection. Like many promises, its hopes might not be fully realized, but even so it could hardly leave refugees worse off than they are now. In view of both the deplorable status quo and the potential for human rights gains, can we afford not to try?

www.ingramcontent.com/pod-product-compliance
Ingram Content Group UK Ltd.
Pitfield, Milton Keynes, MK11 3LW, UK
UKHW041840270426
5426IPUK00014B/50